Teacher Edition

LANGUAGE!®

EVERYDAY ENGLISH

FOR NON-ENGLISH SPEAKERS

Sopris West®
EDUCATIONAL SERVICE

A Cambium Learning Compar

D1318897

ISBN 13: 978-1-60218-719-1
ISBN: 1-60218-719-3

Printed in the United States of America

Published and distributed by

Sopris West™
EDUCATIONAL SERVICES

A Cambium Learning Company

4093 Specialty Place • Longmont, CO 80504 • (303) 651-2829
www.sopriswest.com

170157/4-08

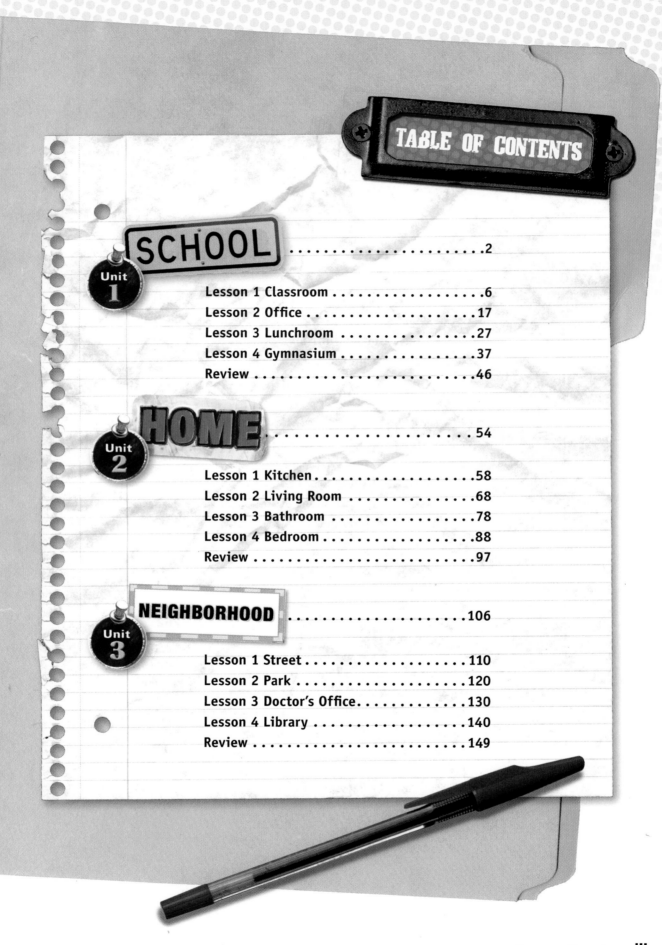

TABLE OF CONTENTS

Why do newcomers need *LANGUAGE!* Everyday English for Non-English Speakers?

Research has shown that English language learners need focused instruction in discrete English language skills, phonology, oral language skills, vocabulary, and grammatical structures. *Everyday English for Non-English Speakers* builds these abilities so that English language newcomers gain a foundation upon which to develop English language proficiency.

Everyday English for Non-English Speakers is a six-unit course that provides an entry point for non-English speakers by increasing their oral fluency, introducing them to the sounds of the English language, strengthening their use of everyday words, fostering their knowledge of core vocabulary, and presenting to them key characteristics of how English works.

These topics are presented in a series of six everyday scenarios that connect directly to the lives of the students: School, Home, Neighborhood, Grocery Store, the Mall, and My Day.

The *LANGUAGE!* Process

Everyday English for Non-English Speakers utilizes the step-by-step curricular process developed in *LANGUAGE!* and applies it to the needs of newcomers. This method not only ensures students' acquisition of foundational English, but also prepares them for the procedures implemented in *LANGUAGE! Focus on English Learning.*

The Interactive Text

Everyday English for Non-English Speakers supports students with an interactive text that provides a basis for daily instructions while serving as a pictorial reference piece that assists newcomers as they navigate through their daily lives.

Newcomers learn the English skills necessary to interact with their social and academic environments.

Unit Opener

Attractive introductions to each scenario set a familiar context for the content of each unit.

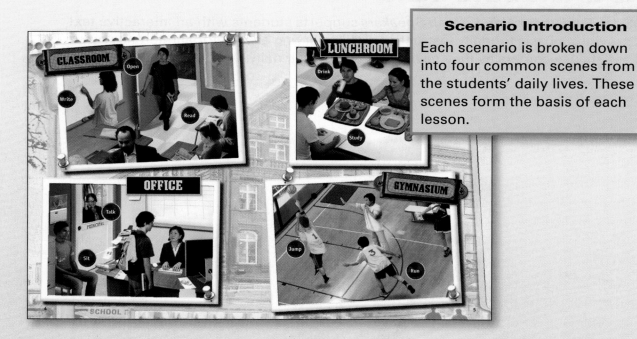

Scenario Introduction

Each scenario is broken down into four common scenes from the students' daily lives. These scenes form the basis of each lesson.

Everyday Scenes

Basic vocabulary is introduced to the students by incorporating the visual resources found in each *Everyday English for Non-English Speakers* scene. Students interact with these items in their familiar context.

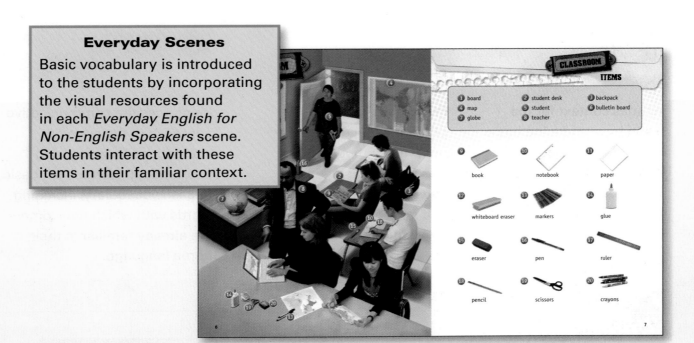

Dialogs and Applications

The students become part of an everyday dialog and then interact with their peers by applying the discrete English skills presented in the lesson as a basis for early conversation.

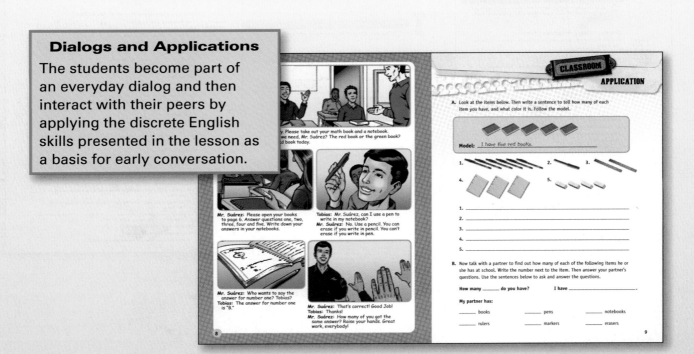

EVERYDAY ENGLISH
FOR NON-ENGLISH SPEAKERS

A comprehensive sequential approach to English-language learning for newcomers

Oral Fluency

STEP 1 Phonemic Awareness

STEP 2 Everyday Words

Provides context for the lesson by introducing basic points of conversational English to be used throughout the lesson's interactions.

Presents English phonemes focused upon throughout the lesson and leads newcomers to identify, and later produce, these phonemes.

Reinforces the communicative approach of the everyday interactions by presenting fundamental words from basic English vocabulary, including words with which newcomers are already familiar in their home language.

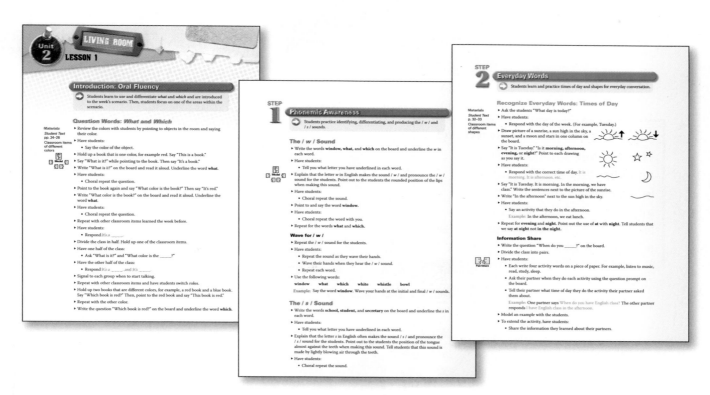

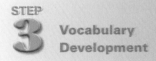

STEP 3 Vocabulary Development

STEP 4 How English Works

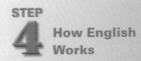

Helps students build their core content vocabulary featured in the everyday scenarios.

Identifies important points of English grammar, syntax, or morphology, and then presents these points in an approachable and appropriate manner for newcomers.

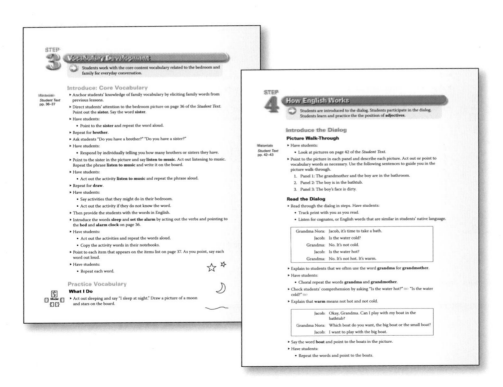

How is daily instruction supported?

The lesson pages in the *Everyday English for Non-English Speakers* bring the objectives, content, activities, and instructional directions together to guide and support teachers.

The **Transition Statement** identifies the focus for the activity and provides links from lesson to lesson.

Materials for each activity are listed at point of use.

The **level of scaffolding** is signaled by icons.

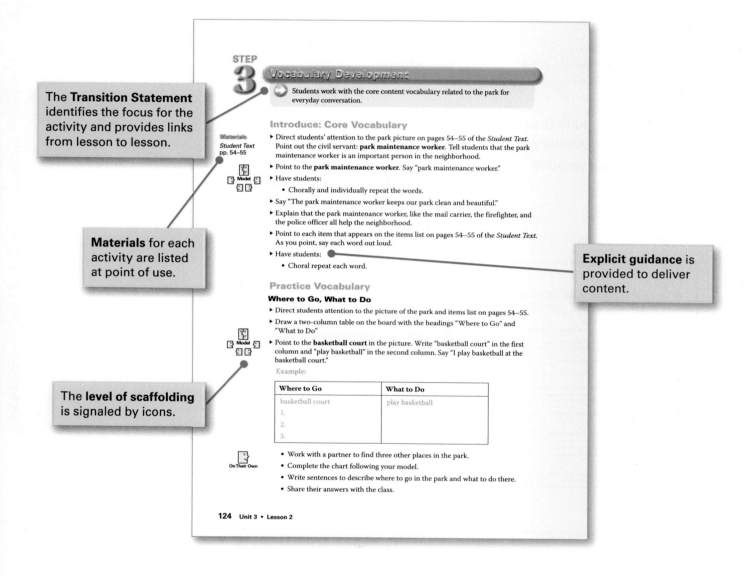

STEP 3

Vocabulary Development

Students work with the core content vocabulary related to the park for everyday conversation.

Materials
Student Text
pp. 54–55

Model

Introduce: Core Vocabulary

▸ Direct students' attention to the park picture on pages 54–55 of the *Student Text*. Point out the civil servant: **park maintenance worker**. Tell students that the park maintenance worker is an important person in the neighborhood.

▸ Point to the **park maintenance worker**. Say "park maintenance worker."

▸ Have students:
  • Chorally and individually repeat the words.

▸ Say "The park maintenance worker keeps our park clean and beautiful."

▸ Explain that the park maintenance worker, like the mail carrier, the firefighter, and the police officer all help the neighborhood.

▸ Point to each item that appears on the items list on pages 54–55 of the *Student Text*. As you point, say each word out loud.

▸ Have students:
  • Choral repeat each word.

Practice Vocabulary

Where to Go, What to Do

▸ Direct students attention to the picture of the park and items list on pages 54–55.

▸ Draw a two-column table on the board with the headings "Where to Go" and "What to Do"

Model

▸ Point to the **basketball court** in the picture. Write "basketball court" in the first column and "play basketball" in the second column. Say "I play basketball at the basketball court."

Example:

Where to Go	What to Do
basketball court	play basketball
1.	
2.	
3.	

On Their Own

  • Work with a partner to find three other places in the park.
  • Complete the chart following your model.
  • Write sentences to describe where to go in the park and what to do there.
  • Share their answers with the class.

124   Unit 3 • Lesson 2

Explicit guidance is provided to deliver content.

Scope and Sequence by Unit

Scenarios	Step	Unit 1 School	Unit 2 Home	Unit 3 Neighborhood	Unit 4 Grocery Store	Unit 5 The Mall	Unit 6 My Day
Introduction: Oral Fluency	☼	Greetings, requests, responses	Likes/dislikes, this/that, What?, Which?	Who?, How?	Where?, directions (left/right), qualities	Where?, here/there, ordering	Time, sequence, telling
Phonemic Awareness	STEP 1	Long vowels	/s/, /t/, /k/, /m/, /w/	/b/, /p/, /d/, /l/, /n/	Short vowels	/r/, /f/, /j/, /h/, /v/	/th/, /sh/, /ch/, /g/, /ng/
Everyday Words	STEP 2	Numbers, colors, letters	Days of the week, times of day, shapes and sizes	Feelings, weather, temperature, seasons	Placement (in, on, at), calendar, money, senses	Placement (in front of, behind, over, under), sequencing words (before, after, then)	Cumulative review of first five weeks.
Vocabulary Development	STEP 3	Classroom items, areas of a school	Family members, appliances, home activities	Important places, civil servants	Foods, household items	Clothing, food court, movies	Cumulative review of first five weeks
How English Works	STEP 4	Plural -s, contractions	Infinitives, adjectives	Pronouns	Verb conjugations, noncount nouns	Prepositions	Sentence structure

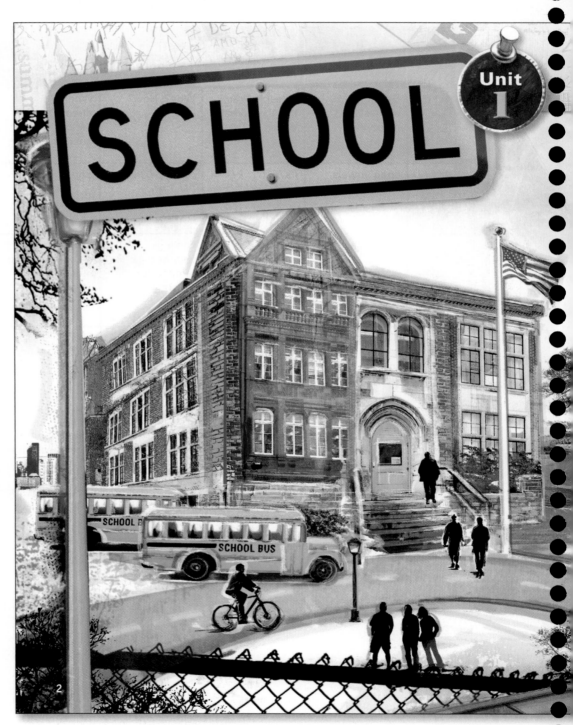

Unit 1

Everyday English Student Text

CLASSROOM

Open

Write

Read

OFFICE

Talk

PRINCIPAL

Sit

Everyday English Student Text

Introduction: Oral Fluency

 Students learn everyday greetings and are introduced to the week's scenario. Then, students focus on one of the areas within the scenario.

Greetings

Materials

Student Text
pp. 2–7

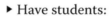
Model
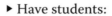

- ▶ Greet the class with "Hello." Wave as you say hello.
- ▶ Have students:
  - • Choral repeat "Hello."
- ▶ Greet the class with "Good morning." Draw a sunrise on the board.
- ▶ Have students:
  - • Choral repeat "Good morning."
- ▶ Repeat with a drawing of a sun high in the sky for "Good afternoon," and a drawing of a moon for "Good evening."
- ▶ Say "Goodbye." Wave and walk away from the class.
- ▶ Have students:
  - • Choral repeat "Goodbye."
- ▶ Greet individual students with one of the greeting expressions.
- ▶ Have individual students:
  - • Repeat the greeting.

Pair/Share

  - • Work in pairs to say and repeat greetings to each other.
- ▶ Point to a window or your watch. Gesture to students to choose the appropriate greeting for that time of day by pointing to one of the drawings on the board.
- ▶ Have students:
  - • Greet you with the appropriate greeting for that time of day.

Unit Overview: School

- ▶ Direct students' attention to the pictures on pages 2 and 3. Say "school."
- ▶ Have students:
  - • Choral repeat the word.
  - • Identify any parts of the school they know in English.
  - • Share the words with the class.
- ▶ Direct students to the photo collage on pages 4–5. Point out the **classroom**. Say "classroom."

- ▸ Have students:
  - • Point to the picture of the classroom.
  - • Choral repeat the word.
- ▸ Repeat for **office**, **lunchroom**, and **gymnasium**. When you say **gymnasium**, say "physical education."
- ▸ Have students:
  - • Say the words **classroom**, **office**, **lunchroom**, **gymnasium**, and **physical education** aloud as you point to the pictures.

Introduction to the Classroom

- ▸ Direct students' attention to the picture of the classroom on page 6 of the *Student Text*.
- ▸ Point out the board in the picture. Point out the board in your classroom if you have one. Say the word **board** aloud.
- ▸ Have students:
  - • Choral repeat the word.
  - • Point to the object and word on the items list on page 7.
- ▸ Repeat with **eraser** and **pen**.
- ▸ If the item is in your classroom, hold it up or point to it for the class to see. Repeat the word.
- ▸ Elicit items that students know in English that are in the picture and ask students to:
  - • Share the words with the class.

STEP 1

Phonemic Awareness

➡ Students practice identifying, differentiating, and producing long vowel sounds.

Long / ā / Vowel Card

Materials
Student Text
pp. 6–7
Blank cards
Eraser
Book
Crayons

- ▸ Give each student a blank card and write the letter *a* on the board.
- ▸ Tell students the name of the letter in English.
- ▸ Have students:
  - • Write the letter *a* on one side of their card.
- ▸ Prepare a card for yourself. Pronounce the long / ā / sound.
- ▸ Point out that the sound has the same pronunciation as the name of the letter.
- ▸ Have students:
  - • Choral repeat the sound.
- ▸ Write the word **eraser** on the board. Hold up the *Student Text* and point out the picture of an eraser. Underline the *a*. Say the word aloud.

- ▸ Have students:
  - Choral repeat the word.
  - Point to the picture of the eraser on page 6 of the *Student Text*.
  - Write the word **eraser** on the other side of their card.
- ▸ Repeat with the words **page**, **crayons**, and **paper**. Hold up the items or draw them on the board. Students should have a list of words with the long / ā / on the back of their card.
- ▸ Pronounce each word slowly. Have students:
  - Hold up their card when they hear the long / ā / sound in each word.
  - Choral repeat each word with you.
- ▸ Tell students to save their cards in a folder for future use.

STEP 2

Everyday Words

Students learn and practice numbers and colors for everyday conversation.

Recognize Everyday Words: Numbers

Materials
Student Text
pp. 6–7

- ▸ Count from 1 to 10. Hold up your fingers to indicate you are counting.
- ▸ Have students:
  - Choral count from 1 to 10 with you.
- ▸ Write the words on the board. Draw a table like the one below to indicate the quantity that each number represents. Say each number.

•	••	•••	••••	•• ••	••• •••	••• ••••	•••• ••••	••• ••• •••	••• •••• •••
1 one	**2** two	**3** three	**4** four	**5** five	**6** six	**7** seven	**8** eight	**9** nine	**10** ten

- ▸ Select any number between 1 and 10 and say it aloud.
- ▸ Have students:
  - Choral repeat the number.
  - Hold up their fingers to indicate the number that you say.
- ▸ Confirm student answers by pointing to the correct numeral.
- ▸ Repeat until you have used all ten numbers.

Everyday Words Seek and Find: Numbers

- ▸ Have students:
  - Look at the picture of the classroom on page 6 of the *Student Text*.
- ▸ Find items for each number in the classroom. Point out the item and say the number. For example, point to the chalkboard and say **one**.

▸ Have students:

  • Repeat the number.

▸ Invite a volunteer to:

  • Find an item on the page that represents **two**.

  • Come to the front of the room, point to the item, and say the number two.

▸ Have students:

  • Students repeat the number.

▸ Continue through all of the numbers until you reach **ten**.

Work with Numbers

▸ Draw a two-column chart on the board. Locate an object in the classroom that also appears on pages 6–7 of the *Student Text*. Draw the object in the first column of the chart. Then write the number for the quantity of that object that you have in the classroom. Say the number out loud for students to hear.

▸ Have students:

  • Copy the chart on a piece of paper.

  • Look around the classroom for four other objects that also appear on pages 6–7 of the *Student Text*.

  • Follow your model to fill in their charts.

Recognize Everyday Words: Colors

▸ Find objects of different colors around the classroom.

▸ Hold up one of the objects and name the color.

▸ Have students:

  • Repeat the colors after you.

▸ Repeat for **white**, **orange**, **red**, **green**, **purple**, **yellow**, **blue**, **black**, and **brown**.

▸ Point to a green object in the room and say "green."

▸ Point to other objects around the room and have students:

  • Say the color.

STEP 3

Vocabulary Development

➡ Students work with the core content vocabulary related to the classroom for everyday conversation.

Introduce: Core Vocabulary

Materials

Student Text
pp. 6–7

Classroom
objects

3-by-3 grid
worksheets

Marker chips
for game

▸ Direct students' attention to the classroom picture on page 6 of the *Student Text*. Point out the verb **open**. Act out opening the door. Say "open."

▸ Have students:

  • Act out the verb **open** and repeat the word aloud.

▸ Repeat for **read** and **write**.

▸ Point to each item that appears on the items list on page 7. As you point, say each word out loud.

▸ Have students:

  • Repeat each word.

▸ Locate objects in your classroom. Hold up or point to the objects. If the item is not in your classroom, have students:

  • Point to the item on the picture on page 6.

  • Repeat the words aloud.

Model

▸ Hold up a ruler for the class to see and say, "What is this?" "This is a ruler."

▸ Have students:

  • Repeat the sentence. This is a ruler.

▸ Repeat with the words **pencil**, **book**, **pen**, and **chalkboard**.

Pair/Share

▸ Have students:

  • Take turns with a partner to find two more objects in the classroom.

  • Take turns showing each other the objects and asking what they are.

Practice Vocabulary

Count and Say

▸ Hold up a pencil for the class to see. Say "I have a pencil."

▸ Have students:

  • Repeat the sentence.

▸ Model the question "Do you have a pencil?"

▸ Model the answer "Yes, I have a pencil."

▸ Model the answer "No, I do not have a pencil."

▸ Model the mini-dialog with a student volunteer.

  Do you have a _____?

  Yes I have a _____.

  No, I do not have a _____.

Three in a Row

▶ Prepare a three-square-by-three-square grid worksheet and hand copies out to the class.

▶ Have students:

  • Choose nine classroom objects and draw one in each square of the grid.

▶ Call out objects from the list on page 7 of the *Student Text*. Keep track of the objects that you call out.

▶ Have students:

  • Put a marker chip on their grid if they have the object that is called out.

  • If students place marker chips on three objects in a row, or diagonally, have them call out "Three in a row!"

  • Say "I have _____." when they have three in a row.

▶ Repeat the game. Invite student volunteers to:

  • Call out the classroom objects.

STEP 4

How English Works

Students are introduced to the dialog. Students participate in the dialog and take their first steps communicating in English. Students learn and practice the plural -**s**, and the contraction **don't**.

Introduce the Dialog

Picture Walk-Through

Materials
Student Text
pp. 8–9
Classroom objects

▶ Have students:

  • Look at the pictures on page 8 of the *Student Text*.

▶ Point to the picture in each panel and describe each picture. Act out or point to vocabulary words as necessary. Use the following sentences to guide you in the picture walk-through.

  1. Panel 1: The students and teacher are in the classroom.
  2. Panel 2: The boy has a red book and a green book.
  3. Panel 3: The boy has a pen.
  4. Panel 4: The two students talk.
  5. Panel 5: The boy opens his math book and his notebook.
  6. Panel 6: The students raise their hands.

Read the Dialog

▶ Read through the dialog in steps.

▶ Have students:

  • Track print with you as you read.

- Listen for and share cognates, or English words that are similar in students' native language.

Mr. Suárez:	Hello, everybody. Please take out your math book and a notebook.
Tobias:	Which math book do we need, Mr. Suárez? The red book or the green book?
Mr. Suárez:	You need the red book today.

▸ Check student's comprehension by asking "Is Mr. Suárez a student or a teacher?" a teacher

▸ Ask "Do the students need the red book or the green book?" the red book

| Mr. Suárez: | Please open your books to page 6. Answer questions one, two, three, four, and five. Write down your answers in your notebooks. |

▸ Check students' comprehension by asking "Do the students open their books to page 5 or 6?" 6

▸ Have students:

- Hold up their fingers to show the correct page number.

| Tobias: | Mr. Suárez, can I use a pen to write in my notebook? |
| Mr. Suárez: | No. Use a pencil. You can erase if you write in pencil. You can't erase if you write in pen. |

▸ Check students' comprehension by asking "Does Tobias have a pencil or a pen?" pen

▸ Have students:

- Point to the pen in the picture.

| Mr. Suárez: | Who wants to say the answer for number one? Tobias? |
| Tobias: | The answer for number one is "B." |

▸ Check students' comprehension by asking "Is the correct answer A or B?" B

Mr. Suárez:	That's correct! Good job!
Tobias:	Thanks!
Mr. Suárez:	How many of you got the same answer? Raise your hands. Great work, everybody!

▸ Check students' comprehension by asking "Was Tobias correct?" yes

Practice the Dialog

- ▸ Read through the dialog line by line.
- ▸ Have students:
  - • Repeat each line after you.
- ▸ Assign students one role of the dialog.
- ▸ Read the other role out loud.
- ▸ Have students:
  - • Choral read the other role of the dialog.

Variation:

- ▸ Divide the class in half.
- ▸ Assign one role to each half of students.
- ▸ Have students:
  - • Choral read each half of the dialog as a group.
- ▸ Check students' comprehension of the dialog by revisiting the questions from Read the Dialog.

One or More

- ▸ Hold up a pencil and say "How many pencils do you have?"
- ▸ Have students:
  - • Repeat the question.
- ▸ Model the answer by saying "I have one pencil."
- ▸ Have students:
  - • Repeat the answer.
- ▸ Get another pencil and say "I have two pencils."
- ▸ Have students:
  - • Repeat **pencil** and **pencils**.
- ▸ Hold up a book and ask "How many books do you have?"
- ▸ Invite a student volunteer to:
  - • Answer the question using the model.
- ▸ Repeat with other items of different quantities.

  Examples: **3 books, 1 desk, 10 crayons, 5 erasers**

How Many?

- ▸ Direct students' attention to Application A on page 9 of the *Student Text*.
- ▸ Have students:
  - • Write sentences to identify the color and number of each object.
- ▸ Check answers.
- ▸ Direct students to Application B on page 9 of the *Student Text*.

Pair/Share

▸ Have students:
- Work with a partner to complete the activity.
- Share their answers with the class.

No, I Don't

▸ Hold up a book for the students to see. Say "I have a book."

▸ Place the book down and say "I do not have a book." Write on the board:

I do not have a book.

▸ Repeat the sentence aloud.

▸ Have students:
- Choral repeat the sentence.

▸ Cross out the words "do not" on the sentence. Write the word "don't" above the crossed out words. Say "I don't have a book."

▸ Have students:
- Choral repeat the sentence.

▸ Model the use of **don't** by saying "I do not have a book. I don't have a book."

▸ Have students:
- Choral repeat the sentences.

▸ Repeat with **eraser**, **pen**, and **ruler**.

▸ Have students:
- Identify classroom objects that they **don't** have using the model.

On Their Own

▸ Have students:
- Write each sentence using **don't**.
  1. I do not have a pen.   I don't have a pen.
  2. I do not have a notebook.   I don't have a notebook.
  3. I do not have an eraser.   I don't have an eraser.

Revisit the Dialog

▸ Direct students' attention again to the dialog on page 8 of the *Student Text*.

▸ Have students:
- Read the dialog out loud with a partner.

Your Turn

▸ Have students:

- Create a dialog for role play between Tobias and another student in the class, in which the other student asks Tobias for certain objects.
- Take turns playing the two roles. (The objects that the other student asks for are: **paper**, a **blue pen**, an **eraser**, and a **green notebook**.)

  Example: Classmate: Do you have paper?
  Tobias: I don't have paper.

▸ Invite volunteers to:

- Perform their dialog in front of the class.

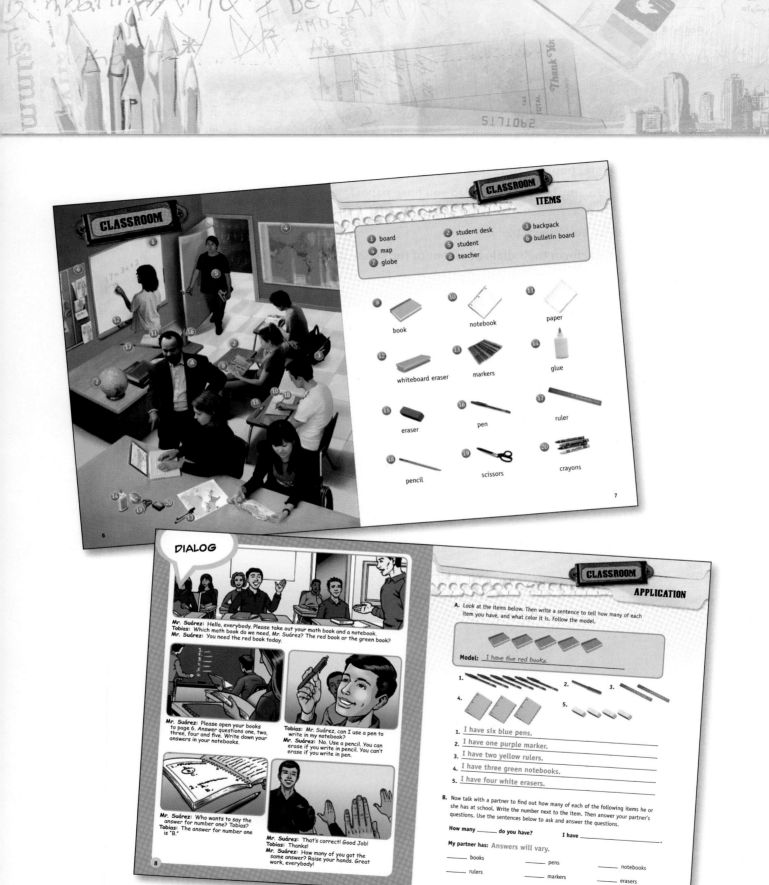

Introduction: Oral Fluency

 Students practice everyday greetings and are reintroduced to the week's scenario. Then, students focus on one of the areas within the scenario.

Greetings

Materials

Student Text
p. 4, p. 10

▶ Greet the class with "Hello." Wave as you say hello.

▶ Have students:

   • Choral repeat "Hello."

▶ Greet one student with the appropriate greeting. If it is morning, say "Good morning." If it is afternoon, say "Good afternoon." If it is evening say "Good evening."

▶ Have students:

   • Answer with the appropriate greeting. (Good morning, Good afternoon, or Good evening.)

   • Turn to another student and greet him or her.

▶ Repeat until all students have greeted another student.

Review: School

▶ Direct students' attention to the pictures on page 4. Point out the classroom in the picture and elicit the words **classroom** from students.

▶ Point out the office in the picture and say "office."

▶ Have students:

   • Say the word aloud.

   • Repeat the word as necessary for pronunciation.

Introduction to the Office

▶ Direct students' attention to the picture of the office on page 10.

▶ Point to the **secretary** and **principal** in the picture.

▶ Have students:

   • Choral repeat the words.

▶ Point out the computer in the picture. Point out the computer in your classroom if you have one. Say the word **computer** aloud.

▶ Have students:

   • Choral repeat the word.

   • Tell you how many computers are in the picture of the office.

- ▸ Repeat with **folder**, **paper clip**, and **stapler**.
- ▸ If the item is in your classroom, hold it up or point to it for the class to see. Repeat the word.
- ▸ Elicit items that students know in English that are in the picture and ask them to share the words with the class.

STEP 1

Phonemic Awareness

 Students practice identifying, differentiating, and producing long vowel sounds.

Long / ē / Vowel Card

Materials

Student Text p. 10

Blank cards

- ▸ Give each student a card and write the letter *e* on the board.
- ▸ Tell students the name of the letter in English.
- ▸ Write the words **screen**, **keyboard** and **green** on the board. Underline the vowels that make the long / ē / sound.
- ▸ Have students:
    - • Write the letter *e* on one side of their card.
- ▸ Prepare a card for yourself. Pronounce the long / ē / sound.
- ▸ Have students:
    - • Choral repeat the sound.
- ▸ Point out that the sound has the same pronunciation as the name of the letter.
- ▸ Point to and say the word screen. Point to the picture of the screen on page 10 of the *Student Text*.
- ▸ Have students:
    - • Choral repeat the word.
    - • Write the word screen on the other side of their card.
- ▸ Repeat with the words **keyboard** and **green**. Point to a green object in the classroom for the word **green**.
- ▸ Pronounce the words **teacher**, **he**, **needs**, **keyboard**, and **eraser** slowly.
- ▸ Have students:
    - • Hold up their card when they hear the long / ē / sound in each word.
    - • Choral repeat each word with you.
- ▸ Tell students to save their cards in a folder for future use.

Everyday Words

 Students practice numbers and letters for everyday conversation.

Recognize Everyday Words: Numbers

Materials
Student Text
pp. 10–11

▶ Say "Let's count from 1 to 10." To review the numbers from 1 to 10, start counting aloud with students but stop counting as they count without you to ten. Hold up your fingers as they count.

▶ Have students:
  • Choral count from 1 to 10.

▶ Show a number on your fingers.

▶ Have a student volunteer:
  • Say the number aloud.
  • Lead the class in choral repetition of the number.
  • Show the next number on his or her fingers.
  • Choose another student volunteer to say the number aloud and lead the class in choral repetition of that number.

▶ Repeat until all numbers between 1 and 10 have been used.

How Many?

▶ Have students:
  • Look at the picture of the office on page 10 of the *Student Text*.

▶ Point to the stapler. If you have a stapler in your classroom, point to it or hold it up for students to see. Say "stapler."

▶ Have students:
  • Choral repeat the word.

▶ Say "How many staplers are there in the office?" Gesture on your fingers to count.

▶ Have a volunteer:
  • Say the number of staplers in the office. one

▶ Write the sentence on the board and say:

There is one stapler in the office.

▶ Underline the verb is.

▶ Have students:
  • Choral repeat the sentence.

▶ Point to the paper clips. If you have paper clips in your classroom, point to them or hold them up for students to see. Say "paper clips."

▶ Have students:
  • Choral repeat the word.

▶ Say "How many paper clips are there in the office?" Gesture on your fingers to count.

▶ Have a volunteer:

• Say the number of paper clips in the office. five

▶ Write the sentence on the board and say:

There are five paper clips in the office.

▶ Underline the verb *are*.

▶ Repeat with **telephone**, **pushpins**, **rubber bands**, and **copy machine**.

Pair/Share

▶ Have students:

• Work in pairs to choose other objects from the picture and items list on pages 10–11.

• Ask each other how many of each object they see in the picture on page 10.

Example: How many folders are there in the office? There are two folders.

Everyday Words: Letters

▶ Write out the alphabet on the board. Point to each letter and say it out loud.

▶ Have students:

• Repeat each letter aloud.

▶ Say "How do you spell your name? I spell my name…" Write your name on the board. Spell your name for students. Point to each letter in your name as you spell it.

▶ Have students:

• Choral repeat the letters.

▶ Ask individual students "How do you spell your name?"

▶ Have a student:

• Write his or her name on the board.

• Point to each letter and say it aloud.

▶ Then, have students:

• Work in pairs to ask each other the spelling of their partner's name.

• Spell their name aloud.

• Write out their partner's name.

STEP 3

Vocabulary Development

Students work with the core content vocabulary related to the office for everyday conversation.

Introduce: Core Vocabulary

Materials

Student Text
pp. 10–11

Office supplies

Blank cards

Set of prepared
cards

▸ Direct students' attention to the office picture on page 10 of the *Student Text*. Point out the verb **talk**. Act out talking on the telephone. Say "talk."

▸ Have students:

- Act out the verb **talk** and repeat the word aloud.

▸ Point to each item that appears on the items list on pages 10–11. As you point, say each word out loud.

▸ Have students:

- Repeat each word.

▸ Locate office supplies. Hold up or point to the supplies. If the item is not in your classroom, point to the item in the picture on page 10.

▸ Have students:

- Repeat the words aloud.

▸ Hold up a folder for the class to see and say, "What is this?" "This is a folder."

▸ Have students:

- Repeat the sentence. This is a folder.

▸ Hold up two folders for the class to see and say, "What are these?" "These are folders."

▸ Have students:

- Repeat the sentence. These are folders.

▸ Repeat with the words **envelope**, **rubber band**, **file cabinet**, and **tape**.

Practice Vocabulary

Draw a Number

▸ Start with twenty blank cards. Prepare ten cards with the numbers from 1 to 10. Write down one number per index card. Choose ten items from pages 10–11 of the *Student Text* and draw one item per card. Your cards will be the model for students to follow.

▸ Divide the class into pairs. Provide each pair with twenty blank cards.

▸ Have students:

- Prepare cards with the numbers from 1 to 10, just like the set you prepared.

- Choose ten items from pages 10–11 of the *Student Text* and draw one item per card.

▸ Keep your cards in two separate stacks: a stack of numbers and a stack of pictures. Shuffle each stack and turn them face down. Pick up the first card in each stack. Show it to students and say how many of the item you have.

Example: You pick up the number 9 from the numbers pile and a picture of a rubber band from the items pile. Model the sentence by saying "I have nine rubber bands."

▶ Pick up the next two cards in each stack and show them to the class.

▶ Have students:

Pair/Share

- Follow your model by using the number to say how many of the object you have.

- Take turns with a partner to pick cards and say how many of each object they have.

- Continue to the end of their stack.

STEP 4

How English Works

 Students are introduced to the dialog. Students participate in the dialog and take their first steps communicating in English. Students learn and practice the plural **-s** and more **contractions**.

Introduce the Dialog
Picture Walk-Through

Materials
Student Text
pp. 12–13

▶ Have students:

- Look at pictures on page 12 of the *Student Text*.

▶ Point to the picture in each panel and describe each picture. Act out or point to vocabulary words as necessary. Use the following sentences to guide you in the picture walk-through.

1. Panel 1: The student and the secretary are in the office.

2. Panel 2: Look at the folder, pushpin and the envelope.

3. Panel 3: There are three folders, six pushpins, and two envelopes.

4. Panel 4: The secretary gives the student the folders, the pushpins, and the envelopes.

5. Panel 5: The secretary gives the student a stapler.

Read the Dialog

▶ Read through the dialog in steps.

▶ Have students:

- Track print with you as you read.

- Listen for and share cognates, or English words that are similar in students' native language.

| Ms. Foley: | Hello, Raj. How can I help you? |
| Raj: | Mr. Suárez needs some things for the classroom. |

▶ Point to the picture of the student. Check students' comprehension by asking "What is the student's name?" Raj

▸ Ask "Who is Raj's teacher? Mr. Suárez

Ms. Foley:	What does he need?
Raj:	He needs some folders, pushpins, and some envelopes.

▸ Check students' comprehension by having them:

- Point out the words for the items on the items list on page 11 of the *Student Text*.

Ms. Foley:	How many does he want?
Raj:	He wants three blue folders, six pushpins, and two envelopes.

▸ Check students' comprehension by asking "How many of each thing does Mr. Suárez need?" 3 folders, 6 pushpins, 2 envelopes
▸ Have students:

- Hold up their fingers to show how many of each item Mr. Suárez needs.
- Say the each number aloud together.

Ms. Foley:	Here you are. Anything else?
Raj:	Oh, yes! I forgot. He also needs a stapler.

▸ Point to the picture of the stapler. Ask "How many staplers does Mr. Suárez need? one

Ms. Foley:	Here you are. Is that all?
Raj:	Yes. That's it. Thanks, Ms. Foley.
Ms. Foley:	You're welcome.

▸ Check students' comprehension by asking "Does Mr. Suárez need other objects?" no

Practice the Dialog

▸ Read through the dialog line by line.
▸ Have students:

- Repeat each line after you.

▸ Assign students one role of the dialog.
▸ Read the other role out loud.
▸ Have students:

- Choral read the other role of the dialog.

Variation:

▸ Divide the class in half.
▸ Assign one role to each half of students.
▸ Have students:

- Choral read each half of the dialog as a group.

▸ Check students' comprehension of the dialog by revisiting the questions from Read the Dialog.

Contraction Action

I Need

▸ Write the sentences on the board. Say "I need a computer." Read each sentence aloud and point to them:

I do not have a computer.

I don't have a computer.

I need a computer.

▸ Have students:
  • Choral repeat the sentences.
▸ Say "I need a computer. What do you need?"
▸ Have students:
  • Choose an item from pages 10–11 that they need or they don't have.
  • Name items they need.
▸ Record the items on the board.
▸ Point to the first item on the list and model the sentence by saying "I need (item). I don't have a(n) (item)."
▸ Have students:
  • Follow your model to name the things they need and do not have.
▸ Repeat with all of the items on the list.

Can't, Don't, Isn't, Won't

▸ Write the following verb pairs on the board.

cannot	*can't*
do not	*don't*
is not	*isn't*
will not	*won't*

▸ Read each verb pair aloud.
▸ Have students:
  • Choral repeat the verb pairs.
▸ Write the following sentences on the board. Read them aloud. As you read them, cross out the verb and rewrite the corresponding contraction over the verb. Repeat the sentence with the contraction. Act out the sentences. Say "I cannot see the chalkboard. I can't see the chalkboard."

▸ Repeat with the sentences:

I do not have a copy machine. I don't have a copy machine.

Raj is not a teacher. Raj isn't the teacher.

Mr. Suárez will not need a rubber band. Mr. Suárez won't need a rubber band.

▸ Say each sentence aloud.

She can't talk on the telephone. She cannot talk on the telephone.

I don't need a printer. I do not need a printer.

Mr. Suárez is not the principal. Mr. Suárez isn't the principal.

The principal won't need a computer. The principal will not need a computer.

▸ Have students:

• Repeat each sentence with the complete verb form.

Revisit the Dialog

▸ Direct students' attention to Application A on page 13 of the *Student Text*.

• Write the number of each item that Mr. Suárez needs.

▸ Check answers.

▸ Direct students to Application B on page 13 of the *Student Text*.

On Their Own

▸ Have students:

• Complete the sentences by writing out the number and items that Mr. Suárez needs.

• Share their answers with the class.

Your Turn

▸ Have students:

• Create a dialog for role play between Raj and Ms. Foley, in which Raj asks Ms. Foley for certain objects. (Raj asks for **tape**, **folders**, and **rubber bands**. Ms. Foley has a **stapler** and **two rubber bands**, and **four pushpins**.)

• Take turns playing the two roles.

• Use **contractions** and **numbers**.

Example: Raj: Ms. Foley, do you have folders?
Ms. Foley: No, I don't. I have two rubber bands.

▸ Invite volunteers to:

• Perform their dialog in front of the class.

Everyday English Student Text

Introduction: Oral Fluency

 Students practice everyday greetings and are reintroduced to the week's scenario. Then, students focus on one of the areas within the scenario.

Greetings

Materials
Student Text
pp. 4–5, p. 14

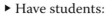
Model

▸ Greet the class with the appropriate greeting. (Good morning, Good afternoon, or Good evening.) Ask "What is your name?"

▸ Have students:

• Choral repeat "What is your name?"

▸ Say "My name is…"

▸ Have students:

• Choral repeat "My name is…"

▸ Say your name. Ask "How are you?"

▸ Have students:

• Choral repeat "How are you?"

▸ Smile and say "I'm fine, thank you."

▸ Have students:

• Choral repeat "I'm fine, thank you."

▸ Turn to a student and say "Good morning (or afternoon, or evening)." Ask "What is your name?"

▸ Have student:

• Respond with his or her name.

▸ Ask the same student "How are you?"

▸ Have student:

• Respond with "I'm fine, thank you."

• Turn to another student and greet him or her.

• Ask "What is your name?"

• Ask "How are you?"

▸ Repeat until all students have had the chance to have the mini-dialog with another student.

Review: School

▸ Direct students' attention to the pictures on pages 4–5. Point out the classroom and the office in the picture and elicit the words **classroom** and **office** from students.

▸ Point out the lunchroom in the picture and say "lunchroom."

▸ Have students:

- Say the word aloud.

- Repeat the word as necessary for pronunciation.

Introduction to the Lunchroom

▸ Direct students' attention to the picture of the lunchroom on page 14 of the *Student Text*.

▸ Point to the **lunch** and **line** in the picture.

▸ Have students:

- Choral repeat the words.

▸ Elicit items that students know in English that are in the picture and ask them to share the words with the class.

STEP 1

Phonemic Awareness

 Students practice identifying, differentiating, and producing long vowel sounds.

Long / ī / Vowel Card

Materials
Student Text
pp. 14–15
Blank cards

▸ Give each student a card and write the letter *i* on the board. Write the words **knife** and **line** on the board. Underline the *i* in each word.

▸ Tell students the name of the letter in English.

▸ Have students:

- Write the letter *i* on one side of their card.

▸ Prepare a card for yourself. Pronounce the long / ī / sound.

▸ Have students:

- Choral repeat the sound.

▸ Point out that the sound has the same pronunciation as the name of the letter.

▸ Point to and say the word **knife**. Point to the picture of the knife on pages 14–15 of the *Student Text*.

▸ Have students:

- Choral repeat the word.

- Write the word knife on the other side of their card.

▸ Repeat with **line** and **I**. Point to yourself for **I**.

▸ Pronounce the words **knife**, **line**, **white**, and **I** slowly.

▸ Have students:

- Hold up their card when they hear the long / ī / sound in each word.
- Choral repeat each word with you.

▸ Tell students to save their cards in a folder for future use.

STEP 2

Everyday Words

➡ Students practice letters and numbers for everyday conversation.

Recognize Everyday Words: Letters

Hangman

Materials
Copies of numbers worksheet

▸ Say "Let's say the alphabet." Start students off reciting the alphabet.

▸ Have students:

- Recite the alphabet together.

▸ Choose a word from this week's vocabulary list. Draw a line for each letter of the word to play Hangman. Draw a hook:

▸ Have students:

- Name letters to try to identify the word.

▸ If the letter that students name is in the word, fill in the letter in the appropriate blank. If the letter that the students name is not in the word, then draw each part of the body, head, arms, torso, legs, etc. Students try to fill in enough letters to identify the word before the man's body on the hangman hook is complete, or before he is 'hanged.'

▸ Have students:

- Use the word in a sentence, once they have identified it.

▸ Have a volunteer:

- Think of a word and lead the next round of the game.

Spelling Bee

▸ Hold a class spelling bee. Choose a vocabulary word that students have learned this week.

Pair/Share

▸ Have students:

- Spell out the word.
- Take turns giving each other vocabulary words to spell.

Recognize Everyday Words: Numbers

▸ Write numerals 1 through 10 on the board. Point to the numbers in random order.

▸ Have students:

- Say the number that you point to aloud.

- Spell the number.

  Example: eight: E-I-G-H-T

▸ Write the numerals **20**, **30**, **40**, **50**, **60**, **70**, **80**, **90**, and **100** on the board.

▸ Point to each numeral and say it out loud.

▸ Have students:

- Choral repeat the number.

▸ Point to the number twenty. Say "twenty." Write the numeral **21** on the board. Say "twenty-one." Repeat until you reach 29.

▸ Have students:

- Repeat the numbers aloud.

▸ Point to the number 30.

▸ Have students:

- Count chorally.

▸ Repeat for all of the numbers to 100.

1, 2, Skip, 4

▸ Tell students that they will play a counting game. Have students:

- Stand in a big circle in the room.

- Take turns counting. The first student says "one," the second student says, "two," etc.

- Say "skip" if their number is a multiple of three.

▸ Tell students that multiples of three will not be said out loud.

▸ Have students:

- Resume the count with the number that comes after the multiple of three.

  Example: one, two, skip, four, five, skip, seven, eight, skip, ten, eleven, skip

- Sit down if they say the number that is the multiple of three instead of saying "skip."

- Play until they reach 100, or until one person is left standing.

STEP 3

Vocabulary Development

 Students work with the core content vocabulary related to the lunchroom for everyday conversation.

Introduce: Core Vocabulary

Materials

Student Text pp. 14–15

Prepared cards

▸ Direct students' attention to the lunchroom picture on page 14 of the *Student Text*. Point out the verb **drink**. Act out drinking something from a glass. Say "drink."

▸ Have students:

- Act out the verb **drink** and repeat the word aloud.

▸ Repeat for **eat** and **study**.

- Point to each item that appears on the item list on page 15. As you point, say each word out loud.
- Have students:
  - Repeat each word.

Practice Vocabulary

Picture This

- Prepare one set of cards with the words from page 15 and the words **eat**, **drink**, and **study**. Write one word on each card.
- Take a card from the stack.

  Example: fork
- Draw a picture of the word on the board.
- Have students:
  - Identify the word.
  - Spell the word and use it in a sentence.
  - Take turns taking a card from the stack and drawing a picture of the word.
- Repeat the game until all of the cards have been used.

STEP 4

How English Works

Students are introduced to the dialog. Students participate in the dialog and take their first steps communicating in English. Students practice the plural **-s** and **contractions.**

Introduce the Dialog

Picture Walk-Through

Materials
Student Text
pp. 16–17
Copies of worksheet

- Have students:
  - Look at pictures on page 16 of the *Student Text*.
- Point to the picture in each panel and describe each picture. Act out or point to vocabulary words as necessary. Use the following sentences to guide you in the picture walk-through.
  1. Panel 1: The students are in line in the lunchroom.
  2. Panel 2: The students have trays.
  3. Panel 3: The students get their lunch.
  4. Panel 4: This girl gets something to drink.
  5. Panel 5: The students are eating.

Read the Dialog

▸ Read through the dialog in steps.

▸ Have students:

- Track print with you as you read.

- Listen for and share cognates, or English words that are similar in students' native language.

> Anika: How is your first day of school going, Trisha?
>
> Trisha: It's good. I like my teacher and everyone is really nice.
>
> Anika: Well, lunch at school is pretty good. We need to get trays.

▸ Point to the picture of the students. Check students' comprehension by asking "Which girl is a new student at the school?" Trisha

▸ Ask "What do the girls need? trays

> Anika: You can get forks and spoons there.
>
> Trisha: What about a knife and napkin?
>
> Anika: Here they are.

▸ Check students' comprehension by having them:

- Point out the words for the items mentioned on the items list on page 15 of the *Student Text*.

> Trisha: Lunch looks good.
>
> Anika: It smells good too!
>   Don't forget dessert!

▸ Check students' comprehension by asking "How does lunch look?" good

> Anika: Do you want some water, Trisha?
>
> Trisha: No, thanks. I'm going to drink milk.

▸ Point to the picture of the milk and water. Ask "What do the girls drink for lunch? milk, water

> Anika: Let's sit here. Hey, everybody. This is Trisha. Today is her first day at school.
>
> Trisha: Hi, everyone. Nice to meet you!

▸ Explain that "Hi" is another way to say "Hello."

▸ Check students' comprehension by asking "Where do the girls sit?" at a table

Practice the Dialog

▸ Read through the dialog line by line.

▸ Have students:

  • Repeat each line after you.

▸ Assign students one role of the dialog.

▸ Read the other role out loud.

▸ Have students:

  • Choral read the other role of the dialog.

Variation:

▸ Divide the class in half.

▸ Assign one role to each half of students.

▸ Have students:

  • Choral read each half of the dialog as a group.

▸ Check students' comprehension of the dialog by revisiting the questions from Read the Dialog.

Find Someone Who Can...

▸ Prepare a worksheet with the following:

Activity	Signature
1. write with left hand	
2. study with music	
3. read upside down	
4. talk fast	
5. drink with a straw	
6. _____	

▸ Hand out copies to students. Go over the vocabulary with students. Say each phrase. Act out or draw its meaning.

▸ Say "write with left hand." Act out writing with your left hand.

▸ Say "study with music." Act out listening to music and studying.

▸ Say "read upside down." Hold up a book, turn it upside down, and act out reading.

▸ Say "drink with a straw." Act out drinking through a straw.

▸ Have students:

  • Write down an original phrase on the blank in the last cell of the table.

▸ Approach a student. Ask "Can you write with your left hand?"

▸ Have student:

  • Answer "yes" or "no."

- ▶ If a student answers "no," model the sentence by saying "No, I can't write with my left hand."
- ▶ Have students:
  - Repeat the sentence.
- ▶ Continue asking individual students the question until someone answers "yes." If a student answers "yes," model the sentence by saying "Yes, I can write with my left hand."
- ▶ Have student:
  - Use your model to say "Yes, I can write with my left hand."
  - Sign your chart in the appropriate blank.
- ▶ Have students:
  - Follow your model.
  - Ask other students the remaining questions on the table until they have a signature for every item.
  - Share who **can** or **can't** do each activity.

    Example: John can't read upside down. Karen can read upside down.
  - Share what they wrote for number 6, and who **can** or **can't** do the activity.

    Example: Elsa can't eat soup with a fork.

Don't and Doesn't

- ▶ Say "I need a spoon. I don't have a spoon." Ask the class "Who needs a spoon?"
- ▶ Have students:
  - Raise their hands.
- ▶ Point to yourself and say "I don't have a spoon. Don't."
- ▶ Point to a student who had raised his or her hand and say "(Student's name) does not have a spoon." Write the sentence on the board.
- ▶ Point to the sentence. Read it aloud. Then cross out "does not" and write "doesn't" above it. Say "(Student's name) doesn't have a spoon."
- ▶ Have students:
  - Choral repeat the sentence.
- ▶ Draw a two column chart on the board with the headings "Name" and "Object."
- ▶ Have students:
  - Name some objects from the lunchroom, office and classroom.
- ▶ Record the objects in the chart.
- ▶ Have students:
  - Copy the chart.

Example:

Name	Object
Sara	straw
	napkin
	salad

- ▶ Write down the name of the objects in the correct column in the chart. Write down the name of a student in the first column. Turn to that student and ask if he or she has the object. For example, ask "Sara, do you have a straw?"
- ▶ Have student:
  - Say either "Yes I have a straw" or "No, I don't have a straw."
  - Write a "Yes" or a "No" in the chart next to the object to indicate whether or not the person has the object.
- ▶ Have students:
  - Write out whether or not the students they asked have the object.
  - Use the contraction **doesn't**.

    Example: Sara doesn't have a straw.

Revisit the Dialog

- ▶ Direct students' attention to the items list on page 15 and the dialog on page 16 of the *Student Text*.
- ▶ Read the dialog aloud. As you read the dialog have students:
  - Write a list of the items that the girls put on their trays.
- ▶ Check answers. Then, count the number of students in your class. Divide by two.
- ▶ Have students:
  - Count off from 1 to the number of half of the students.

    Example: There are 14 students in class. Have students count off from 1 to 7. Approach a student. Ask "What number are you?"
- ▶ Have student:
  - Respond with "I am number __."
  - Look for the person with the same number to be his or her partner.
- ▶ If there are an odd number of students in the class, you will be that student's partner.
- ▶ Have students:
  - Read the dialog out loud with their partner.
  - Practice intonation and natural conversational tone.
- ▶ Ask one pair of students to:
  - Volunteer to perform the dialog in front of the class.

Your Turn

My Lunch Tray

On Their Own

- ▶ Direct students' attention to the Application on page 17 of the *Student Text*.
- ▶ Have students:
  - Draw the items that they want to put on their lunch tray.
  - Present their lunch tray to a partner and say the name and how many of each of the items they want on their tray aloud to their partners.
  - Say out loud what their partner **has** or **doesn't have** on his or her lunch tray.

LUNCHROOM ITEMS

1. lunch table
4. line
7. pitcher
10. lunch
2. bench
5. cook
8. milk
11. salad
3. exit
6. tray
9. dessert

12. juice
13. napkin
14. spoon
15. straw
16. cup
17. plate
18. bowl
19. fork
20. knife

15

DIALOG

Anika: How is your first day of school going, Trisha?
Trisha: It's good. I like my teacher and everyone is really nice.
Anika: Well, lunch at school is pretty good. We need to get trays.

Anika: You can get forks and spoons there.
Trisha: What about a knife and napkin?
Anika: Here they are.

Trisha: Lunch looks good.
Anika: It smells good too! Don't forget dessert!

Anika: Do you want some water, Trisha?
Trisha: No, thanks. I'm going to drink milk.

Anika: Let's sit here. Hey, everybody. This is Trisha. Today is her first day at school.
Trisha: Hi, everyone. Nice to meet you!

16

LUNCHROOM APPLICATION

The tray below is empty. Draw the things you want to put on your tray. Then label each item. Use words from the box below. You do not have to use all of the words.

plate	juice	cup	napkin
fork	bowl	spoon	straw
lunch	knife	dessert	milk carton

Answers will vary.

17

Everyday English Student Text

Introduction: Oral Fluency

 Students practice everyday greetings and are reintroduced to the week's scenario. Then, students focus on one of the areas within the scenario.

Greetings

Materials
Student Text
pp. 4–5, p. 18

▸ Turn to one student. Greet him or her by name and with the appropriate greeting. (Good morning, Good afternoon, or Good evening.) Shake his or her hand. Ask "How are you?" Pause after each step and cue student to respond.

▸ Have student:

• Greet you and shake your hand.

• Say how he or she is.

• Ask you how you are.

▸ Say "I am fine, thank you."

▸ Have student:

• Turn to another student.

• Greet that student and shake his or her hand.

• Ask how he or she is.

▸ Repeat until all students have had the chance to have the mini-dialog with another student.

Review: School

▸ Direct students' attention to the pictures on pages 4–5. Point out the classroom, the office, and the lunchroom in the picture and elicit the words **classroom, office,** and **lunchroom** from students.

▸ Point out the gymnasium in the picture and say "gymnasium." Then say "physical education."

▸ Have students:

• Say the words aloud.

• Repeat the words as necessary for pronunciation.

Introduction to Physical Education

▸ Direct students' attention to the picture on page 18 of the *Student Text*.

▸ Point to the basketball game, the volleyball game, and the track. Say "sports."

▸ Have students:

  • Choral repeat the word.

▸ Elicit items that students know in English that are in the picture and ask them to share the words with the class.

STEP 1

Phonemic Awareness

 Students practice identifying, differentiating, and producing long vowel sounds.

Long / ō / and / ū / Vowel Cards

Materials
Student Text
pp. 18–19
Blank cards

▸ Give each student two cards and write the letters **o** and **u** on the board. Write the words **ropes**, **notebook**, and **envelope** underneath the letter **o**. Write the words **computer** and **use** underneath the letter **u**. Underline the **o** in each of the **o** words. Underline the **u** in each of the **u** words.

▸ Tell students the name of the letters in English. Point out that the sound has the same pronunciation as the name of the letter.

▸ Have students:

  • Write the letter **o** on one side of one card.

  • Write the letter **u** on one side of the other card.

▸ Prepare two cards for yourself. Pronounce the long / ō / and / ū / sound.

▸ Have students:

  • Choral repeat the sounds.

▸ Point to and say the word **ropes**. Point to the picture of the ropes on pages 18 and 19 of the *Student Text*.

▸ Have students:

  • Choral repeat the word.

  • Write the word **ropes** on the other side of their *o* card.

▸ Repeat with **notebook** and **envelope**.

▸ Say the word **computer**.

▸ Have students:

  • Choral repeat the word.

  • Write the word **computer** on the other side of their *u* card.

▸ Repeat with **you** and **use**.

▸ Pronounce the words **coach**, **bowl**, **fork**, **computer**, and **use** slowly.

▸ Have students:

  • Hold up their *o* card when they hear the long / ō / sound in each word.

  • Hold up their *u* card when they hear the long / ū / sound in each word.

  • Choral repeat each word with you.

▸ Tell students to save their cards in a folder for future use.

Everyday Words

→ Students practice letters, numbers, and colors for everyday conversation.

Recognize Everyday Words: Letters and Numbers

Break the Code

Materials

Copies of code worksheet

Objects of different colors

▸ Prepare a worksheet with the following tables. Provide students with copies of the worksheet.

A	B	C	D	E	F	G	H	I	J	K	L	M	N	O	P
1	2	3	4	5	6	7	8	9	10	11	12	13	14	15	16

Q	R	S	T	U	V	W	X	Y	Z
17	18	19	20	21	22	23	24	25	26

▸ Copy the following code on the board:

I		P	L	A	Y		F	O	O	T	B	A	L	L
9		16	12	1	25		6	15	15	20	2	1	12	12

▸ Have students:

- Copy the code in their notebooks.

▸ Point to the number 9. Ask "What number is this?" nine

▸ Point to the number 9 on the alphabet chart. Ask "What letter goes with number 9?" I

▸ Write the letter **I** above the number 9.

▸ Have students:

- Use the code worksheet to find and write the letters in the spaces.
- Break the code to figure out the sentence: I PLAY FOOTBALL
- Share the answer with the class.

▸ Divide the class into pairs.

▸ Have students:

- Make up a new sentence code and write the code on a piece of paper.

▸ Exchange codes with another pair of students.

- Say the number with their partners and identify each letter to decode the sentences.

Recognize Everyday Words: Colors

▶ Gather objects of different colors: **red**, **orange**, **yellow**, **green**, **blue**, **purple**, **black**, **white**, and **brown**. Hold one object up for the class to see.

> Example: Hold up a piece of white chalk. Ask "What color is this?"

▶ Have students:
  - Say the color "white."

▶ Repeat until they have named all of the colors of the objects that you hold up.

▶ Ask "Who can find a blue object in our classroom?"

▶ Have students:
  - Look around the classroom.
  - Point to the blue object.
  - Say the English word if they know it.

▶ If necessary, provide the English words for objects that students point out.

▶ Have students:
  - Choral repeat the word.

▶ Repeat for the rest of the colors.

STEP 3

Vocabulary Development

Students work with the core content vocabulary related to physical education for everyday conversation.

Introduce: Core Vocabulary

Materials
Student Text
pp. 18–21

▶ Direct students' attention to the physical education picture on page 18 of the *Student Text*. Point out the verb **jump**. Act out jumping. Say "jump."

▶ Have students:
  - Act out the verb **jump** and repeat the word aloud.

▶ Point to yourself. Jump, and say "I jump."

▶ Have students:
  - Repeat the sentence.

▶ Point to the picture of the student jumping on page 18 of the *Student Text*. Say "The student jumps."

▶ Have students:
  - Repeat the sentence.

▶ Repeat for **run**.

▶ Point to each item that appears on the items list on pages 18–19. As you point, say each word out loud.

▶ Have students:
  - Repeat each word.

Practice Vocabulary

Which One is Different?

▸ Direct students' attention to Application A on page 21 of the *Student Text*.

▸ Have students:

- Look at each group of words.
- Decide which word does not belong in the group.
- Circle the word.

▸ Check answers.

▸ As an extension, have students:

- Look at the items list on page 19 of the *Student Text*.
- Write down one more list of words to share with the class.
- Present their list for the class to identify the word that does not belong in the group of words.

Study the Picture

On Their Own

▸ Direct students' attention to Application B on page 21 of the *Student Text*.

▸ Have students:

- Work with a partner.
- Look at the picture on page 18 of the *Student Text*.
- Complete Application B, based on the picture.

▸ Check answers.

STEP 4

How English Works

Students are introduced to the dialog. Students participate in the dialog and take their first steps communicating in English. Students practice the plural **-s** and **contractions**.

Introduce the Dialog

Picture Walk-Through

Materials
Student Text
pp. 18–21

▸ Have students:

- Look at pictures on page 20 of the *Student Text*.

▸ Point to the picture in each panel and describe each picture. Act out or point to vocabulary words as necessary. Use the following sentences to guide you in the picture walk-through.

1. Panel 1: The football player talks to the coach.
2. Panel 2: The football player has a number.
3. Panel 3: There are cheerleaders and a mascot.
4. Panel 4: The boy wants to win.

Read the Dialog

▸ Read through the dialog in steps.

▸ Have students:

- Track print with you as you read.
- Listen for and share cognates, or English words that are similar in students' native language.

> Coach: Hi, Trevor. Are you ready for the game today?
>
> Trevor: Yes. I think I'm ready. We practiced a lot.

▸ Check students' comprehension. Ask "When is the game?" today

▸ Check students' comprehension. Point to the picture of the coach. Ask "Who is this?" the coach

▸ Point to the picture of the boy. Ask "Is the boy a player or a mascot?" a player

> Coach: Don't forget to pass to Jason. He runs fast with the ball.
>
> Trevor: Yes, he's a good player.

▸ Check students' comprehension. Point to the picture of player number 2, Jason. Ask "What is this player's name?" Jason

▸ Ask "What is Jason's number?" 2

> Trevor: Are the cheerleaders and the mascot going to be at the game?
>
> Coach: Yes. And a lot of people are coming to watch the game. Are you nervous?
>
> Trevor: No. I love to play football!

▸ Point to the people in the bleachers in the picture. Check students' comprehension by asking "Who is coming to the game?" a lot of people

> Trevor: I hope we win!
>
> Coach: I hope we win, too! Run fast and jump to catch the ball!

▸ Check students' comprehension. Ask "What does the coach tell Trevor to do?" run, jump

Practice the Dialog

▸ Read through the dialog line by line.

▸ Have students:

- Repeat each line after you.

▸ Assign students one role of the dialog.

▸ Read the other role out loud.

▶ Have students:

  • Choral read the other role of the dialog.

Variation:

▶ Divide the class in half.

▶ Assign one role to each half of students.

▶ Have students:

  • Choral read each half of the dialog as a group.

▶ Check students' comprehension of the dialog by revisiting the questions from Read the Dialog.

Class Survey

▶ Copy the following chart on the board:

Sport	Do	Do not
football		

▶ Have students:

  • Name different sports that are in the picture on page 18 of the *Student Text*.

  • Name any other sports that they know the English words for.

▶ Record the names of the sports in the Sports column of the chart. Draw or act out any additional sports that the students name and that are not depicted on page 18 of the *Student Text*.

▶ Ask the class "How many of you play football?"

▶ Have students:

  • Raise their hands if they play football.

  • Count out loud how many students play football.

▶ Record the number of students who play football in the **Do** column of the chart.

▶ Ask the class "How many of you do not play football?"

▶ Have students:

  • Raise their hands if they do not play football.

  • Count out loud how many students do not play football.

▶ Record the number of students who do not play football in the **Do not** column of the chart.

▶ Repeat until the table is completely filled out.

▶ Point to the information for football on the chart. Say "(Number of) students play football." Write the sentence on the board. Then, say "(Number of) students don't play football. Write the sentence on the board.

On Their Own

▶ Have students:

  • Work with a partner to write complete sentences with the information for the other sports on the table.

  • Share their answers with the class.

Revisit the Dialog

▸ Direct students' attention to the dialog on page 20 of the *Student Text*.

▸ Have students:

- Read the dialog out loud with their partner.

- Practice intonation and natural conversational tone.

▸ Ask one pair of students to:

- Volunteer to perform the dialog in front of the class.

Your Turn

Pair/Share

▸ Have students:

- Interview each other about what sports they do or do not play.

- Include different sports that can be seen on page 18 of the *Student Text*.

- Use **contractions**.

  Example: Student 1: Do you play football.
  Student 2: No, I don't play football

GYMNASIUM

GYMNASIUM

ITEMS

1. gymnasium
2. sports
3. field
4. track
5. players
6. mascot
7. bleachers
8. lockers
9. coach
10. cheerleaders
11. gym bag

12. mat
13. net
14. rope
15. weights
16. helmet
17. drinking fountain
18. basketball hoop
19. balls
20. whistle

19

18

DIALOG

Coach: Hi, Trevor. Are you ready for the game today?
Trevor: Yes. I think I'm ready. We practiced a lot.

Coach: Don't forget to pass to Jason. He runs fast with the ball.
Trevor: Yes, he's a good player.

HOME 17
VISITORS 10

Trevor: Are the cheerleaders and the mascot going to be at the game?
Coach: Yes, and a lot of people are coming to watch the game. Are you nervous?
Trevor: No. I love to play football!

Trevor: I hope we win!
Coach: I hope we win, too! Run fast and jump to catch the ball!

20

GYMNASIUM

APPLICATION

A. Look at each group of words. Circle the word that does not belong in the group.

1. cheerleader   mascot   (locker)   player

2. (bleachers)   run   jump   win

3. net   (coach)   ropes   mat

4. field   (drinking fountain)   track   gymnasium

B. Look at the picture on page five. Work with a partner to find the answers to the questions below.

1. What color is the mascot?   yellow

2. Who has a whistle?   the coach

3. How many balls are there?   three

4. What are the school colors?   blue and yellow

21

Everyday English Student Text

Unit 1 • Lesson 4   **45**

Introduction: Oral Fluency

 Students review everyday greetings and review this week's scenarios. Then, students revisit the Unit Overview.

Review Greetings

Materials
Student Text
pp. 4–5

▸ Draw a sunrise on the board.

▸ Draw a sun high in the sky on the board.

▸ Draw a moon in the sky on the board.

▸ Say "Hello." Point to one of the drawings.

▸ Have students:

  • Say the appropriate greeting.

▸ Ask the class "How are you?" Gesture for students to:

  • Turn to another student and ask "How are you?"

  • Greet that student and shake his or her hand.

Unit Review: School

▸ Direct students' attention to the picture on pages 4–5. Point out the classroom, the office, and the lunchroom in the picture and elicit the words **classroom**, **office**, and **lunchroom** and **gymnasium** from students.

▸ Have students:

  • Say the words aloud as you point.

STEP

1

Phonemic Awareness

 Students practice identifying, differentiating, and producing long vowel sounds.

Vowel Flip Cards
Review Phonemes

Materials
Prepared cards
with long vowel
sound from the
week

▸ Have students:

  • Arrange their vowel cards from the week in a row on their desk, with the vowel facing up.

▸ Hold up the long / $\bar{a}$ / card. Elicit the sound from students.

▸ Have students:

  • Say the long / $\bar{a}$ / sound.

  • Turn the card over to see the words that they have written on the back.

  • Say the words aloud.

▸ Repeat with the remaining vowel cards.

Practice Phonemes

▸ Pronounce each of the following words from the dialog on page 22 of the *Student Text*: **name**, **you**, **I**, **go**, **nice**, **meet**, and **later**.

▸ Have students:

  • Hold up the vowel card to show which vowel sound it is.

  • Repeat the word aloud.

  • Add it to the back of the corresponding card.

▸ Say the word **green**. Hold up the long / $\bar{e}$ / card.

▸ Repeat until all long vowel sounds have been practiced.

Produce Phonemes

▸ Hold up a card with one of the long vowel sounds on it.

▸ Have students:

  • Say a word with that sound.

▸ Hold up the long / $\bar{o}$ / card.

▸ Have students:

  • Say a word that they have practiced that has a long / $\bar{o}$ / sound.

  • Make a chart with words with the long vowel sounds from the dialog.

  • Add words that they know to the list.

  • Then, play a guessing game in pairs where one student says a word with a long vowel sound and the other student holds up the corresponding long vowel card.

STEP 2 Everyday Words

➡ Students review letters, numbers, and colors for everyday conversation.

Recognize Everyday Words: Numbers and Colors

I Spy

Materials
Student Text
pp. 7, 11, 15, 19

▸ Divide the class into groups of three.

▸ Look around the room as if you are searching for something. Locate an object that students have learned this week. Say "I spy" and the number and name of the object.

  Example: I spy five paper clips.

- ► Have a volunteer:
    - • Write the number on the board.
    - • Point to the object in the classroom.
- ► Have students:
    - • Play the game in their groups.
    - • Write down on a piece of paper the list of objects and number of objects that their group spies.
    - • Share their list with the class.

Review Everyday Words: Letters

Letter Categories

- ► Divide the students into groups of three. Divide the alphabet into parts to equal the number of groups that you have. Assign each group a part of the alphabet.
- ► Have students:
    - • Work with pages 7, 11, 15, and 19.
    - • Classify vocabulary words that begin with the same letter.
    - • Write down their words in a letter chart similar to the one below.
- ► Do an example from the chart below for students to see.

Example:

	A	B	C	D
Classroom		backpack	chalk	desk
Office			computer	
Lunchroom		bowl	cup	dessert
Physical education		ball	coach	

- ► Draw a large chart that has all of the letters of the alphabet on it.
- ► Invite students to:
    - • Come to the board.
    - • Write their words in the appropriate boxes in the chart.
    - • Share their words with the sentence frame "_____ begins with the letter _____."

Vocabulary Development

Students review content vocabulary related to school for everyday conversation.

Review: Core Vocabulary

Materials

Student Text
pp. 7–18

One copy of
Student Text
pp. 6, 10, 14,
and 18.

▸ Divide the class into four groups. Appoint a leader of each group. Give each leader one of four pictures face down.

▸ Hold up your watch and say "You have thirty seconds to look at the picture."

▸ Have the group leader:

  • Flip over the picture to show his or her group.

▸ Have students:

  • Study the picture for thirty seconds.

▸ After thirty seconds, say "Stop!"

▸ Have the group leader:

  • Turn the picture face down again.

▸ Give students three minutes to:

  • Write down a list of all of the items that they see in the picture.

▸ After three minutes, have students:

  • Flip over the picture and compare their list to the picture.

  • Work with a partner to say what items they **don't have** on their list but are in the picture.

    Example: I don't have an eraser on my list. There is an eraser in the picture.

▸ Have groups switch pictures and repeat.

Practice Vocabulary

Word Associations

▸ Act out the verb **open**.

▸ Have students:

  • Identify the action.

▸ Write **open** on the chalkboard in a chart similar to the one below.

▸ Repeat with the rest of this week's called out verbs from pages 6, 10, 14, and 18 on the board: **write**, **read**, **talk**, **drink**, **eat**, **study**, **jump**, and **run**.

open	write	read	talk	drink	eat	study	jump	run

▸ Divide the class into pairs.

▸ Have students:

- Look through the week's vocabulary and write down words that are associated with each of the actions.

Model

▸ Model an example by turning to page 7. Point to the book. Act out opening a book. Say "I open a book." Write "book" in the **open** column.

▸ Write **open** on the chalkboard in a chart similar to the one above.

▸ Have students:

- Share their word associations with the class.

STEP 4

How English Works

 Students are introduced to the review dialog. Students participate in the dialog and take their first steps communicating in English. Students review the plural **-s** and **contractions**.

Introduce the Dialog

Picture Walk-Through

Materials
Student Text
pp. 22–23

▸ Have students:

- Look at pictures on page 22 of the *Student Text*.

▸ Point to the picture in each panel and describe each picture. Act out or point to vocabulary words as necessary. Use the following sentences to guide you in the picture walk-through.

1. Panel 1: This student has a book and a notebook. This student has a backpack. There are lockers.
2. Panel 2: This girl talks about her class.
3. Panel 3: This girl talks about lunch.
4. Panel 4: This girl shows her books.
5. Panel 5: This girl talks about sports. The other girl talks about the office.
6. Panel 6: The girls say goodbye.

Read the Dialog

▸ Read through the dialog in steps.

▸ Have students:

- Track print with you as you read.
- Listen for and share cognates, or English words that are similar in students' native language.

> Sara: Hi. I'm Sara. You're a new student, right?
>
> Trisha: Yes, I am. Today's my first day.
>
> Sara: What's your name?
>
> Trisha: I'm Trisha.

▸ Check students' comprehension. Ask "What are the students' names?" Trisha and Sara

> Trisha: Who's your teacher? I'm in Ms. Anderson's class.
>
> Sara: I'm in Mr. Suárez's class. He's really nice.

▸ Check students' comprehension. Ask "Who is Trisha's teacher?" Ms. Anderson Ask "Who is Sara's teacher?" Mr. Suárez

> Sara: What do you think of the school lunch?
>
> Trisha: It's good. I like it.
>
> Sara: Yes, it isn't bad.

▸ Check students' comprehension. Ask "Does Trisha like the school lunch?" yes

> Sara: Do you have all of your books?
>
> Trisha: I don't have all of them. I have this red book. I have four books in my locker.

▸ Check students' comprehension. Ask "How many books does Trisha have in her locker? four

> Sara: Do you have a class now?
>
> Trisha: I'm going to the gymnasium. I'm going to practice.
>
> Sara: I'm going to the office. My teacher needs some tape from the secretary.

▸ Check students' comprehension. Ask "Where are the girls going?" Sara is going to the office. Trisha is going to the gymnasium.

> Trisha: It was nice to meet you, Sara.
>
> Sara: It was nice to meet you, too. See you later!

▸ Check students' comprehension. Ask "Is this the first time Sara met Trisha?" yes

Practice the Dialog

▸ Read through the dialog line by line.

▸ Have students:

• Repeat each line after you.

▸ Assign students one role of the dialog.

- ▸ Read the other role out loud.
- ▸ Have students:
  - • Choral read the other role of the dialog.

Variation:

- ▸ Divide the class in half.
- ▸ Assign one role to each half of students.
- ▸ Have students:
  - • Choral read each half of the dialog as a group.
- ▸ Check students' comprehension of the dialog by revisiting the questions from Read the Dialog.

Revisit the Dialog

- ▸ Direct students' attention to the dialog on page 22 of the *Student Text*.
- ▸ Have students:
  - • Read the dialog out loud with their partner.
  - • Practice intonation and natural conversational tone.
- ▸ Ask one pair of students to:
  - • Volunteer to perform the dialog in front of the class.

Your Turn

- ▸ Direct students' attention to Application A on page 23 of the *Student Text*.
- ▸ Read the instruction and model with students.

On Their Own

- ▸ Have students:
  - • Work in pairs to identify each item and where it belongs.
  - • Take turns asking and answering each question.
  - • Check answers.
- ▸ Direct students' attention to Application B on page 23 of the *Student Text*.
- ▸ Have students:
  - • Work individually to write out complete sentences.
  - • Share their answers with the class.

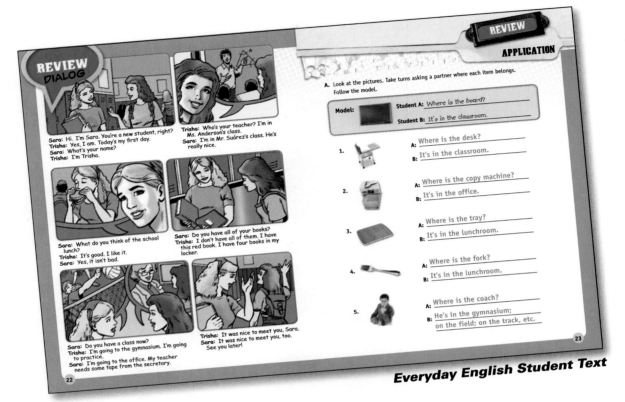

Everyday English Student Text

HOME

Unit
2

24

25

Everyday English Student Text

LIVING ROOM

grandfather

dog

mother

KITCHEN

father

baby

cat

26

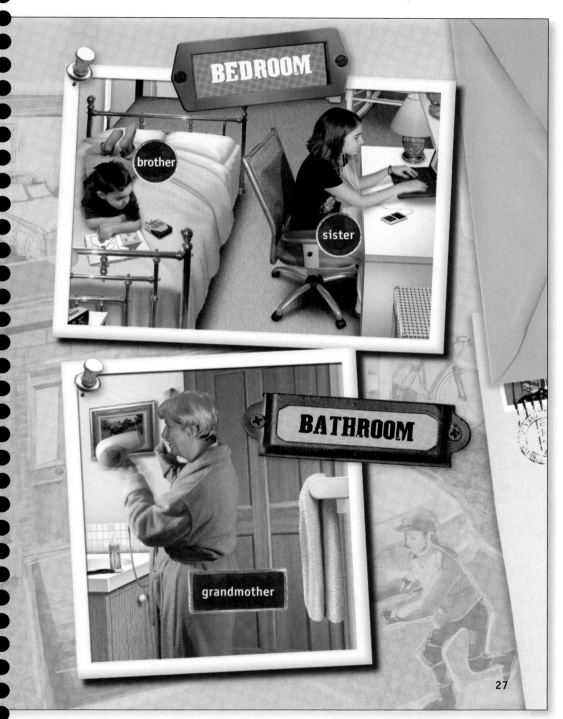

BEDROOM

brother

sister

BATHROOM

grandmother

27

Everyday English Student Text

Introduction: Oral Fluency

 Students learn to use and differentiate *what* and *which* and are introduced to the week's scenario. Then, students focus on one of the areas within the scenario.

Question Words: *What* and *Which*

Materials

Student Text
pp. 24–28

Classroom items
of different
colors

▶ Review the colors with students by pointing to objects in the room and saying their color.

▶ Have students:

　• Say the color of the object.

▶ Hold up a book that is one color, for example red. Say "This is a book."

▶ Say "What is it?" while pointing to the book. Then say "It's a book."

▶ Write "What is it?" on the board and read it aloud. Underline the word **what**.

▶ Have students:

　• Choral repeat the question.

▶ Point to the book again and say "What color is the book?" Then say "It's red."

▶ Write "What color is the book?" on the board and read it aloud. Underline the word **what**.

▶ Have students:

　• Choral repeat the question.

▶ Repeat with other classroom items learned the week before.

▶ Have students:

　• Respond It's a _____.

▶ Divide the class in half. Hold up one of the classroom items.

▶ Have one half of the class:

　• Ask "What is it?" and "What color is the _____?"

▶ Have the other half of the class:

　• Respond It's a _____. and It's _____.

▶ Signal to each group when to start talking.

▶ Repeat with other classroom items and have students switch roles.

▶ Hold up two books that are different colors, for example, a red book and a blue book. Say "Which book is red?" Then, point to the red book and say "This book is red."

▶ Repeat with the other color.

▶ Write the question "Which book is red?" on the board and underline the word **which**.

▸ Have students:

- Choral repeat the question.

▸ Repeat with other classroom items and other colors.

▸ Monitor comprehension by holding up an item and asking "What is it?" "What color is the _____?" Then hold up a second item to ask "Which _____ is _____?"

Unit Overview: Home

▸ Direct students' attention to the picture on pages 24–25. Say "home." Have students:

- Choral repeat the word.

▸ Have students:

- Identify any parts of the house they may know in English by sharing the words with the class.

▸ Direct students' attention to the picture collage on pages 26–27. Point to the **living room**. Say "living room."

▸ Have students:

- Point to the picture of the living room.
- Choral repeat the word.

▸ Repeat for **kitchen, bedroom,** and **bathroom.**

▸ Direct students' attention again to pages 24–25.

▸ Have students:

- Say the words **living room, kitchen, bedroom,** and **bathroom** aloud as you point to them.

Introduction to the Living Room

▸ Direct students' attention to the picture of the living room on page 28.

▸ Elicit words that students know in English that are in the picture and share them with the class.

▸ Have students:

- Choral repeat the words.

▸ Elicit items that students know in English that are in the picture, and ask students to:

- Share the words with the class.

STEP

Phonemic Awareness

→ Students practice identifying, differentiating, and producing the / w / and / s / sounds.

The / **w** / Sound

▸ Write the words **window, what,** and **which** on the board and underline the *w* in each word.

▸ Have students:

- Tell you what letter you have underlined in each word.

▸ Explain that the letter *w* in English makes the sound / w / and pronounce the / w / sound for the students. Point out to the students the rounded position of the lips when making this sound.

▸ Have students:

- Choral repeat the sound.

▸ Point to and say the word **window.**

▸ Have students:

- Choral repeat the word with you.

▸ Repeat for the words **what** and **which.**

Wave for / **w** /

▸ Repeat the / w / sound for the students.

▸ Have students:

- Repeat the sound as they wave their hands.
- Wave their hands when they hear the / w / sound.
- Repeat each word.

▸ Use the following words:

window   what   which   white   whistle   bowl

Example: Say the word **window.** Wave your hands at the initial and final / w / sounds.

The / **s** / Sound

▸ Write the words **school, student,** and **secretary** on the board and underline the *s* in each word.

▸ Have students:

- Tell you what letter you have underlined in each word.

▸ Explain that the letter *s* in English often makes the sound / s / and pronounce the / s / sound for the students. Point out to the students the position of the tongue almost against the teeth when making this sound. Tell students that this sound is made by lightly blowing air through the teeth.

▸ Have students:

- Choral repeat the sound.

- ▶ Point to the students and say the word **students.**
- ▶ Have students:
  - Choral repeat the word with you.
- ▶ Repeat for the words **school** and **secretary.**

Snake Hands for / s /

- ▶ Repeat the / s / sound for the students.
- ▶ Have students:
  - Repeat the sound as they make a wavy S, like a snake, in the air.
  - Make a wavy S in the air when they hear the / s / sound.
  - Repeat each word.
- ▶ Use the following words:

    school   secretary   students   Sunday   Saturday

    Example: Say the word **school**. Make a wavy S like a shape with your hands at the initial / s / sounds.

STEP 2

Everyday Words

Students learn and practice the days of the week for everyday conversation.

Recognize Everyday Words: Days of the Week

Materials
Blank cards

Model

- ▶ Write the days of the week in a table like the one below.

Sunday	Monday	Tuesday	Wednesday	Thursday	Friday	Saturday

- ▶ Say each word as you point to it.
- ▶ Have students:
  - Choral repeat each word.
- ▶ Point to today's day, for example Monday, and say "Today is Monday."
- ▶ Have students:
  - Choral repeat the sentence.
  - Copy each day of the week on blank cards.

Unscramble the Week

On Their Own

- ▶ Have students:
  - Shuffle their days-of-the-week cards.
  - Put the days of the week in order, starting with Sunday.
- ▶ Check the students' order by having the class say the days of the week aloud in order as you prompt them.

What Day?

▸ Say one of the days of the week.

▸ Have students:

- Hold up the card with that day of the week.
- Say the day of the week.

▸ Ask students: "Is today _____?"

▸ Have students:

- Respond with Yes, today is _____. or No, today is _____.

STEP 3

Vocabulary Development

 Students work with the core content vocabulary related to the living room and family for everyday conversation.

Introduce: Core Vocabulary

Materials

Student Text
pp. 28–29

Old magazines
that include
pictures of target
vocabulary

Scissors

Glue

Model collage

▸ Direct students' attention to the living room picture on pages 28–29 of the *Student Text*. Point out the family members **mother, grandfather** and **dog.** Tell students these are members of the family. Say **mother**.

▸ Have students:

- Choral repeat the word.

▸ Repeat with the words **grandfather** and **dog.**

▸ Point to the grandfather watching television. Say "The grandfather is watching television." Act out watching. Write the word **watch.**

▸ Have students:

- Act out the activity and repeat the word **watch** aloud.

▸ Repeat with the actions of **play piano** and **sleep.**

▸ Point to the **books** in the **bookcase** on pages 28–29. Say "I can **read a book** in the living room." Act out reading a book. Write **read a book** on the board.

▸ Have students:

- Repeat the sentence.

▸ Repeat with the actions **play games, play the piano,** and **listen to music.**

▸ Have students:

- Act out the activities and repeat the words aloud.
- Copy the activity words in their notebooks.

▸ Point to each item that appears on the items list on pages 28–29. As you point, say each word out loud.

▸ Have students:

- Repeat each word.

Practice Vocabulary

Design-A-Living-Room

▸ Prepare a collage of a living room with cut out pictures as a model. Divide the class into pairs. Explain to students that they are going to design their own living room by cutting out items that they would like to include in their living room and making a collage.

Pair/Share

▸ Have students:

- Look through magazines to cut out pictures of living room items.
- Label 10 items in their living room.
- Share their collages with the class and point out the items.

What Do I Need?

▸ Act out one of the actions from the Introduce: Core Vocabulary section.

▸ Have students:

- Say the action.
- Tell you what items from pages 28–29 you need to do the activity.

▸ Repeat for all of the actions.

STEP 4

How English Works

⮕ Students are introduced to the dialog. Students participate in the dialog. Students learn and practice **adjectives**.

Introduce the Dialog

Picture Walk-Through

Materials
Student Text
pp. 28–31

▸ Have students:

- Look at pictures on page 30 of the *Student Text*.

▸ Point to the picture in each panel and describe each picture. Act out or point to vocabulary words as necessary. Use the following sentences to guide you in the picture walk-through.

1. Panel 1: The grandfather and the boy are in the living room.
2. Panel 2: The remote control is on the table.
3. Panel 3: This grandfather talks to the mother.
4. Panel 4: The mom leaves today.
5. Panel 5: The boy and the grandfather sit on the couch.
6. Panel 6: There is a stereo in the living room.

Read the Dialog

▸ Read through the dialog in steps. Have students:

- Track print with you as you read.

- Listen for cognates, or English words that are similar in students' native language.

> Jacob: Hi, Grandpa. What are you doing?
>
> Grandpa Jose: I'm watching television, but I can't find the remote control.

▸ Explain to students that we often use the word **grandpa** for **grandfather**.

▸ Have students:

- Choral repeat the words **grandpa** and **grandfather**.

▸ Check students' comprehension by asking "What problem does Grandpa have?" He can't find the remote control.

> Jacob: It's on the table.
>
> Grandpa Jose: On the coffee table or the round table?
>
> Jacob: The coffee table. Can I watch television?

▸ Check students' comprehension by asking "On which table is the remote control?" the coffee table

▸ Have students:

- Point to the coffee table in the picture.

> Grandpa Jose: Well, we have to say goodbye to your mom. She's leaving soon.
>
> Jacob: When will she come home?

▸ Explain to students that we often use the word **mom** for **mother**.

▸ Have students:

- Point to the **mom** in the picture and say the words **mom** and **mother**.

> Grandpa Jose: She will come home on Friday.
>
> Jacob: What day is it today?
>
> Grandpa Jose: Today is Sunday.

▸ Check students' comprehension by asking "What day is it in the dialog?" It's Sunday.

> Jacob: What will we do without Mom?
>
> Grandpa Jose: Don't worry. We can do a lot of things.
>
> Jacob: What can we do?

▸ Check students' comprehension by asking "Is Oscar happy or sad?" Act out happy and sad. sad

Grandpa Jose:	Well, we can read a book together and listen to music on the stereo.
Jacob:	Can we play games, too?
Grandpa Jose:	Of course!
Jacob:	You're right, Grandpa. We can do a lot of things.

▸ Check students' comprehension by asking "What can Oscar and Grandpa do together?" They can read a book, listen to music, and play games.

Practice the Dialog

▸ Read through the dialog line by line.

▸ Have students:

- Repeat each line after you.

▸ Assign students one role of the dialog.

▸ Read the other role out loud.

▸ Have students:

- Choral read the other role of the dialog.

Variation:

▸ Divide the class in half.

▸ Assign one role to each half of students.

▸ Have students:

- Choral read each half of the dialog as a group.

▸ Check students' comprehension of the dialog by revisiting the questions from Read the Dialog.

What's It Like?

▸ Point to the picture of the living room on page 28 of the *Student Text*. Ask students "Are there a lot of things on the floor?" no Say "The floor is **clean**." Act out running your fingers over a surface and rubbing your fingers together as though they are clean as you make a face. Write the word **clean** on the board. Then, act out running your fingers over a surface and rubbing your fingers together as though they are dirty as you make a face. Write the word **dirty** on the board.

▸ Have students:

- Choral repeat the word.

▸ Introduce the adjectives **clean, dirty, young, old, tall,** and **short** by pointing to examples in the pictures or acting them out. Write each word on the board.

▸ Have students:

- Repeat each word.

▸ Ask yes/no and embedded questions to practice the vocabulary using items and people that are familiar to the students.

Example: Is Grandpa **old** or **young**? Is the chalkboard **clean** or **dirty**?

▶ Have students:

- Make sentences about the items and people used in the questions.
- Write their sentences on the board.

  Example: Grandpa is old. The chalkboard is dirty.

- Write their own sentences to describe people and items using the new adjectives.

Revisit the Dialog

▶ Direct students' attention to Application A on page 31 of the *Student Text*.

▶ Read the dialog on page 30 of the *Student Text* aloud for the students.

On Their Own

▶ Have students:

- Listen to the dialog to check the boxes in Application A.

▶ Go over the answers with the students.

Have students:

- Complete Application B on page 31 of the *Student Text*.
- Share their sentences with the class.

Your Turn

Pair/Share

▶ Have students:

- Ask each other if they can complete the activities listed in Application A on page 31 of the *Student Text*.
- Take turns asking and answering questions.

▶ Model an example for the students by asking "Can you play the piano?" and responding to the question with "Yes, I can play the piano." or "No, I can't play the piano."

▶ Have student volunteers:

- Share what things their partner can or can't do.

▶ Have students:

- Write their sentences on the line in Application B on page 31 of the *Student Text*.

Unit 2

KITCHEN

LESSON 2

Introduction: Oral Fluency

→ Students learn to talk about likes and dislikes and are reintroduced to the week's scenario. Then, students focus on one of the areas within the scenario.

Likes and Dislikes

Materials
Student Text
pp. 24–27, p. 32

▸ Begin the class by reviewing the activity words, **read a book, watch television, play the piano, play games,** and **sleep** from the **Living Room** lesson. Call out one activity.

▸ Have students:

  • Act out the activity.

▸ Write the activities on the board in one column. Point to **read a book** and say "I like to read a book at home." Draw a happy face next to the phrase on the board.

▸ Have students:

  • Choral repeat the sentence.

▸ Point to the word **sleep** and say "I don't like to sleep." Draw a sad face next to the word on the board.

▸ Have students:

  • Choral repeat the sentence.

▸ Write "I like _____." next to the happy face. Write "I don't like _____." next to the sad face. Point to each phrase and read it out loud.

▸ Have students:

  • Choral repeat the phrases.

▸ Prompt students to:

  • Tell you what they like and don't like by asking "Do you like _____?"

▸ Model an example for the students.

  Example: "Do you like to watch television?" Yes. I like to watch television. or No. I don't like to watch television.

▸ Repeat using other activity words and incorporate other words that students know, such as **Saturday, books, sports,** etc. that may come from other lessons.

Review: Home

▸ Direct students' attention to the picture on pages 24–25. Say "home." Have students:

  • Choral repeat the word.

▸ Point out the living room in the picture and elicit the word **living room** from the students.

- ▸ Direct students to the pictures on pages 26–27.
- ▸ Point out the kitchen in the picture and say "kitchen."
- ▸ Have students:
  - Say the word aloud.
  - Repeat the word as necessary for pronunciation.

Introduction to the Kitchen

- ▸ Direct students' attention to the picture of the kitchen on page 32.
- ▸ Elicit items that students know in English that are in the picture and ask them to share the words with the class.
- ▸ Have students:
  - Choral repeat the words.

STEP 1

Phonemic Awareness

Students practice identifying, differentiating, and producing the / t / sound.

The / t / Sound

- ▸ Write the words **Tuesday, television** and **plant** on the board and underline the *t* in each word.
- ▸ Have students:
  - Tell you what letter you have underlined in each word.

- ▸ Explain that the letter *t* in English makes the sound / t / and pronounce the / t / sound for the students. Point out to the students the position of the tongue against the front part of the roof of the mouth when making this sound.
- ▸ Have students:
  - Choral repeat the sound.
- ▸ Point to and say the word **Tuesday.**
- ▸ Have students:
  - Choral repeat the word with you.
- ▸ Repeat for the words **television** and **plant.**

Tap for / t /

- ▸ Repeat the / t / sound for the students.
- ▸ Have students:
  - Repeat the sound as they tap their feet.
  - Tap their feet when they hear the / t / sound.
  - Repeat each word.

▸ Use the following words:

Tuesday   **television**   **plant**   **remote control**   **teacher**

Example: Say the word **Tuesday**. Tap your foot at the initial / *t* / sound.

STEP 2

Everyday Words

Students learn and practice times of day and shapes for everyday conversation.

Recognize Everyday Words: Times of Day

Materials

Student Text
p. 32–33

Classroom items of different shapes

▸ Ask the students "What day is today?"

▸ Have students:

• Respond with the day of the week. (For example, Tuesday.)

▸ Draw picture of a sunrise, a sun high in the sky, a sunset, and a moon and stars in one column on the board.

▸ Say "It is Tuesday." "Is it **morning, afternoon, evening,** or **night**?" Point to each drawing as you say it.

▸ Have students:

• Respond with the correct time of day. It is morning. It is afternoon. etc.

▸ Say "It is Tuesday. It is morning. In the morning, we have class." Write the sentences next to the picture of the sunrise.

▸ Write "In the afternoon" next to the sun high in the sky.

▸ Have students:

• Say an activity that they do in the afternoon.

Example: In the afternoon, we eat lunch.

▸ Repeat for **evening** and **night**. Point out the use of **at** with **night**. Tell students that we say **at night** not **in the night.**

Information Share

▸ Write the question "When do you _____?" on the board.

▸ Divide the class into pairs.

Pair/Share

▸ Have students:

• Each write four activity words on a piece of paper. For example, listen to music, read, study, sleep.

• Ask their partner when they do each activity using the question prompt on the board.

• Tell their partner what time of day they do the activity their partner asked them about.

Example: One partner says When do you have English class? The other partner responds I have English class in the afternoon.

▸ Model an example with the students.

▸ To extend the activity, have students:

- Share the information they learned about their partners.

Recognize Everyday Words: Shapes

▸ Find objects around the classroom that are **round, square,** and **rectangular.**

▸ Hold up a round object and say "This is round."

▸ Have students:

- Repeat the word **round** after you.

▸ Repeat for **square** and **rectangular.**

▸ Hold up a round item and ask "Is it round or square?" round

▸ Repeat with other object of different shapes.

Practice: Shapes

▸ Hold up a **rectangular** item.

▸ Have students:

- Tell you what shape it is.

▸ Point to other objects around the room.

▸ Have students:

- Say the shape.
- Find other items in the room to point out to the class.
- Describe the shape by saying "It is _____."

▸ To extend the activity, have students:

- Name other items they have learned in previous lessons for the class to describe.

STEP 3

Vocabulary Development

 Students work with the core content vocabulary related to the kitchen and family for everyday conversation.

Introduce: Core Vocabulary

Materials
Student Text
pp. 32–33

▸ Anchor students' knowledge of family vocabulary.

▸ Have students:

- Provide family words from the previous day's lesson. (**mother, mom, grandfather, grandpa** and **dog**)

▸ Direct students' attention to the kitchen picture on page 32 of the *Student Text.* Point out the **father.** Say the word **father.**

► Have students:

  • Point to the **father** and repeat the word aloud.

► Repeat for **baby** and **cat**.

► Point to the **cat** in the picture.

► Have students:

  • Tell you what action the **cat** is doing. eat

► Point to the **baby** in the picture.

► Have students:

  • Tell you what action the **baby is** doing. drink

► Point to the **father** in the picture. Say "The father cooks for the family." Act out the verb cooking for the students to see. Write the verb **cook** on the board.

► Have the students:

  • Repeat the word **cook.**

► Introduce the verbs **wash, put,** and **walk** (the dog) by acting them out for the students and write each verb on the board.

► Have students:

  • Act out the activities and repeat the phrases aloud.

  • Copy the activity words in their notebooks.

► Point to each item that appears on the items list on page 33. As you point, say each word out loud.

► Have students:

  • Repeat each word.

Practice Vocabulary

What Do You Use It For

► Point to the **pot** in the picture. Say "I use a pot **to cook**."

► Have students:

  • Repeat the sentence.

► Repeat with the word **stove.**

► Write on the board:

I use _____ to cook.

► Have students:

  • Find other items that are used for cooking.

  • Share their responses.

  • Form a complete sentence by using the sentence frame on the board.

What Is It?

► Invite a student volunteer to:

  • Come to the front of the class.

  • Draw an item from the kitchen.

▸ Have students:

- Guess what the item is.

- Choral repeat the word when the word has been correctly guessed.

- Take turns choosing and drawing an item for the class to guess.

STEP

How English Works

 Students are introduced to the dialog. Students participate in the dialog. Students learn and practice **adjectives** and the use of an **infinitive** with the word **need**.

Introduce the Dialog

Picture Walk-Through

Materials

Student Text
pp. 34–35

Copies of
prepared chart

▸ Have students:

- Look at pictures on page 34 of the *Student Text*.

▸ Point to the picture in each panel and describe each picture. Act out or point to vocabulary words as necessary. Use the following sentences to guide you in the picture walk-through.

1. Panel 1: The family is in the kitchen.
2. Panel 2: The boy and the girl take care of the dog and the cat.
3. Panel 3: The brother and sister clean the house.
4. Panel 4: This is an old refrigerator. This is a new refrigerator.
5. Panel 5: It is time to eat.
6. Panel 6: The mother says goodbye.

Read the Dialog

▸ Read through the dialog in steps.

▸ Have students:

- Track print with you as you read.

- Listen for cognates, or English words that are similar in students' native language.

Mom:	I have to go away on business this week. I need you to help Dad while I am gone. I made a list.
Jessica:	What do we have to do?

▸ Explain to students that we often use the word **dad** for **father**.

▸ Have students:

- Choral repeat the words **dad** and **father**.

▸ Check students' comprehension by asking "Who is going away, Mom or Dad? Mom

> Mom: You and your brother need to walk the dog. You have to walk the dog in the morning and in the evening.
>
> Jessica: Okay. Jacob can put out food for the cat and dog in the afternoon.

▶ Check students' comprehension by asking "When do Jessica and Jacob have to walk the dog? in the morning and the evening

> Mom: Good. I want you and your brother to make your beds every day. And, you need to help Dad clean the house and wash the dishes. Can you do that?
>
> Jessica: Yes, Mom. What does Dad have to do?

▶ Check students' comprehension by asking "What do Jessica and Jacob have to do every day?" make the beds, clean house, wash dishes

> Mom: On Monday, your father has to buy a new refrigerator. The old refrigerator is broken.
>
> Jessica: Yes. It's not cold! It's hot!

▶ Check students' comprehension by asking "Is the refrigerator in the kitchen old?" yes

▶ Have students:

- Point to the old refrigerator in the picture.

> Mom: You can help Dad cook dinner. All of you have to help take care of the baby, too.
>
> Jessica: Okay, Mom. When are you coming home?

▶ Check students' comprehension by asking "Who will cook dinner, Dad or Grandpa?" Dad "Can Jessica help Dad?" yes

> Mom: I'm coming home on Friday night. I will miss you all!
>
> Jessica: We will miss you too!

▶ Check students' comprehension by asking "What day is Mom coming home?" Friday

Practice the Dialog

▶ Read through the dialog line by line.

▶ Have students:

- Repeat each line after you.

▶ Assign students one role of the dialog.

▶ Read the other role out loud.

▶ Have students:

- Choral read the other role of the dialog.

Variation:

‣ Divide the class in half.

‣ Assign one role to each half of students.

‣ Have students:

• Choral read each half of the dialog as a group.

‣ Check students' comprehension of the dialog by revisiting the questions from Read the Dialog.

Working with Adjectives

‣ Review previously learned adjectives such as **clean, dirty, old, young, short, tall, round, square,** and **rectangular** with the students by asking them yes/no and embedded questions about the picture on page 32 of the *Student Text.*

Example: Point to the picture of the baby and say "Is the baby young or old?" (young) Point to the picture of the table and say "Is the table clean?" (yes)

‣ Point to the picture of the old refrigerator and say "The refrigerator is old. It is broken." Act out breaking an object to demonstrate the meaning of the word **broken.**

‣ Have students:

• Repeat the word **broken.**

‣ Point to the new refrigerator in panel 4 on page 34 of the *Student Text.* and say "This refrigerator is **new**."

‣ Have students:

• Repeat the word **new.**

‣ Introduce the words **cold** and **hot** by acting out being cold and hot.

‣ Have students:

• Repeat the words **cold** and **hot.**

Practice Adjectives

‣ Direct students' attention to the Application on page 35 of the *Student Text.*

‣ Have students:

• Match the picture to adjectives that describe the item.

• Write a sentence to describe each item using the adjective chosen.

• Share their sentences with the class.

Infinitives with *Need*

‣ Teach students to use **need** with the infinitive form of the verbs for obligation.

‣ Direct students to panel 2 on page 34 of the *Student Text.*

‣ Say "Jessica and Jacob need to walk the dog."

‣ Write the sentence on the board. Circle the word **need** and underline the infinitive.

‣ Point to the picture of Jacob putting out food for the cat and dog and say "Jacob needs to put out food for the cat and dog."

‣ Circle the word **needs** and underline the infinitive. Point out the use of **needs** with the singular subject.

▸ Have students:

- Tell you other things that Jessica, Jacob, and Dad need to do.

▸ Write their responses on the board in complete sentences. Circle **need** or **needs** and underline the infinitive in each sentence.

Chore Share

Pair/Share

▸ Prepare a blank chart worksheet and hand out to the students.

	YES	NO

▸ Elicit six home activities from the students and write them on the board.

▸ Have students:

- Copy the activities in the left column on the chart.
- Tell their partner which activities they need to do at home.
- Mark **yes** or **no** in the column next to the activity according to their partners' statements.

  Example: One partner will say "I need to wash the dishes." The other partner will make a mark in the "yes" column next to the activity. If students do not need to do the activity mentioned, they may say who in their family needs to do it.

▸ Model an example with the students.

▸ When students have finished, have volunteers:

- Share the information they learned about their partner with the class.

Revisit the Dialog

▸ Direct students' attention again to the dialog on page 34 of the *Student Text*.

▸ Have students:

- Read the dialog out loud with a partner.

Your Turn

▸ Have students:

- Create a dialog for role play between Jessica and Jacob, in which the two are reminding each other what they need to do while their mom is away.
- Take turns playing the two roles.
- Use the structure **need** with the infinitive.

Example:

Jessica:	Jacob, you need to put out food for the dog and cat this afternoon.
Jacob:	I know. We need to walk the dog in the evening and the morning.

▸ Invite volunteers to:

- Perform their dialog in front of the class.

Introduction: Oral Fluency

 Students learn to use and differentiate *this* and *that* and are reintroduced to the week's scenario. Then, students focus on one of the areas within the scenario.

Demonstratives: *This* and *That*

Materials
Student Text pp. 24–25, 36
Various classroom items

Model

▸ Prepare the classroom by placing items that students know in English both near and far from you. For example, place a red book near you and blue book far from you.

▸ Hold up the red book. Point to it and say "**This** is a book. **This** book is red."

▸ Write the sentences on the board and repeat the sentences.

▸ Have students:

• Choral repeat the sentence.

▸ Point to the blue book and say "**That** is a book. **That** book is blue."

▸ Write the sentence on the board and repeat the sentence.

▸ Have students:

• Choral repeat the sentence.

▸ Underline **this** in the first two sentences.

▸ Point to the word **this.** Then point to red book again and say **this.**

▸ Have students:

• Choral repeat the word.

▸ Underline **that** in the second two sentences.

▸ Point to the word **that.** Then point to blue book again and say **that.**

▸ Have students:

• Choral repeat the word.

▸ Repeat with two other items in the room.

▸ Invite student volunteers to:

• Point out objects in the room to say what they are and describe them using **this** and **that.**

Review: Home

▸ Direct students' attention to the picture on pages 24–25. Say "home." Have students:

• Choral repeat the word.

▸ Point out the living room and elicit the words **living room** from the students.

- ▶ Point out the bedroom in the picture and say "bedroom."
- ▶ Have students:
  - • Say the word aloud.
  - • Repeat the word as necessary for pronunciation.

Introduction to the Bedroom

- ▶ Direct students' attention to the picture of the bedroom on page 36.
- ▶ Elicit items that students know in English that are in the picture and ask them to share the words with the class.
- ▶ Have students:
  - • Choral repeat the words.

STEP

1

Phonemic Awareness

Students practice identifying, differentiating, and producing the / k / sound.

The / k / Sound

- ▶ Direct students' attention to the picture of the living room on page 28.
- ▶ Write the words **couch** and **coffee table** on the board and underline the initial *c* in each word.
- ▶ Have students:
  - • Tell you what letter you have underlined in each word.

- ▶ Explain that the letter *c* in English often makes the sound / k / and pronounce the / k / sound for the students. Point out to the students the position of the back of the tongue against the roof of the mouth when making this sound.
- ▶ Have students:
  - • Choral repeat the sound.
- ▶ Point to and say the word **cabinet.**
- ▶ Have students:
  - • Choral repeat the word with you.
- ▶ Repeat for the word **couch.**
- ▶ Write the words **kitchen** and **clock** on the board and underline the letters that make the / k / sound in each word (*k* in kitchen and the *c* and *ck* in clock). Point out to students that these letters and letter combinations also often make the / k / sound.
- ▶ Repeat the routine for these words.

Clap for / k /

- ▶ Repeat the / k / sound for the students.
- ▶ Have students:
  - • Repeat the sound as they clap their hands.

- Clap their hands when they hear the / k / sound.
- Repeat each word.

▸ Use the following words:

cabinet   couch   kitchen   clock   curtain

Example: Say the word **cabinet**. Clap your hands at the initial / k / sound.

STEP 2

Everyday Words

➡ Students learn and practice ways to combine days and times of day for everyday conversation.

Recognize Everyday Words: Days and Times of Day

▸ Review the days of the week with the students. Ask them "What day is it today?"

▸ Have students:

- Tell you the day.
- Recite the rest of the days of the week starting from today.

▸ Ask students "Is it morning, afternoon, evening, or night?"

▸ Have students:

- Tell you the time of day.

▸ Write day of the week and the time of the day on the board next to each other in complete sentences.

Example: It is Wednesday. and **It is afternoon.**

Model

▸ Read the sentences aloud as you point to them. Then say "It is Wednesday afternoon." Write the sentence under the two sentences on the board and draw a line from the first two sentences to the new sentence.

▸ Have students:

- Choral repeat the new sentence.

▸ Model another example for the students with a different day of the week and time of day.

Day and Time Combinations

Pair/Share

▸ Divide the students into pairs.

▸ Have students:

- Choose one partner to write down three days of the week on a piece of paper.
- Choose one partner to write down the times of day on a piece of paper.
- Work with their partner to combine their lists and write three sentences using both the day of the week and time of day.

  Example: One partner wrote **Monday.** The other partner wrote **morning.** The pair will write the sentence: It is Monday morning.

▸ Have students:

- Share one sentence with the class.

STEP 3

Vocabulary Development

→ Students work with the core content vocabulary related to the bedroom and family for everyday conversation.

Introduce: Core Vocabulary

Materials
Student Text
pp. 36–37

▸ Anchor students' knowledge of family vocabulary by eliciting family words from previous lessons.

▸ Direct students' attention to the bedroom picture on page 36 of the *Student Text*. Point out the **sister.** Say the word **sister**.

▸ Have students:

- Point to the **sister** and repeat the word aloud.

▸ Repeat for **brother**.

▸ Ask students "Do you have a brother?" "Do you have a sister?"

▸ Have students:

- Respond by individually telling you how many brothers or sisters they have.

▸ Point to the sister in the picture and say **listen to music**. Act out listening to music. Repeat the phrase **listen to music** and write it on the board.

▸ Have students:

- Act out the activity **listen to music** and repeat the phrase aloud.

▸ Repeat for **draw**.

▸ Have students:

- Say activities that they might do in their bedroom.
- Act out the activity if they do not know the word.

▸ Then provide the students with the words in English.

▸ Introduce the words **sleep** and **set the alarm** by acting out the verbs and pointing to the **bed** and **alarm clock** on page 36.

▸ Have students:

- Act out the activities and repeat the words aloud.
- Copy the activity words in their notebooks.

▸ Point to each item that appears on the items list on page 37. As you point, say each word out loud.

▸ Have students:

- Repeat each word.

Practice Vocabulary

What I Do

▸ Act out sleeping and say "I sleep at night." Draw a picture of a moon and stars on the board.

▸ Have students:

- Repeat the sentence.

▸ Model the question "When do you study?"

▸ Model the answer "I study in the evening." Draw a picture of a sunset.

▸ Model the mini dialog with a student volunteer.

When do you _____?

I _____ in the/at _____.

▸ Have students:

- Work with a partner to create mini-dialogs to ask and answer when they do certain activities.

- Use the activities **listen to music, draw, study, set the alarm,** and **study.**

- Volunteer to perform one of their dialogs for the class.

What I Need

▸ Assign each pair one of the following activities: **listen to music, draw, study, set the alarm,** and **study.**

▸ Have students:

- Look at the picture and items list on pages 36–37.

- Choose the items in the bedroom that they need or would use to do these activities.

- Make a list of the items.

    Example: For **sleep,** students choose **bed, pillow, sheets,** and **blanket.**

▸ Have students:

- Share their activities and list with the class.

STEP 4

How English Works

Students are introduced to the dialog. Students participate in the dialog. Students learn and practice the use of infinitives for obligation.

Introduce the Dialog

Picture Walk-Through

Materials

Student Text
pp. 38–39

▸ Have students:

- Look at pictures on page 38 of the *Student Text*.

▶ Point to the picture in each panel and describe each picture. Act out or point to vocabulary words as necessary. Use the following sentences to guide you in the picture walk-through.

1. Panel 1: The girl is in her bedroom.
2. Panel 2: She has a laptop computer and a telephone.
3. Panel 3: The girl cleans her room.
4. Panel 4: The grandmother has clothes to wash.

Read the Dialog

▶ Read through the dialog in steps. Have students:

- Track print with you as you read.
- Listen for cognates, or English words that are similar in students' native language.

Jessica:	Hi, Mai. This is Jessica.
Mai:	Hi, Jessica. What are you doing?
Jessica:	Oh, I'm studying in my bedroom right now.

▶ Check students' comprehension by asking: "Is Jessica studying?" yes What is she using to help her study? her laptop computer

▶ Have students:

- Point to the laptop computer.

Mai:	Are you working on the science project?
Jessica:	Yes. I'm using my new laptop computer to find information.
Mai:	We have to work together on the project. Can we meet after school tomorrow afternoon?

▶ Check students' comprehension by asking, "Does Mai want to meet Jessica today or tomorrow?" tomorrow

▶ Have students:

- Tell you if it Mai wants to meet tomorrow in the morning, afternoon, or evening. afternoon

Jessica:	Well, my mother isn't here this week. I have to clean my room and put my clean clothes in the closet.
Mai:	What about tomorrow morning? We can meet before school.

▶ Check students' comprehension by asking "Can Jessica meet Mai tomorrow afternoon?" no "What does Jessica have to do tomorrow afternoon?" clean her room and put her clean clothes in the closet

▶ Have students:

- Tell you when Mai wants to meet tomorrow. in the morning

> Jessica: Well, my mom wants me to wash the sheets. Maybe my grandma can do that.
>
> Mai: Okay. You need to set your alarm clock. Don't forget! You always sleep late!
>
> Jessica: I won't forget. See you tomorrow!
>
> Mai: Bye! See you tomorrow!

▸ Check students' comprehension by asking "What does Jessica have to do?" set the alarm clock

▸ Point out the expression "See you tomorrow."

▸ Have students:

   • Repeat the expression.

Practice the Dialog

▸ Read through the dialog line by line.

▸ Have students:

   • Repeat each line after you.

▸ Assign students one role of the dialog.

▸ Read the other role out loud.

▸ Have students:

   • Choral read the other role of the dialog.

Variation:

▸ Divide the class in half.

▸ Assign one role to each half of students.

▸ Have students:

   • Choral read each half of the dialog as a group.

▸ Check students' comprehension of the dialog by revisiting the questions from Read the Dialog.

Infinitives for Obligation

▸ Direct students' attention to panel 3 on page 38 of the *Student Text*. Point to the picture of Jessica cleaning her bedroom.

▸ Ask students "What does Jessica need to do?" Jessica needs to clean her bedroom.

▸ Write the sentence "Jessica needs to clean her bedroom." Circle the word **needs** and underline the infinitive in the sentence. Say the sentence.

▸ Write an equal sign (=) next to the sentence. Then write and say "Jessica has to clean her bedroom." Circle the word **has** and underline the infinitive.

▸ Explain to students that the sentences are similar in meaning.

▸ Explain the use of **have** versus **has** by giving an example of what both Mai and Jessica have to do.

- ▸ Have students:
  - • Tell you other things that Jessica has to do.
- ▸ Write their responses on the board in complete sentences. Circle **have** or **has** and underline the infinitive in each sentence.
- ▸ Explain to students that we can also talk about things that are not necessary to do using **don't have** or **doesn't have** with the infinitive.
- ▸ Point to the sentence "Jessica has to clean her bedroom."
- ▸ Have students:
  - • Imagine that two days have passed and Jessica's bedroom is clean.
- ▸ Ask "Does Jessica have to clean her bedroom?" no
- ▸ Next to the sentence, write "Jessica doesn't have to clean her bedroom." Circle the words **doesn't have** and underline the infinitive in the sentence.
- ▸ Have students:
  - • Choral repeat both sentences.
  - • Transform the other sentences on the board to make them negative.
- ▸ Explain the use of **don't have** with plural subjects by giving an example of something Mai and Jessica do not have to do.

What I Have to Do

- ▸ Direct students' attention to Application B on p. 39 of the *Student Text*.
- ▸ Have students:

On Their Own

  - • Write sentences to tell what they have to do at home.
  - • Share what they do not have to do at home.
- ▸ Check answers.

Revisit the Dialog

- ▸ Direct students' attention to Application A on page 39 of the *Student Text*.
- ▸ Read the dialog aloud for the students.
- ▸ Have students:
  - • Listen to the dialog to circle *true* or *false* for the statements in Application A.
- ▸ Repeat the dialog a second time if necessary.
- ▸ Review the answers with the students.
- ▸ Have students:
  - • Explain why the statements are false by correcting the information in the false statement.
  - • Read the dialog out loud with a partner.

Pair/Share

Your Turn

▸ Have students:

- Create a dialog for role play between Jessica and Mai, in which Jessica calls Mai to suggest an alternative day of the week and time of day.

- Take turns playing the two roles. (The alternatives Jessica suggests are **Wednesday morning** or **afternoon**, or **Thursday morning**.)

Example:

Jessica:	Hi, Mai. We have to meet on a different day.
Mai:	Okay. When do you want to meet?
Jessica:	Can you meet on Wednesday morning?
Mai:	Okay. I can meet on Wednesday morning.

▸ Invite volunteers to:

- Perform their dialog in front of the class.

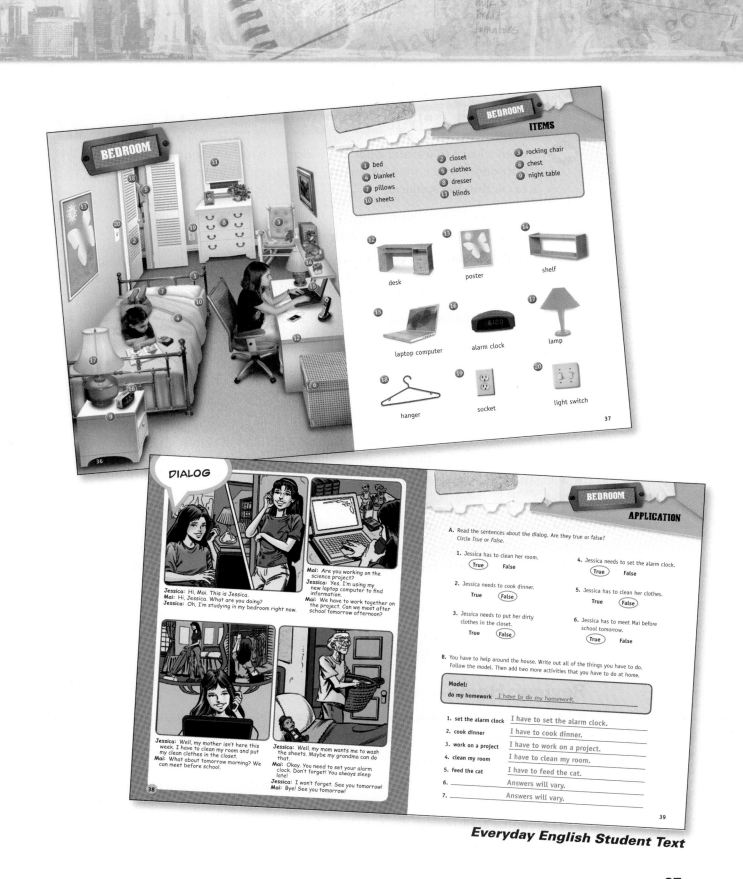

Everyday English Student Text

Introduction: Oral Fluency

 Students learn to use and *what* and *which* with *this* and *that* and are reintroduced to the week's scenario. Then, students focus on one of the areas within the scenario.

What and *Which* with *This* and *That*

Materials

Student Text p. 24–25, 40

Various vocabulary items

Model

▸ Gather items that students know the names of in English. Choose similar items that are either different shapes, sizes, or colors. For example, a clock that is round and a clock that is square.

▸ Review the use of *what* by holding up the round clock and asking "What is this?" It's a clock.

▸ Review the use of *which* by holding up both clocks and asking "Which clock is round?"

▸ Have students:

   • Point to the round clock.

▸ Then place the round clock far away from you. Point to the clock and ask "What is that?" Answer the question by saying "That is a clock."

▸ Write the following question and answer on the board.

▸ Have students:

   • Choral repeat the question and answer.

▸ Ask "Which clock is square, this clock or that clock?" Point to the nearby square clock as you say **this clock** and point to the far round clock as you say **that clock**. that clock

▸ Write the question and answer on the board.

▸ Have students:

   • Choral repeat the question and answer.

Review: Home

▸ Direct students' attention to the picture on pages 24–25. Say "home."

▸ Have students:

   • Choral repeat the word.

▸ Point out the living room, kitchen, and bedroom in the picture and elicit these words from the students.

▸ Point out the bathroom in the picture and say "bathroom."

▸ Have students:

  • Say the word aloud.

  • Repeat the word as necessary for pronunciation.

Introduction to the Bathroom

▸ Direct students' attention to the picture of the bathroom on page 40.

▸ Elicit items that students know in English that are in the picture and ask them to share the words with the class.

▸ Have students:

  • Choral repeat the words.

STEP 1

Phonemic Awareness

Students practice identifying, differentiating, and producing the / *m* / sound.

The / *m* / Sound

▸ Write the words **Monday, mother,** and **microwave** on the board and underline the *m* in each word.

▸ Have students:

  • Tell you what letter you have underlined in each word.

▸ Explain that the letter *m* in English makes the sound / *m* / and pronounce the / *m* / sound for the students. Point out to the students the position of the lips pressed against each other when making this sound.

▸ Have students:

  • Choral repeat the sound.

▸ Point to and say the word **Monday.**

▸ Have students:

  • Choral repeat the word with you.

▸ Repeat for the words **mother** and **microwave.**

Make Up a Movement for / *m* /

▸ Repeat the / *m* / sound for the students.

▸ Have students:

  • Repeat the sound as they make up a movement for the sound.

  • Make their movement when they hear the / *m* / sound.

  • Repeat each word.

▸ Use the following words:

Monday   **mother**   **microwave**   **map**   **marker**

STEP

2 Everyday Words

 Students learn and practice shape sizes for everyday conversation.

Recognize Everyday Words: Sizes

Materials

Various objects of different sizes

▸ Gather objects of different sizes, big and small. Use objects that students know in English. If possible, use two similar items that are different sizes. There should be at least one item per student.

▸ Hold up a small item. For example, a cup. Say "This cup is small."

▸ Have students:

  • Choral repeat the sentence.

▸ Hold up the big item. Say "This is big."

▸ Have students:

  • Choral repeat the sentence.

▸ Write the words **small** and **big** on the board. Point to and say each word.

▸ Have students:

  • Choral repeat both words.

▸ Hold up another small item and ask "Is it big?" no "Is it small?" yes

▸ Hold up another big item and ask "Is it big or small?" It's big.

▸ Hold up other items and ask similar yes/no and embedded questions.

Everyday Words Sorting: Shapes

▸ Distribute the items evenly among the students.

▸ Draw a line down the board to separate it in half. Write the word **small** at the top of one half and **big** in the other half.

▸ Have students:

  • Come to the board with their item.

  • Stand under the words **small** or **big** according to the size of their item.

  • Hold up their item and describe their item. This _____ is _____.

  • Say that they agree or disagree with how their classmates sorted each item.

STEP 3

Vocabulary Development

 Students work with the core content vocabulary related to the bathroom and family for everyday conversation.

Introduce: Core Vocabulary

Materials
Student Text
pp. 40–41

▸ Anchor students' knowledge of family vocabulary by eliciting family words from previous lessons.

▸ Direct students' attention to the bathroom picture on page 40 of the *Student Text*. Point out the **grandmother**. Say the word **grandmother**. Have students:

- Point to the **grandmother** and repeat the word aloud.

▸ Point to the grandmother in the picture and say **comb**. Act out combing your hair. Repeat the word and write it on the board.

▸ Have students:

- Act out brushing their hair and repeat the word **comb** aloud.

▸ Repeat for **dry**.

▸ Point out the **sink**, the **shower**, and the **bathtub**.

▸ Introduce the phrases **brush teeth, wash face, take a bath,** and **take a shower** by acting out the activities.

▸ Have students:

- Act out the activities and repeat the phrases aloud.
- Copy the activity words in their notebooks.

▸ Point to each item that appears on the items list on page 41. As you point, say each word out loud.

▸ Have students:

- Repeat each word.

Practice Vocabulary

Items Search

▸ Act out brushing your teeth. Say "I brush my teeth in the morning."

▸ Have students:

- Repeat the sentence.

▸ Ask students "What do I need to brush my teeth?"

▸ Model the answer "I need the sink, a toothbrush, toothpaste, and a towel to brush my teeth" Point to each item in the picture as you say it.

▸ Act out how you use each item mentioned as you repeat the sentence.

▸ Write the sentence on the board.

Example: For sink, act out turning on the sink. For toothbrush and toothpaste, act out picking up a toothbrush and squeezing out toothpaste to it. Then act out brushing your teeth. For towel, act out wiping your mouth.

- Divide the class into pairs.
- Assign each pair one of the bathroom activities (**dry hair, brush teeth, wash face, take a bath,** and **take a shower**).

Pair/Share

- Have students:
  - Choose the items they will need to do their activity.
  - Write a sentence. I need _____ to _____.
  - Act out how they will use each item to do the activity.
- Invite student volunteers to share their activities. One partner will read the sentence as the other acts out how the items are used.

STEP 4

How English Works

Students are introduced to the dialog. Students participate in the dialog. Students learn and practice the the position of **adjectives**.

Introduce the Dialog

Picture Walk-Through

Materials
Student Text
pp. 42–43

- Have students:
  - Look at pictures on page 42 of the *Student Text*.
- Point to the picture in each panel and describe each picture. Act out or point to vocabulary words as necessary. Use the following sentences to guide you in the picture walk-through.
  1. Panel 1: The grandmother and the boy are in the bathroom.
  2. Panel 2: The boy is in the bathtub.
  3. Panel 3: The boy's face is dirty.

Read the Dialog

- Read through the dialog in steps. Have students:
  - Track print with you as you read.
  - Listen for cognates, or English words that are similar in students' native language.

Grandma Nora:	Jacob, it's time to take a bath.
Jacob:	Is the water cold?
Grandma:	No. It's not cold.
Jacob:	Is the water hot?
Grandma:	No. It's not hot. It's warm.

- Explain to students that we often use the word **grandma** for **grandmother**.
- Have students:
  - Choral repeat the words **grandma** and **grandmother**.

▸ Check students' comprehension by asking "Is the water hot?" no "Is the water cold?" no

▸ Explain that **warm** means not hot and not cold.

Jacob:	Okay, Grandma. Can I play with my boat in the bathtub?
Grandma Nora:	Which boat do you want, the big boat or the small boat?
Jacob:	I want to play with the big boat.

▸ Say the word **boat** and point to the boats in the picture.

▸ Have students:

  • Repeat the words and point to the boats.

▸ Check students' comprehension by asking "Which boat does Jacob want, the big boat or the small boat?" the big boat

▸ Have students:

  • Point to the big boat in the picture.

Grandma Nora:	You can play with the big boat, but I want to wash your face. It's dirty. Give me the soap, please.
Jacob:	It's not dirty! It's clean!
Grandma Nora:	Okay. We're done. It's time to get out of the bathtub. Here's a towel.
Jacob:	Can you dry my hair with the hairdryer?
Grandma Nora:	Of course!

▸ Check students' comprehension by asking "What does Grandma want?" the soap

▸ Have students:

  • Point to the soap in the picture.

  • Predict what items Jacob and Grandma will need next. a towel, the hairdryer, a robe, a comb

Practice the Dialog

▸ Read through the dialog line by line.

▸ Have students:

  • Repeat each line after you.

▸ Assign students one role of the dialog.

▸ Read the other role out loud.

▸ Have students:

  • Choral read the other role of the dialog.

Variation:

▸ Divide the class in half.

▸ Assign one role to each half of students.

▶ Have students:

- Choral read each half of the dialog as a group.

▶ Check students' comprehension of the dialog by revisiting the questions from Read the Dialog.

Describing with Adjectives

On Their Own

▶ Direct students to page 43 of the *Student Text*.

▶ Have students:

- Complete the chart in Application A with items from pages 40–41 of the *Student Text*.

- Share some of their responses with the class.

- Complete Application B by writing sentences using their completed charts from Application A.

▶ Check answers.

Position of Adjectives

▶ Write the words **hot, cold, warm, big, small, dirty,** and **clean** on the board.

▶ Point to the picture in panel 1 of the dialog and ask "Is the water hot, cold, or warm?" The water is warm.

▶ Write on the board:

The water is warm.

▶ Say the sentence aloud.

▶ Ask students "What is warm?" the water

▶ Circle the word **water** and underline the word **warm.**

▶ Point to the water in panel 1 of the dialog and ask "What is this?" Answer the question by saying "It is warm water."

▶ Write the sentence on the board under the first sentence.

▶ Circle the word **water** and underline the word **warm.**

▶ Point out the changed positions of the words.

▶ Model another example with the students.

Example: "The boat is big." It is a big boat.

Transform Sentences

▶ Direct students to the sentences they wrote in Application B on page 43 of the *Student Text*.

▶ Have students:

- Transform each sentence by using your model and starting each sentence with It is _____.

▶ Check answers.

Revisit the Dialog

▸ Direct students' attention again to the dialog on page 42 of the *Student Text*

▸ Have students:

- Read the dialog out loud with a partner.

Your Turn

▸ Have students:

- Create a dialog between Grandma and Jacob after Jacob gets out of the bath in which Grandma asks Jacob: what size towel he wants, and if he wants the hairdryer to be hot, cold, or warm.

- Take turns playing the two roles.

Example:

Grandma:	Do you want a big towel or a small towel?
Jacob:	I want a big towel.

▸ Invite volunteers to:

- Perform their dialog in front of the class.

BATHROOM

BATHROOM
ITEMS

1. bathtub
2. shower
3. toilet
4. robe
5. towel
6. mirror
7. medicine
8. shampoo
9. hamper
10. medicine cabinet
11. scale

12. tissue
13. toilet paper
14. soap
15. toothbrush
16. toothpaste
17. razor
18. comb
19. brush
20. hairdryer

41

DIALOG

Grandma Nora: Jacob, it's time to take a bath.
Jacob: Is the water cold?
Grandma: No. It's not cold.
Jacob: Is the water hot?
Grandma: No. It's not hot. It's warm.

Jacob: Okay, Grandma. Can I play with my boat in the bathtub?
Grandma Nora: Which boat do you want, the big boat or the small boat?
Jacob: I want to play with the big boat.

Grandma Nora: You can play with the big boat, but I want to wash your face. It's dirty. Give me the soap, please.
Jacob: It's not dirty! It's clean!
Grandma Nora: Okay. We're done. It's time to get out of the bathtub. Here's a towel.
Jacob: Can you dry my hair with the hairdryer?
Grandma Nora: Of course!

42

BATHROOM
APPLICATION

A. Use information from the pictures on pages 40 and 41 and the dialog from page 42. Write words that fit each category. Answers will vary.

clean	small	wet	big

B. Write sentences with the following sentence frames for each of the objects in your chart. Answers will vary.

The _____ is _____

1. _____

2. _____

3. _____

4. _____

43

Everyday English Student Text

Introduction: Oral Fluency

 Students review the uses of *what* and *which, this* and *that,* and how to talk about likes and dislikes. Students revisit the Unit Overview.

Question Words, Demonstratives, and Likes and Dislikes

Materials
Student Text pp. 24–25

Various objects or pictures of object of different shapes, sizes, and colors

‣ Gather objects that the students know in English that are of different shapes, sizes and colors, for example, a big book and a small book. Place the items either near you or far from you and the students.

‣ Hold up the small book and ask "What is this?" a book

‣ Point to the big book that you have placed far away and ask "What is that?" a book.

‣ Point to both books and ask "Which book is big?" That book is big.

‣ Point to both books and ask "Which book do you like?" I like this / that book..

‣ Repeat with other objects that you have prepared. Vary the questions by asking about the shape or color of the objects.

Unit Review: Home

‣ Direct students' attention to the pictures on pages 26–27. Say "home." Have students:

 • Choral repeat the word.

‣ Point out the living room in the picture. Elicit the word **living room** from the students.

‣ Repeat for **kitchen, bedroom,** and **bathroom.**

STEP 1

Phonemic Awareness

 Students practice identifying, differentiating, and producing the / w /, / s /, / t /, / c /, and / m / sounds.

Review of the / w /, / s /, / t /, / c /, and / m / sounds.

Materials
Prepared cards

‣ Write the words **wash, soap, table, couch** and **mirror** on the board and say each word.

‣ Have students:

 • Repeat each word with you.

Model

- Underline the *w* in **wash**, the *s* in **soap**, the *t* in **table**, the *c* in **couch**, and the *m* in **mirror**.
- Have students:
  - Identify each letter that you underlined.
  - Pronounce each sound that the letter makes in each word.
- Review the gestures for each sound with the students as practiced throughout the week. Wave your hands when you make the / *w* / sound. Make an S like a snake with your hand when you make the / *s* / sound. Tap your foot when you make the / *t* / sound, and clap your hand when you make the / *k* / sound and make your individual movement that you made up the day before when you make the / *m* / sound.
- Say each word with the students.
- Have the students:
  - Make the gesture associated with each sound in the word.

A Symphony of Sounds

- Prepare cards for the students with words from the week's lesson that include the week's sounds. Prepare enough cards so that each student has at least five cards.
- Write one word or phrase for each card and underline the sounds that you want the students to focus on.

  Example: Write **coffee maker** on one card. Underline the *c*, the *m*, and the *k*.
- Divide the students into pairs.
- Shuffle the cards and give each student five prepared cards.

Pair/Share

- Have students:
  - Read their cards to their partners, one by one.
  - Make the correct gesture to their partner when they hear one of the five sounds in the words.
- Model an example for the students.
- Have student volunteers:
  - Demonstrate their words for the class.

STEP 2

Everyday Words

Students review and practice days of the week, times of day, and shapes and sizes for everyday conversation.

Review Everyday Words: Days of the Week and Times of Day

Materials

Student Text p. 28, 32, 36, and 40

Objects of different shapes and sizes

Copies of prepared chart

▸ Prepare a table with eight columns and five rows as shown and hand out to the students:

	Sunday		Tuesday				Saturday
morning							
evening							

On Their Own

▸ Have students:

  • Complete the missing days of the week and times of day in the chart.

▸ Check answers.

My Week

▸ Have students

  • Name activities that they do during the day that were learned from the unit or from the previous week's lesson.

▸ Write their responses on the board.

▸ Have students:

  • Choose five activities to write into their charts.

  • Write a sentence for each activity to say what day and time of day they have to do that activity. Have them start the sentences with I have to _____.

▸ Model an example for the students.

  Example: The chart is filled in with **play piano** in the Sunday morning box. Write the following sentence on the board: I have to play piano on Sunday morning.

Recognize Everyday Words: Shapes and Sizes

▸ Gather objects of different shapes and sizes. If possible, find some objects that are similar in either shape, but differ in size or vice versa. For example, a small ball and a big ball.

▸ Hold up a small round object and ask students "Is it round?" yes "Is it big or small?" It's small.

▸ Repeat with other objects of different shapes and sizes to practice **square, rectangular, big,** and **small.**

Everyday Words Seek and Find: Shapes and Sizes

Pair/Share

▸ Divide the class into pairs.

▸ Have students:

- Individually choose one scenario picture from pages 28, 32, 36, and 40 of the *Student Text* and choose three items that are either **round, square,** or **rectangular** to describe to their partner.
- Tell their partner what room the item is in and to describe the shape, and the size.
- Give more detail if they can.
- Guess the item that their partner has described.

▸ Model an example for the students.

Example: Describe the table in the kitchen on page 32 of the *Student Text*. Say "It is in the kitchen. It is round. It is big." More advanced students may add more information such as "It is brown. I sit here when I eat. I put my plate here."

▸ Invite volunteers to:

- Describe an item for the class to guess.

STEP 3

Vocabulary Development

Students work with the core content vocabulary related to the home and family for everyday conversation.

Review: Core Vocabulary

Materials
Student Text
p. 45

▸ Direct students to Application A on page 45 of the *Student Text.*

▸ Have students:

- Draw a room in their house.
- Label the items in the room.
- Share their pictures with a partner and point out the items in the room.
- Volunteer to present their pictures to the class.

Practice Vocabulary

Family Talk

▸ Review the names of family members learned during the week.

▸ Write the words on the board.

▸ Have students:

- Write the names of their family members on a piece of paper.
- Write the family word next to each person's name.
- Tell a partner about the members of their family.
- Volunteer to tell the class about the members of their family.

How English Works

 Students are introduced to the dialog. Students participate in the dialog. Students review and practice **infinitives** and **adjectives.**

Introduce the Dialog

Picture Walk-Through

Materials

Student Text
p. 44

▸ Have students:

   • Look at pictures on page 44 of the *Student Text*.

▸ Point to the picture in each panel and describe each picture. Act out or point to vocabulary words as necessary. Use the following sentences to guide you in the picture walk-through.

   1. Panel 1: The mother comes home.
   2. Panel 2: The brother and sister want to talk to the mother.
   3. Panel 3: The brother tells the mother about the refrigerator.
   4. Panel 4: The boy talks about taking a bath.

Read the Dialog

▸ Read through the dialog in steps. Have students:

   • Track print with you as you read.

   • Listen for cognates, or English words that are similar in students' native language.

Mom:	Hi, everybody! I'm home!
Jessica:	Hi, Mom! We missed you!

▸ Check students' comprehension by asking "Where is Mom now?" at home

Mom:	Tell me about your week. What did you do?
Jacob:	We made our beds every day!
Jessica:	You didn't make your bed on Wednesday. Grandma made your bed.
Jacob:	You didn't walk the dog on Tuesday afternoon. I walked the dog with Dad.
Jessica:	I had to meet Mai to work on the science project!

▸ Check students' comprehension by asking "Did Jessica make the bed?" yes

"What did Jessica do on Tuesday afternoon?" She met Mai to work on the science project.

> Mom: It's okay. Did Dad buy a new refrigerator?
>
> Jacob: Yes! He bought a big, new refrigerator. It's cold now, not hot!
>
> Mom: Did you help your Dad?
>
> Jessica: Yes. We helped cook dinner and we washed the dishes every evening. Well, we put the dishes in the dishwasher.

▸ Check students' comprehension by asking the students to describe the new refrigerator. It's new, big, and cold.

▸ Have students:

  • Point to the new refrigerator.

> Jacob: And I took a bath every night! Grandma dried my hair with the hairdryer, too.
>
> Mom: Great! Thank you, kids. I am happy to be home.

Check students' comprehension by asking "What activity did Jacob do at night?" take a bath

Practice the Dialog

▸ Read through the dialog line by line.

▸ Have students:

  • Repeat each line after you.

▸ Assign students one role of the dialog.

▸ Read the other role out loud.

▸ Have students:

  • Choral read the other role of the dialog.

Variation:

▸ Divide the class in half.

▸ Assign one role to each half of students.

▸ Have students:

  • Choral read each half of the dialog as a group.

▸ Check students' comprehension of the dialog by revisiting the questions from Read the Dialog.

Describe Your Room

▸ Review the week's adjectives with the students by writing them on the board and acting out or pointing to examples that illustrate each adjective.

▸ Draw students' attention to the completed Application A on page 45 of the *Student Text*.

▸ Have students:

  • Choose five items to describe.

  • Write two sentences for each item using adjectives.

• Share their descriptions with a partner.

▸ Invite volunteers to share their pictures and descriptions with the class.

Revisit the Dialog

Pair/Share

▸ Direct students' attention again to the dialog on page 44 of the *Student Text*.

▸ Have students:

• Read the dialog out loud with a partner.

• Practice intonation and natural conversational tone.

▸ Ask one pair of students to:

• Volunteer to perform the dialog in front of the class.

Your Turn

▸ Direct students' attention to Application B on page 45 of the *Student Text*.

▸ Have students:

• Work with a partner to fill in the chart.

• Ask their partners what activities they do at home.

• Respond to their partners' questions.

▸ Invite volunteers to:

• Share the information they learned about their partners with the class.

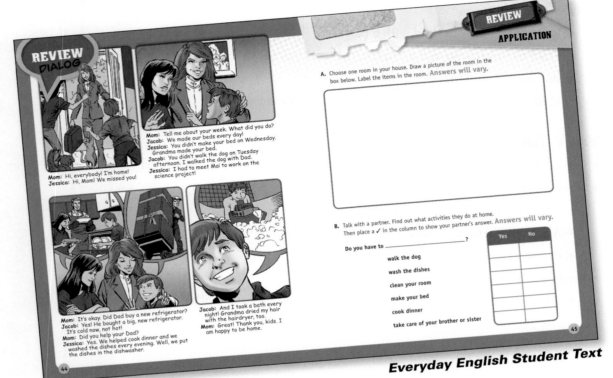

Mom: Hi, everybody! I'm home!
Jessica: Hi, Mom! We missed you!

Mom: Tell me about your week. What did you do?
Jacob: We made our beds every day!
Jessica: You didn't make your bed on Wednesday. Grandma made your bed.
Jacob: You didn't walk the dog on Tuesday afternoon. I walked the dog with Dad.
Jessica: I had to meet Mai to work on the science project!

Mom: It's okay. Did Dad buy a new refrigerator?
Jacob: Yes! He bought a big, new refrigerator. It's cold now, not hot!
Mom: Did you help your Dad?
Jessica: Yes. We helped cook dinner and we washed the dishes every evening. Well, we put the dishes in the dishwasher.

Jacob: And I took a bath every night! Grandma dried my hair with the hairdryer, too.
Mom: Great! Thank you, kids. I am happy to be home.

44

A. Choose one room in your house. Draw a picture of the room in the box below. Label the items in the room. Answers will vary.

B. Talk with a partner. Find out what activities they do at home. Then place a ✓ in the column to show your partner's answer. Answers will vary.

Do you have to _____?

	Yes	No
walk the dog		
wash the dishes		
clean your room		
make your bed		
cook dinner		
take care of your brother or sister		

45

Everyday English Student Text

NEIGHBORHOOD

Unit 3

Everyday English Student Text

THE STREET

firefighter

POST OFFICE

mail carrier

police officer

PARK

park maintenance worker

48

DOCTORS OFFICE

waiting room

receptionist

examination room

LIBRARY

KID'S CORNER

RESTROOMS

PERIODICALS

librarian

REFERENCE

INFORMATION

CHECKOUT

BOOK RETURN

49

Everyday English Student Text

Introduction: Oral Fluency

 Students learn to use and differentiate *who* and *how* and are introduced to the week's scenario. Then, students focus on one of the areas within the scenario.

Question Words: *Who* and *How*

Materials

Student Text
pp. 46–49

▸ Start class by greeting students.

▸ Approach one student, point to yourself and say "My name is (name). I am (name)." Point to the student and say "What's your name? Who are you?"

▸ Prompt student to:

• Answer the question with the sentence frame I am (name).

▸ Say "My name is (name). I am the teacher. Who are you?" Write "Who are you?" on the board and read it aloud. Underline the word **who**. Say "You are students."

▸ Have students:

• Repeat the word **who** and answer "We are students."

▸ Point to an individual student and ask "Who are you?" Prompt the student to:

• Say "I am a student."

• Ask another student "Who are you?"

• Repeat until all students have had the opportunity to ask and answer the question.

▸ Ask the class "How are you?" Write "How are you?" on the board and read it aloud. Underline the word **how**. Then, smile and say "I am fine. I am happy."

▸ Have students:

• Chorally and individually repeat the phrases.

▸ Frown and say "I am sad."

▸ Have students:

• Chorally and individually repeat the phrase.

▸ Ask one student "How are you?" and have him or her:

• Respond with how he or she feels and ask another student "How are you?"

▸ Repeat until all students have had a chance to answer and ask another student.

Unit Overview: Neighborhood

▸ Direct students' attention to the picture on pages 46–47. Say "neighborhood."

▸ Have students:

- Chorally and individually repeat the word.

- Identify any parts of the neighborhood they may know in English by sharing the words with the class.

▸ Point to the **street.** Say "street."

▸ Have students:

- Point to the street and chorally and individually repeat the word.

▸ Direct students' attention to pages 48–49. Ask students "Where is the street?"

▸ Have students:

- Point to the street picture and repeat the word **street**.

▸ Repeat for **park, doctor's office,** and **library**.

Introduction to the Street

▸ Direct students' attention to the picture of the street on page 48.

▸ Elicit words that students know in English that are in the picture and share them with the class.

▸ Point out the words and pictures of the **mail carrier,** the **police officer,** and the **firefighter**.

▸ Have students:

- Chorally and individually repeat the words.

STEP
1

Phonemic Awareness

 Students practice identifying, differentiating, and producing the / *b* / and / *p* / sounds.

The / *b* / Sound

▸ Write and draw words **bicycle, bus,** and **book** on the board and underline the *b* in each word.

▸ Have students:

- Tell you what letter you have underlined in each word.

Model

▸ Explain that the letter *b* in English makes the sound / *b* / and pronounce the / *b* / sound for the students. Show them how to form the b sound by putting your lips together and releasing the puff of air while you say the / *b* / sound.

▸ Have students:

- Chorally and individually repeat the sound.

▸ Point to your picture of the **bicycle** and say "bicycle."

▸ Have students:

- Chorally and individually repeat the word with you.

▸ Repeat for the words **bus** and **book**.

Box Your Buddy for / *b* /

▸ Repeat the / *b* / sound for the students. Punch the air very lightly with your hands as if you are boxing. Say "**Box your buddy!**" Explain that **buddy** is another word for **friend** in English.

▸ Have students:

- Repeat "box your buddy" as they make the motion.
- Turn to a partner and make the boxing motion when they hear the sound.

▸ Write the following tongue twister on the board and say it aloud as you make the boxing motion. Clarify the meaning of the tongue twister by drawing or acting out the words. Bobby buys big books.

▸ Have students:

- Choral repeat the tongue twister and turn to a partner and make the boxing motion when they hear the sound.

The / *p* / Sound

▸ Write the words **police, park,** and **post office** on the board and underline the *p* in each word.

▸ Have students:

- Tell you what letter you have underlined in each word.

▸ Explain that the letter *p* in English often makes the sound / *p* / and pronounce the / *p* / sound for the students. Point out that the position of your mouth to make / *p* / sound is the same for the / *b* / sound, except you don't make a sound with your voice. Tell students that this sound is made by pushing air through their lips.

▸ Have students:

- Hold their hand up to their lips to feel the puff of air that comes out of their mouth while pronouncing the / *p* / sound.
- Choral repeat the / *p* / sound.
- Compare the / *b* / and / *p* / sound by putting their hands on their throat to feel their vocal chords vibrate when pronouncing the / b /. When they pronounce the / p / they should not feel their vocal chords vibrate.

▸ Point to the picture of the police department on page 48 of the *Student Text.* Point to the word **police** and say "police."

▸ Have students:

- Chorally and individually repeat the word.

▸ Repeat for the words **park** and **post office**.

Point your Pinky for / *p* /

▸ Repeat the / *p* / sound for the students. Hold up your pinky finger and say "pinky." Point with your pinky to the class. Say "**Point your pinky!**"

▸ Have students:

- Choral repeat "point your pinky" as they make the motion.

▸ Write the following tongue twister on the board and say it aloud as you point your pinky. Clarify the meaning of the tongue twister by drawing or acting out the words. Paula paints pretty pictures.

▸ Have students:

- Choral repeat the tongue twister and point their pinky when they hear the / *p* / sound.

Practice the Sounds

▸ Point to the / *b* / sound tongue twister. Say "Box your buddy!" and do the boxing motion.

▸ Prompt students to:

- Turn to another student, and say the tongue twister out loud while doing the boxing motion.

▸ Repeat with the / *p* / sound.

STEP 2 — Everyday Words

Students learn and practice the seasons and weather for everyday conversation.

Recognize Everyday Words: Seasons

Materials
Calendar photos to represent the seasons

▸ Bring pictures of typical scenes from each season. These can be found in many calendars. Draw a chart on the board like the one below. Write the names of the seasons in the boxes.

winter	spring
summer	fall

▸ Show the picture for winter. Point to and say the word "winter."

▸ Have students:

- Copy the chart on a piece of paper and write the words in each square.
- Chorally and individually repeat the season.

▸ Repeat for **spring, summer,** and **fall**.

Recognize Everyday Words: Weather

▸ Direct students' attention to your seasons chart on the board. Make a shivering motion. Draw a picture of a snowman and snowflakes in the winter square of the chart. Point to the **winter** square and say "In the winter, it is cold. It's snowing."

▶ Have students:

  • Chorally and individually repeat the sentences.

▶ Draw an umbrella and raindrops in the spring square of the chart. Act out opening an umbrella and holding it above your head. Point to the **spring** square and say "In the spring, it is warm. It's raining."

▶ Have students:

  • Chorally and individually repeat the sentences.

▶ Draw a hot summer sun and a glass of lemonade in the summer square of the chart. Act out fanning yourself in the heat. Point to the **summer** square and say "In the summer, it is hot."

▶ Have students:

  • Chorally and individually repeat the sentence.

▶ Draw a tree losing its leaves in the fall square of the chart. Act out shielding yourself and walking against the wind. Say "In the fall, it is cool. It's windy."

▶ Have students:

  • Chorally and individually repeat the sentences.

How's the Weather?

▶ Hold up one of the seasons photos that you brought to class for students to see. Ask "What season is it? "How's the weather?"

▶ Have students:

  • Identify the season and describe the weather that occurs typically in that season.

▶ Repeat with the remaining photos.

STEP 3

Vocabulary Development

Students work with the core content vocabulary related to the street for everyday conversation.

Introduce: Core Vocabulary

Materials
Student Text
pp. 50–51

▶ Direct students' attention to the street picture on pages 50–51 of the *Student Text.* Point out the civil servants: **mail carrier**, **firefighter**, and **police officer**. Tell students these people are all important people in our neighborhood.

▶ Point to the **mail carrier**. Say "mail carrier."

▶ Have students:

  • Chorally and individually repeat the words.

▶ Say "The mail carrier brings us letters and packages that people send us." Draw pictures and act out as necessary to help students understand the concept.

▶ Repeat with the words **firefighter** and **police officer**.

▶ For **firefighter**, say "The firefighter puts out fires in our neighborhood."

▶ For **police officer**, say "The police officer protects our neighborhood."

- Explain that the mail carrier, the firefighter, and the police officer all help the neighborhood.
- Point to each item that appears on the items list on pages 50–51. As you point, say each word out loud.
- Have students:
  - Choral repeat each word.

Practice Vocabulary

Person, Place or Thing

- Draw a three column chart like the one below on the board.

Person	Place	Thing

Pair/Share

- Have students:
  - Copy the chart in their notebooks.
  - Work with a partner to categorize all of the items on pages 50–51 into their proper categories.
- Check answers by having students identify the items with the sentence frames:

  A(n) _____ is a person.   A(n) _____ is a place.   A(n) _____ is a thing.

  Example: A restaurant is a place.

STEP 4

How English Works

Students are introduced to the dialog. Students participate in the dialog. Students learn and practice **pronouns**.

Introduce the Dialog

Picture Walk-Through

Materials
Student Text
pp. 52–53

- Have students:
  - Look at pictures on page 53 of the *Student Text*.
- Ask students simple questions about the pictures to predict the main idea of the dialog.
- Point to the picture in each panel. Act out or point to vocabulary words as necessary. Ask:
  1. Panel 1: Who is talking? a boy and the mail carrier
  2. Panel 2: What does the mail carrier give the boy? letters
  3. Panel 3: Where are the boy and the mail carrier? on the corner
  4. Panel 4: What does the boy show the mail carrier? his bicycle

5. Panel 5: Does the go with the mail carrier? no

▸ Record student responses on the board.

Read the Dialog

▸ Read through the dialog in steps. Have students:

- Track print with you as you read.
- Listen for cognates, or English words that are similar in students' native language.

Trang:	Hi, Mr. Curtiss!
Mr. Curtiss:	Well, good morning, Trang! Today must be a special day.
Trang:	Today is my birthday! How did you know?

▸ Point to the mail carrier in the picture. To check comprehension, ask students "Who is Mr. Curtiss?" the mail carrier

▸ Ask students "Why is the day special for Trang?" It is Trang's birthday.

▸ Explain that **birthday** is the day that you are born.

Mr. Curtiss:	Well, I have several letters for you. They must be birthday cards. How old are you today?
Trang:	I'm twelve. I feel very happy today. Are all of these cards for me?

▸ Check students' comprehension by asking "How does Trang feel today?" happy Ask "How do you know Trang is happy?" He is smiling. Mr. Curtiss brings him letters.

▸ Have students:

- Point to the places on the picture to show how they know Trang is happy.

Mr. Curtiss:	They sure are! So what are your plans for the day? It's a beautiful fall day. The weather is just right.
Trang:	The temperature is perfect! I'm glad I wasn't born in the winter!

▸ Explain to students that **glad** is another word for **happy**.

▸ Have students:

- Repeat the word **glad**.

▸ Check students' comprehension by asking "What season is it?" fall

Mr. Curtiss:	Did you get anything special for your birthday?
Trang:	Yes! I got this red bicycle. I'm going to the library.
Mr. Curtiss:	Well, Trang, be careful on the street. Make sure you stay on the sidewalk.

▸ Check students' comprehension by asking "What did Trang get for his birthday?" a bicycle "What color is the bicycle?" red "Where is Trang going?" to the library

	Trang:	I will. Thanks, Mr. Curtiss! I'll see you tomorrow.
	Mr. Curtiss:	Happy birthday!

▸ Check students' comprehension by asking "Does Trang say *hello* or *goodbye* to Mr. Curtiss?" goodbye

Practice the Dialog

▸ Assign the class the role of Trang. You will read the role of Mr. Curtiss. Read through the dialog line by line.

▸ Have students:

- Read Trang's part of the dialog aloud.

Variation:

▸ Divide the class in half.

▸ Assign one role to each half of students.

▸ Have students:

- Choral read each half of the dialog as a group.

▸ Check students' comprehension of the dialog by revisiting the questions from the Picture Walk-Through.

Who? English Subject Pronouns

▸ Write the question "Who?" on the board. Point to yourself and say "Who?" Then say "I." Write down the subject pronoun **I** on the board.

▸ Have students:

- Choral repeat the subject pronoun **I**.

▸ Face a student, point to him or her, and say "you." Then, point to all of the students and say "you."

▸ Have students:

- Choral repeat the subject pronoun **you**.

▸ Point to a male student in the class, look at the class and say "he." Point to a female student in the class, look at the class and say "she." Point to an object in the classroom, such as a book or a chair, and say "it."

▸ Have students:

- Choral repeat the pronouns **he**, **she**, and **it**.

▸ Face the class and point to yourself and a student. Say "we."

▸ Have students:

- Choral repeat the subject pronoun **we**.

▸ Face the same student, point to the rest of the class, and say "they" to that student.

▸ Have students:

- Choral repeat the subject pronoun **they**.

▸ Write the pronouns **I, you, he, she, it, we,** and **they** on the board. Then point to yourself and ask the class "Who?"

▸ Have students:

- Say the correct subject pronoun. I

▸ Repeat with the other pronouns. Point to the same person or people when you taught the pronouns to elicit the correct pronoun from the class.

▸ Explain to students that these words all say **who** does an action.

Examples: **I** am happy. **You** go to the post office. **He** rides his bicycle.

Pronoun Practice

On Their Own

▸ Direct students' attention to Application A on page 53 of the *Student Text.*

▸ Have students:

- Match the correct pronoun to the picture.

▸ Direct students' attention to Application B on page 53 of the *Student Text.*

▸ Have students:

- Read each sentence and substitute the underlined word for the correct pronoun.

Revisit the Dialog

▸ Redirect students' attention to the dialog on page 53 of the *Student Text.*

▸ Read the dialog aloud for students.

▸ Have students:

- Clap once every time they hear one of the pronouns that they learned today.

Your Turn

Pair/Share

▸ Have students:

- Role play the roles of Mr. Curtiss and Trang.
- Greet each other in the street and ask how the other one is doing.

Example:

Mr. Curtiss:	Hi, Trang!
Trang:	Hello, Mr. Curtiss!
Mr. Curtiss:	How are you today?
Trang:	I'm happy!

Introduction: Oral Fluency

 Students learn to talk about *who* and *how* and are reintroduced to the week's scenario. Then, students focus on one of the areas within the scenario.

Who and *How*

Materials
Student Text
pp. 46–48

▶ Begin the class by reviewing the question words **who** and **how**.

▶ Remind students that **who** is used to ask about a person.

▶ Point to the picture of the mail carrier in the street scenario on page 48. Ask "Who is this?" the mail carrier

▶ Have students:

• Volunteer to point out other people in the street scene.

• Ask "Who is this?"

• Invite a student volunteer to answer.

▶ Remind students that **how** is used to ask about the way or manner in which someone does something or feels about something.

▶ Smile and act out a joyful expression. Ask the class "How do I feel?" Then say, "I am happy."

▶ Frown and act out a sad expression. Ask the class "How do I feel?" Then say "I am sad."

▶ Have students:

• Have a conversation with a partner to ask and tell **who** they are and **how** they feel.

• Include a greeting.

• Share their conversation with the class.

Review: Neighborhood

▶ Direct students' attention to the pictures on pages 48–49. Say "neighborhood." Point to the street and elicit the word **street** from the students.

▶ Point to the **park** and say "park."

▶ Have students:

• Point to the **park**.

• Choral repeat the word.

▶ Repeat for **park maintenance worker**.

- Direct students' attention to pages 48–49. Point to the park maintenance worker. Ask students "Who is in the park?"
- Have students:
  - Say who they see in the park.

Introduction to the Park

- Direct students' attention to the picture of the park on page 54.
- Elicit words that students know in English that are in the picture and share them with the class.
- Have students:
  - Choral repeat the words.

Phonemic Awareness

 Students practice identifying, differentiating, and producing the / n / sound.

The / n / Sound

- Write the words **neighborhood, night,** and **notebook** on the board and underline the **n** in each word.
- Have students:
  - Tell you what letter you have underlined in each word.

- Explain that the letter **n** in English makes the sound / n / and pronounce the / n / sound for the students. Show them how to form the / n / sound by putting the tip of your tongue behind your upper teeth.
- Have students:
  - Chorally and individually repeat the sound.
- Point to the word **neighborhood** and say "neighborhood."
- Have students:
  - Chorally and individually repeat the word with you.
- Repeat for the words **night** and **notebook.** For **night,** draw a moon and stars on the board. For **notebook,** hold up a notebook for the class to see.

Nod to Your Neighbor for / n /

- Repeat the / n / sound for the students. Turn to a nearby student and nod your head. Say "**Nod to your neighbor.**" Explain that a **neighbor** is someone who lives nearby, in your neighborhood.
- Have students:
  - Repeat "nod to your neighbor" as they make the motion.
  - Turn to a nearby classmate and nod their heads when they hear the sound.

▸ Write the following tongue twister on the board and say it aloud as you nod your head. Clarify the meaning of the tongue twister by drawing or acting out the words. Nancy needs nine new notebooks.

▸ Have students:

• Choral repeat the tongue twister and turn to a nearby student and nod when they hear the sound.

STEP 2

Everyday Words

Students learn and practice seasons, weather, and feelings for everyday conversation.

Recognize Everyday Words: Seasons

Materials

Student Text p. 57

Calendar photos of the four seasons

Photos of different types of weather

▸ Point out the window, and say the appropriate season. Say "It is (season)." Show each of the seasons photos one by one.

▸ Have individual students:

• Say the season by using the sentence frame It is _____.

▸ Draw students' attention to Application A on page 57. Copy the chart on the board.

▸ Have students:

• Draw an activity that they like to do in each season on their chart.

▸ As students are drawing their activities, draw an activity for each season on your chart on the board. For example, biking in the spring, swimming in the summer, football in the fall.

Seasons Charades

▸ Show students the pictures that you drew for each season.

▸ Choose one of the seasons and act out the activity that you drew.

▸ Have students:

• Identify in what season you do the activity.

▸ When they guess correctly, tell them what you like to do in that season.

Example: I like to swim in the summer.

• Play the game with a partner until all of their seasons are identified.

Pair/Share

▸ Walk around the class and help students by providing them with the English words for their activities. Help them to:

• Use the sentence frame to say what they like to do each season. I like to _____ in the _____.

▸ Have students:

• Complete Application B on page 57 of the *Student Text.*

• Share their answers with the class.

Seasons Interview

- Start by having students:
  - Name different activities. play basketball, go to the park, etc.
- Record the activities on the board.
- Choose one of the activities and write it in the "I" column of the table for the season that you do the activity. For example, **play basketball**. Then, turn to a student and ask "What do you do in the winter?" Write that student's name in the header of the chart, and write his or her answer in the chart.

Example:

Season	I	Name _____
Winter **Spring**	play basketball	study
Summer **Fall**		

- Say "In the winter, I play basketball. (Partner's name) studies."
- Have students:
  - Work in pairs to interview each other.
  - Share their answers with the class.
- To extend the activity, have students:
  - Write out the sentences on a sheet of paper.

Recognize Everyday Words: Feelings

- Draw five faces on the board with the following expressions: **happy, sad, mad, scared,** and **surprised**.
- Have students:
  - Give a name to each of the faces.
- Write each of the names under the corresponding face.
- Point to the happy face and say "(Name) is happy."
- Have students:
  - Chorally and individually repeat the sentence.
- Repeat for the other faces.
- Ask the class "Who is happy?" (Name of happy face) is happy.
- Choose another face and ask the class "How does (name of angry face) feel?" (Name of angry face) is angry.
- Repeat until all faces have been used.

Fast Faces

- Call out a feeling. Act out the expression.

  Example: I am happy!

- ▸ Have students:
  - Choral repeat the expression with feeling.
  - Act out the expression.
- ▸ Continue by calling out the feelings in the same manner without acting them out.
- ▸ Have students:
  - Choral repeat the expression with feeling.
  - Act out the expression.
- ▸ Invite volunteers to:
  - Call out the next expression.

STEP 3

Vocabulary Development

➡ Students work with the core content vocabulary related to the park for everyday conversation.

Introduce: Core Vocabulary

Materials
Student Text
pp. 54–55

- ▸ Direct students' attention to the park picture on pages 54–55 of the *Student Text*. Point out the civil servant: **park maintenance worker**. Tell students that the park maintenance worker is an important person in the neighborhood.
- ▸ Point to the **park maintenance worker**. Say "park maintenance worker."
- ▸ Have students:
  - Chorally and individually repeat the words.
- ▸ Say "The park maintenance worker keeps our park clean and beautiful."
- ▸ Explain that the park maintenance worker, like the mail carrier, the firefighter, and the police officer all help the neighborhood.
- ▸ Point to each item that appears on the items list on pages 54–55 of the *Student Text*. As you point, say each word out loud.
- ▸ Have students:
  - Choral repeat each word.

Practice Vocabulary

Where to Go, What to Do

- ▸ Direct students attention to the picture of the park and items list on pages 54–55.
- ▸ Draw a two-column table on the board with the headings "Where to Go" and "What to Do"

- ▸ Point to the **basketball court** in the picture. Write "basketball court" in the first column and "play basketball" in the second column. Say "I play basketball at the basketball court."

Example:

Where to Go	What to Do
basketball court	play basketball
1.	
2.	
3.	

On Their Own

- Work with a partner to find three other places in the park.
- Complete the chart following your model.
- Write sentences to describe where to go in the park and what to do there.
- Share their answers with the class.

STEP 4

How English Works

Students are introduced to the dialog. Students participate in the dialog. Students continue their practice of **pronouns**.

Introduce the Dialog

Picture Walk-Through

Materials
Student Text
pp. 56–57
Blank cards

▶ Have students:
- Look at pictures on page 56 of the *Student Text*.
▶ Ask students simple questions about the pictures to predict the main idea of the dialog.
▶ Point to the picture in each panel. Act out or point to vocabulary words as necessary. Ask:
  1. Panel 1: What season is it? summer
  2. Panel 2: Where do the girls play? at the playground
  3. Panel 3: Where can the kids play? in the fountain
  4. Panel 4: Where are the children playing? in the sandbox
  5. Panel 5: What do the girls do at the pond? feed the ducks
  6. Panel 6: Are the girls going to eat or to play? eat
▶ Record student responses on the board.

Read the Dialog

▶ Read through the dialog in steps.
▶ Have students:
- Track print with you as you read.
- Listen for cognates, or English words that are similar in students' native language.

> | Grace: | Hi, Sophie! It's a great day for your party! |
> | Sophie: | Hi, Grace! Thanks for coming. It's such a nice summer day. The party will be really fun. My dad is making barbecue! |
> | Grace: | He's a good cook. I love barbecue! It's great to have a party in the park. |

▶ Remind students that they learned about adjectives last week. Remind them that adjectives are words that describe people, places and things.

▶ Have students:

- Identify the adjectives. great, nice, fun, good

▶ Check students' comprehension by asking "Who is making barbecue?" Sophie's dad

> | Sophie: | In the summer, the park is so fun, but sometimes the playground is too hot. |
> | Grace: | We can go on the swings and the seesaw, and go down the slide. |

▶ Check students' comprehension by asking "What is the playground like in the summer?" too hot "What does Grace want to do at the playground?" go on the swings, seesaw, and slide

> | Sophie: | If it's too hot, we can go play in the fountain. |

▶ Check students' comprehension by asking "What can Sophie and Grace do if it is hot?" play in the fountain

> | Grace: | Is there a sandbox here at the park? |
> | Sophie: | Yeah, but sometimes there are too many children in it. |

▶ Tell students that **yeah** is another way of saying **yes**. Explain that **yeah** is generally used in conversation among friends.

▶ Check students' comprehension by asking "Is there a sandbox at the park?" yes

> | Grace: | I brought my basketball. Hopefully the basketball court isn't too hot today. |
> | Sophie: | I hope not. My mom gave me some old bread. We can go feed the ducks at the pond after lunch. |

▶ Check students' comprehension by asking "What did Grace bring to the park?" a basketball "What does Sophie want to do after lunch?" feed the ducks

> | Grace: | So, do you want something to eat? |
> | Sophie: | Yes! I'm hungry! Let's go eat lunch! |

▶ Check students' comprehension by asking " How does Sophie feel?" hungry

Practice the Dialog

▶ Assign the class the role of Sophie. You will read the role of Grace. Read through the dialog line by line.

▶ Have students:

- Read Sophie's part of the dialog aloud.

Variation:

▶ Divide the class in half.

▶ Assign one role to each half of students.

▶ Have students:

- Choral read each half of the dialog as a group.

▶ Check students' comprehension of the dialog by revisiting the questions from the Picture Walk-Through.

Working with Subject Pronouns

▶ Review the subject pronouns with students by pointing to various people and eliciting the correct pronoun from students. Point to people as you did in yesterday's lesson.

▶ Have students:

- Identify each pronoun aloud.

▶ Write each subject pronoun on the board in a chart as students identify them: **I, you, he, she, it, we, you**, and **they**.

I	we
you	you
he, she, it	they

Who Is It?

▶ Divide class into pairs. Give each pair a set of six blank cards.

▶ Have students:

- Work with their partners to write the subject pronouns on each card. **He, she,** and **it** should be written on the same card.

▶ Choose a pronoun as a model (for example, he).

▶ Have students:

- Name subjects that can be replaced by the pronoun **he**. Mr. Curtiss, the boy, etc.
- Write down subjects on the back of each card that can be replaced by each pronoun.
- Write down their own name on the back of the **I** card.
- Write down their partner's name on the back of the **you** (singular) card.
- Shuffle their pronoun cards, with the subjects facing up, and the subject pronouns facing down.

- Take turns looking at the subjects and identifying which pronoun it is. For **you** and **I**, each student should point to his or her partner then to himself or herself, respectively.

Example:

Front of card	Back of card
John and I You and I He and I	We

- Exchange **he / she / it, we, you** (plural), and **they** cards with another group and play again.

Revisit the Dialog

▸ Direct students' attention again to the dialog on page 56 of the *Student Text*

▸ Have students:

- Read the dialog out loud with a partner.

Your Turn

▸ Have students:

- Create a dialog for role play between Grace and Sophie in which the two and tell each other what they usually do at the park.
- Use the list of places on page 54 to tell where they play in the park.
- Use **pronouns**.

Example:

Sophie:	Where do you like to play in the park?
Grace:	I like to play at the basketball court. What do you like to do at the park?
Sophie:	I like to feed the ducks at the pond.

▸ Invite volunteers to:

- Perform their dialog in front of the class.

Introduction: Oral Fluency

 Students learn to use and differentiate *who* and *how* and are reintroduced to the week's scenario. Then, students focus on one of the areas within the scenario.

Who and *How*

Materials

Student Text
pp. 46–49,
pp. 58–59

▸ Begin class by making a happy expression on your face. Ask "How are you? Who is happy today?"

▸ Prompt students to:

• Raise their hands.

▸ Repeat with **sad, angry, surprised,** and **scared**.

▸ Approach a student and say "How are you today?"

▸ Have student:

• Answer with the sentence frame I am _____ today.

• Ask another student "How are you today?"

▸ Repeat until all students have had the opportunity to ask and answer the question.

Review: Neighborhood

▸ Direct students' attention to the picture on pages 46–47. Say "neighborhood." Point to the street and elicit the words **street** and **park** from the students.

▸ Point to the **doctor's office** on page 49 and say "doctor's office."

▸ Have students:

• Point to the **doctor's office**.

• Choral repeat the word.

▸ Repeat for **receptionist, examination room,** and **waiting room**.

▸ Direct students' attention to pages 58–59. Point to the receptionist. Ask students "Who is in the doctor's office?" Say "receptionist."

▸ Have students:

• Repeat **receptionist**.

Introduction to the Doctor's Office

- ▸ Direct students' attention to the picture of the doctor's office on page 58.
- ▸ Elicit words that students know in English that are in the picture and share them with the class.
- ▸ Have students:
  - Choral repeat the words.

STEP
1

Phonemic Awareness

 Students practice identifying, differentiating, and producing the / *d* / sound.

The / *d* / Sound

- ▸ Write the words **doctor, ducks,** and **dresser** on the board and underline the *d* in each word.
- ▸ Have students:
  - Tell you what letter you have underlined in each word.
- ▸ Explain that the letter *d* in English makes the sound / *d* / and pronounce the / *d* / sound for the students. Show them how to form the / *d* / sound by putting the tip of your tongue behind your upper teeth.
- ▸ Have students:
  - Chorally and individually repeat the sound.
- ▸ Point to the word **doctor** and say "doctor."
- ▸ Have students:
  - Chorally and individually repeat the word with you.
- ▸ Repeat for the words **ducks** and **dresser**.

Do a Dance for / *d* /

- ▸ Repeat the / *d* / sound for the students. Do a little dance and say "**Do a dance!**"
- ▸ Have students:
  - Repeat "do a dance" as they make the motion.
  - Do a dance when they hear the sound.
- ▸ Write the following tongue twister on the board and say it aloud as you do a dance. Clarify the meaning of the tongue twister by drawing or acting out the words.
  David's doctor dries the dishes.
- ▸ Have students:
  - Choral repeat the tongue twister and do a dance when they hear the sound.

Everyday Words

→ Students learn and practice seasons and weather expressions for everyday conversation.

Recognize Everyday Words: Weather

▸ Review the weather expressions with students. Ask them "How's the weather?"

▸ Have students:

- Describe the weather.

▸ Draw a thermometer on the board.

▸ Draw a line to where the mercury on the thermometer would stop and write 80°. Say "What is the temperature?"

▸ Have students:

- Choral repeat the question.

▸ Point to the number and say "It is eighty degrees."

▸ Prompt students with a season. Then ask the temperature. Say "It is winter. How is the weather? What is the temperature?"

▸ Have student volunteers:

- Answer the questions.

  Example: It is cold. The temperature is 30°.

▸ Accept temperature in Fahrenheit or Celsius.

Recognize Everyday Words: Feelings

▸ Draw the following seasons chart on the board.

winter	spring
summer	fall

▸ Then draw a face with an expression for the way you feel during each season in each box.

Example:

▸ Say "In the summer, I am happy. I like the summer when the temperature is 80°. It is not too hot."

▸ Have students:

- Copy the chart in their notebooks.

- Draw faces for how they feel in each of the squares.

- Interview a partner about how he or she feels during each season.
- Talk about the weather that makes them feel that way.

  Example: How do you feel in the fall?
  I feel happy in the fall. The temperature is 50°. It is not too cold.

▸ Ask volunteers "How do you feel in the (season)? How does (name of volunteer's partner) feel in the (season)?"

▸ Have volunteers:

  - Answer the questions aloud about themselves and their partners.

STEP 3

Vocabulary Development

Students work with the core content vocabulary related to the body and doctor's office for everyday conversation.

Introduce: Core Vocabulary

Materials

Student Text pp. 58–59, p. 61

Blank paper

Colored markers

Scissors

Cards with body parts written on them

Paper bag

Tape or Glue

▸ Direct students' attention to the doctor's office picture on page 58 of the *Student Text*. Point out the **doctor**. Say "doctor."

▸ Have students:

  - Point to the **doctor** and repeat the word aloud.

▸ Repeat for **nurse** and **patient**.

▸ Have students:

  - Point to all of the patients in the picture.

▸ Point to the **waiting room**. Say "The patients wait to see the doctor. They sit in the waiting room." Act out the verb **wait** by sitting down, acting as if you are flipping through a magazine, and looking at your watch.

▸ Have students:

  - Act out waiting in the waiting room.

  - Point to the **waiting room**. Say "The patients wait to see the doctor. They sit in the waiting room." Act out the verb **wait** by sitting down, acting as if you are flipping through a magazine, and looking at your watch.

▸ Point to the **examination room**. Say "The doctor sees me in the examination room." Act out listening to a patient's heartbeat through the stethoscope.

▸ Point to each item that appears on the items list on pages 58–59 of the *Student Text*. As you point, say each word out loud.

▸ Have students:

  - Choral repeat each word.

Body Parts

▸ Direct students' attention again to the items list on page 59 of the *Student Text*. Point to your **head** and point to the word **head** on the items list. Say "head" out loud. Say "I use my head to think."

▸ Have students:

  • Point to their head and choral repeat the word.

▸ Repeat for all of the body parts listed on pages 58–59 of the *Student Text* (**eyes, ear, arm, hand, chest, stomach, leg, knee,** and **foot**.) Point to each body part when presenting each word.

▸ Say "The doctor puts a thermometer in my mouth to check my temperature." Act out putting a thermometer in your mouth. Point to your mouth and say "mouth." Say "I use my mouth to eat." Act out eating.

▸ Have students:

  • Choral repeat the word.

▸ Repeat with **nose**.

Practice Vocabulary

Simon Says

▸ Tell the class you will play a game using the new vocabulary. Explain the rules of Simon Says to the class.

▸ Say "Simon says, touch your nose." Then touch your nose.

▸ Prompt students to:

  • Touch their nose.

▸ Say "Touch your nose." Then put your hand behind your back and shake your head to indicate to students to not touch their nose.

▸ Do one more example as necessary for students to understand how the game works.

▸ Invite student volunteers to:

  • Lead the game.

Paper Doll Factory

▸ Prepare a set of cards. Write one body part on each card. Use the words **head, eyes, ears, arms, hands, chest, stomach, legs, knees, feet, mouth,** and **nose**.

▸ Divide the class into equal groups and distribute the body part cards among the groups. Some groups may have more than one card.

▸ Distribute paper, markers, and a pair of scissors to each group.

▸ Have students:

  • Draw and cut out the body parts for each of the cards that they have.

  • Draw as many body parts for the number of groups in the class that there are. For example, if there are five groups of students, and one group has the card for "arms," have them draw five sets of arms (ten arms).

  • Cut out their body parts and put them in the paper bag. (If students have arms, have them separate the two arms.)

▸ Mix the bag. Explain to students that they will make paper dolls.

▸ Have each group:

  • Pick 19 body parts from the bag.

- Sort through the body parts to make sure they have the parts they need to construct one doll in its entirety. (2 eyes, 2 ears, etc.)

- Take turns telling the class which body parts they have too many of, and which body parts they need. Trade body parts with other groups to complete their doll.

  Example: We have too many legs. We need an eye and an ear.

- Assemble their paper doll once they have all of their body parts.

- Share and describe their doll with the rest of the class.

Body Basics

On Their Own

▸ Direct students' attention to page 61 in the *Student Text*.

▸ Have students:

- Label the body parts on the picture in Application A.

- Fill in the blanks in Application B.

- Share their answers with the class.

STEP 4

How English Works

 Students are introduced to the dialog. Students participate in the dialog. Students learn more about **pronouns**.

Introduce the Dialog

Picture Walk-Through

Materials

Student Text pp. 58–60

Classroom objects

Copies of pronoun worksheet

▸ Have students:

- Look at pictures on page 60 of the *Student Text*.

▸ Ask students simple questions about the pictures to predict the main idea of the dialog.

▸ Point to the picture in each panel. Act out or point to vocabulary words as necessary. Ask:

1. Panel 1: Is Jacob talking to the nurse or the doctor? the doctor

2. Panel 2: What season is it? winter Where is Jacob? at the park

3. Panel 3: What part of Jacob's body hurts? his arm

4. Panel 4: How's the weather? It is cold.

5. What will the doctor do? take X-rays

▸ Record student responses on the board.

Read the Dialog

▸ Read through the dialog in steps. Have students:

- Track print with you as you read.

- Listen for cognates, or English words that are similar in students' native language.

> | Dr. Fielder: | Hi, Trang, what seems to be the problem? |
> |---|---|
> | Trang: | I hurt my arm. |
> | Dr. Fielder: | Tell me what happened. |

▸ Check students' comprehension by asking "Why does Trang go to the doctor?" He hurt his arm.

▸ Have students:

- Point to Trang's arm.

> | Trang: | I was riding my bicycle in the park, and it started to snow. |
> |---|---|
> | Dr. Fielder: | How fast were you going? |

▸ Check students' comprehension by asking "How did Trang hurt his arm?" He fell off of his bicycle. "How was the weather?" It was snowing.

▸ Have students:

- Point to the snow.

> | Trang: | Well, I wanted to get home, so I was going pretty fast. Then, I fell. |
> |---|---|
> | Dr. Fielder: | Well, it looks like you had a pretty bad fall. Does it hurt? |
> | Trang: | At first, it didn't hurt. Now it hurts a lot. |

▸ Check students' comprehension by asking "How does Trang's arm feel?" It hurts.

▸ Have students:

- Act out their arm hurting.

> | Dr. Fielder: | I hope you were wearing a helmet. |
> |---|---|
> | Trang: | I was. |
> | Dr. Fielder: | Well, it is winter. Riding your bike in the snow can be dangerous. A lot of my patients get hurt on the ice and snow. The temperatures go down, but people don't slow down. |
> | Trang: | It was very cold outside. |

▸ Check students' comprehension by asking "Was Trang wearing a helmet?" yes

▸ Have students:

- Point to the helmet.

> | Dr. Fielder: | I will have the nurse clean your arm. Then, I'll take some x-rays. |
> |---|---|
> | Trang: | Did I break my arm? |
> | Dr. Fielder: | No, but I want to make sure everything is okay. |
> | Trang: | I feel okay. Just a little dumb. |
> | Dr. Fielder: | Well, we'll get you all taken care of. |

▶ Check students' comprehension by asking "Who will clean Jacob's arm?" the nurse "How does Jacob feel?" dumb

Practice the Dialog

▶ Assign the class the role of Trang. You will read the role of Dr. Fielder. Read through the dialog line by line.

▶ Have students:

• Read Jacob's part of the dialog aloud.

Variation:

▶ Divide the class in half.

▶ Assign one role to each half of students.

▶ Have students:

• Choral read each half of the dialog as a group.

▶ Check students' comprehension of the dialog by revisiting the questions from the Picture Walk-Through.

Pronoun Practice

▶ Prepare and distribute copies of a worksheet with pictures of the items from the items list on page 59 of the *Student Text*.

▶ Review the pronouns with students by pointing at yourself and others in the class, as you did to teach the subject pronouns on the first day of this week.

▶ Have students:

• Identify the subject pronouns by naming them aloud.

▶ Write **it** and **they** on the board.

▶ Tell students that **it** generally refers to inanimate objects, or things. Hold up a notebook and say "This is a notebook. It is (color)." Write the sentence on the board. Underline the word notebook. Circle the word **It** and draw an arrow to the words **a notebook**.

This is a notebook. It is red.

▶ Tell students that the word **It** represents the words **a notebook**.

▶ Tell students that **they** can refer to people or inanimate objects. Point to the patients in the picture on page 59 of the *Student Text*.

▶ Say "These people are waiting to see the doctor. They are all patients." Write the sentence on the board. Underline the words **These people**. Circle the word **They** and draw an arrow to the underlined words **These people**.

These people are waiting to see the doctor. They are all patients.

▸ Hold up a handful of paperclips. Say "These are paperclips. They are small." Underline the word **paperclips**. Circle the world **They** and draw an arrow to the word **paperclips**.

These are paperclips. They are all small.

▸ Distribute copies of the worksheet and divide the class into pairs.

▸ Have students:

- Work with their partner to write the correct subject pronoun in the blank.

Your Turn

▸ Have students:

- Create a dialog for role play between Dr. Fielder and Trang, in which Trang tells Dr. Fielder what part of his body he hurt.

- Make a list of three body parts that Trang may have hurt when he fell. (**leg, chest, hand,** etc.)

Example:

Dr. Fielder:	Hi Trang. What happened?
Trang:	I hurt my leg.
Dr. Fielder:	How?
Trang:	It was snowing, and I fell.

▸ Invite volunteers to:

- Perform their dialog in front of the class.

Introduction: Oral Fluency

 Students practice *who* and *how* and are reintroduced to the week's scenario. Then, students focus on one of the areas within the scenario.

Who and *How*

Interview

Materials
Student Text
pp. 46–49,
pp. 62–63

▸ Have students write down five questions to interview a classmate.

▸ Have students:

- Use the words **who** and **how**.

  Examples: Who is your favorite teacher?
  How do you feel in the winter?

- Interview a partner using the questions they wrote to guide them.

- Write a short paragraph describing their partner without using their partner's name.

▸ Collect all of the paragraphs and shuffle them in a pile. Invite volunteers to:

- Come to the front of the class and take a paper from the pile.

- Read the paragraph aloud to the class.

▸ Have students:

- Identify the person.

  Example: This person's favorite teacher is (name). She feels sad in the winter. She has five brothers and sisters. She goes to the park every week. Her father is a firefighter. Who is she?

Review: Neighborhood

▸ Direct students' attention to the picture on pages 48–49. Say "neighborhood." Point to the street and elicit the word **street, park,** and **doctor's office** from the students.

▸ Point to the **library** and say "library."

▸ Have students:

- Point to the **library**.

- Choral repeat the word.

▸ Repeat for **librarian**.

▸ Direct students' attention to pages 62–63. Point to the librarian. Ask students "Who is in the library?"

▸ Have students:

  • Repeat **librarian**.

Introduction to the Library

▸ Direct students' attention to the picture of the library on page 62.

▸ Elicit words that students know in English that are in the picture and share them with the class.

▸ Have students:

  • Choral repeat the words.

STEP

1

Phonemic Awareness

 Students practice identifying, differentiating, and producing the / l / sound.

The / l / Sound

▸ Write the words **library, lunch,** and **lamp** on the board and underline the *l* in each word.

▸ Have students:

  • Tell you what letter you have underlined in each word.

▸ Explain that the letter *l* in English makes the sound / l / and pronounce the / l / sound for the students. Show them how to form *the* / l / sound by curling the tip of your tongue behind your upper teeth and releasing.

▸ Have students:

  • Chorally and individually repeat the sound.

▸ Point to the word **library** and say "library."

▸ Have students:

  • Chorally and individually repeat the word with you.

▸ Repeat for the words **lunch** and **lamp**.

Lift Your Legs for / l /

▸ Repeat the / l / sound for the students. Lift your legs and say "**Lift your legs!**"

▸ Have students:

  • Repeat "lift your legs" as they make the motion.

  • Lift their legs when they hear the sound.

▸ Write the following tongue twister on the board and say it aloud as you lift your legs at each / l / sound. Clarify the meaning of the tongue twister by drawing or acting out the words. Liliana likes late lunches.

▸ Have students:

  • Choral repeat the tongue twister and lift their legs when they hear the sound.

Everyday Words

 Students practice weather, seasons and feelings for everyday conversation.

Recognize Everyday Words: Seasons

▸ Ask students "How's the weather today?"

▸ Have students:

  • Volunteer to describe today's weather.

▸ Elicit the names of the seasons from students. Write **winter, spring, summer,** and **fall** on the board.

▸ Say "I am thinking of a season. In this season it is not too hot. It is not too cold. It is warm. I feel happy. I ride my bicycle in the park. I go to school during this season. What season am I thinking of?" spring

▸ Divide the class into pairs.

▸ Have students:

  • Work together to write a description of one of the seasons following your model.

  • Volunteer to share their description with the class.

  • Identify the season.

Recognize Everyday Words: Feelings

▸ Elicit the feelings from students. Write down the feelings on the board in a chart.

happy	sad	angry	surprised	scared

▸ Have students:

  • Write down pictures, places or activities that they associate with each feeling.

  • Share their answers with the class.

    Example: Riding my bicycle in the snow makes me feel scared.

Variation:

▸ Have students:

  • Ask their partner What makes you feel (feeling)?

  • Record their partner's answers in the chart.

  • Present the information to the class.

3

Vocabulary Development

 Students work with the core content vocabulary related to the library for everyday conversation.

Introduce: Core Vocabulary

Materials
Student Text
pp. 62–63, 65

▸ Direct students' attention to the library picture on page 62 of the *Student Text*. Point out the **computer lab**. Say "computer lab."

▸ Have students:

 • Point to the **computer lab** and repeat the word aloud.

▸ Repeat with the different areas around the library: **information desk, check out desk, meeting room, multimedia room,** and **reference area, reading corner,** and **restrooms**.

▸ Have students:

 • Repeat each of the words aloud.

▸ Point to each item that appears on the items list on page 63. As you point, say each word out loud.

▸ Have students:

 • Repeat each word.

Practice Vocabulary

Library Places

▸ Direct students' attention to Application A on page 65 of the *Student Text*.

▸ Have students:

 • Match the object to its place in the library.

▸ Check answers.

4

How English Works

 Students are introduced to the dialog. Students participate in the dialog. Students practice **pronouns**.

Introduce the Dialog

Picture Walk-Through

Materials
Student Text
pp. 62–63
Copies of
library card
worksheet
Pictures cut out
from magazines

▸ Have students:

 • Look at pictures on page 62 of the *Student Text*.

▸ Ask students simple questions about the pictures to predict the main idea of the dialog.

▸ Point to the picture in each panel. Act out or point to vocabulary words as necessary. Ask:

1. Panel 1: Who is in the picture? the librarian and a girl What do you think the girl wants to do? take out library books, get a library card, get information

2. Panel 2: What area in the library does the librarian show the girl? the multimedia room

3. Panel 3: Why do you think the librarian is showing the girl the computer? to see the online catalog

4. Panel 4: Which area in the library does the librarian show the girl? the reference area

5. Panel 5: Which area in the library does the librarian show the girl? the information desk

6. Panel 6: Where does the girl want to go? to the restroom

▸ Record student responses on the board.

Read the Dialog

▸ Read through the dialog in steps. Have students:

- Track print with you as you read.

- Listen for cognates, or English words that are similar in students' native language.

Mrs. Simons:	Good morning. What can I do for you?
Melinda:	Hi. My family just moved here. I want to check out a couple of books.
Mrs. Simons:	Well, the first thing you need is a library card. You can fill out this paper with your name, address, and phone number. Then we'll get you a card.

▸ Point to the library card.

▸ Check students' comprehension by asking "What information do you need fill out in order to get a library card?" name, address, and telephone number

Melinda:	May I check out movies and music, as well as books?
Mrs. Simons:	Of course. I'll show you where they are. This is the multimedia room. It has all of our movies on DVD. You can take out CDs as well. You can even watch movies or listen to music here.

▸ Check students' comprehension by asking "What can people do in the multimedia room?" listen to music, watch movies

Melinda:	Where can I find the library catalog?
Mrs. Simons:	There are several computer terminals in the library.
Melinda:	The library in my old neighborhood has them too!

▸ Check students' comprehension by asking "Where is the library catalog?" on the computer

Mrs. Simons:	Over here is the reference room. You can find dictionaries and encyclopedias here.
Melinda:	When is the library open?
Mrs. Simons:	It's open every day, except on Sundays.

▸ Check students' comprehensions by asking "What books are in the reference room?" dictionaries and encyclopedias "What day of the week is the library closed?" Sunday

| Melinda: | Who can I talk to if I need help finding a book? |
| Mrs. Simons: | The information desk is in the middle of the library. The librarians there can help you find what you need. |

▸ Where can Melinda go if she needs help finding a book? to the information desk

Melinda:	Thank you so much. I have one last question.
Mrs. Simons:	Sure.
Melinda:	Where is the restroom?

▸ Check students' comprehensions by asking "What area of the library does Melinda ask about?" the restroom

Practice the Dialog

▸ Assign the class the role of Melinda. You will read the role of Mrs. Simons. Read through the dialog line by line.

▸ Have students:

- Read Melinda's part of the dialog aloud.

Variation:

▸ Divide the class in half.

▸ Assign one role to each half of students.

▸ Have students:

- Choral read each half of the dialog as a group.

▸ Check students' comprehension of the dialog by revisiting the questions from the Picture Walk-Through.

Pronoun Pictures

▸ Gather various pictures of people and items from magazines. Make sure there are pictures of both singular and plural items and people.

▸ Explain to students that they are going to:

- Call out the pronoun that would be used to substitute the person, people or objects in the picture that you show.

- Call out the pronoun based on their own perspective.

▸ Hold up a picture of a woman. Point to the woman.

- ▶ Have students:
    - Say **she**.
- ▶ Hold up a picture of two people and point to both people in the picture.
- ▶ Have students:
    - Say **they**.
- ▶ Point to the same picture of two people and include yourself by pointing back and forth between the picture and yourself.
- ▶ Have students:
    - Say **you**.
- ▶ Point to an individual student.
- ▶ Have students:
    - Say **I**.
- ▶ Point to yourself.
- ▶ Have students:
    - Say **you**.
- ▶ Point to the whole class.
- ▶ Have students:
    - Say **we**.
- ▶ Hold up a picture of a singular object.
- ▶ Have students:
    - Say **it**.
- ▶ Hold up a picture of a plural object.
- ▶ Have students:
    - Say **they**.
- ▶ Hold up a picture of a group of people.
- ▶ Have students:
    - Say **they**.
- ▶ Hold up a picture of a boy.
- ▶ Have students:
    - Say **he**.

Revisit the Dialog

- ▶ Direct students' attention again to the dialog on page 64 of the *Student Text.*
- ▶ Read the dialog aloud. As you read the dialog have students:
    - Write a list of the items that Melinda can take out of the library or read in the library.
    - Check their answers with the sentence frame Melinda can _____ at the library.

Your Turn

I Need a Library Card

▶ Prepare worksheets that ask students information necessary to get a library card.

PUBLIC LIBRARY
Name _____
Address _____
_____
_____
Phone number _____

▶ Tell students to imagine they want to get a library card at the local library.

▶ Distribute copies of the worksheet.

▶ Have students:

  • Complete the information card.

Library Floor Plan

▶ Direct students' attention to Application B on page 65 of the *Student Text.*

▶ Have students:

  • Draw a floor plan of the school or town library.
  • Label the areas of the library in the floor plan.

▶ Have volunteers:

  • Present their floor plan and point out the different areas of the library.

Everyday English Student Text

Introduction: Oral Fluency

 Students review the uses of *who* and *how*. Students revisit the Unit Overview.

Who and *How*

Who Am I?

Materials

Student Text pp. 46–47 Pictures or line drawings of neighborhood people

▸ Gather pictures from magazines, the Internet, or clip art that depict the neighborhood people from the week's lesson.

▸ Review the vocabulary with students. Hold up the picture of the firefighter. Ask "Who am I?"

▸ Prompt students to:

   • Answer "You are a firefighter."

▸ Repeat with **police officer, mail carrier, park maintenance worker, doctor, nurse, receptionist,** and **librarian**.

▸ Ask students "Who protects the neighborhood?" the police officer

▸ Ask students "Who brings us our letters and packages?" the mail carrier

▸ Ask students "Who takes care of us when we are sick?" the doctor and the nurse

▸ Ask students "Who helps us at the doctor's office?" the receptionist

▸ Ask students "Who keeps our parks clean and safe?" the park maintenance worker

▸ Ask students "Who saves us from a fire?" the firefighter

▸ Ask students "Who helps us at the library?" the librarian

Variation:

▸ Have students:

   • Write a description of the neighborhood people and civil servants to read to the class.

   • Read their description to the class.

Unit Review: Neighborhood

▸ Direct students' attention to the picture on pages 48–49. Say "neighborhood." Have students:

   • Choral repeat the word.

▸ Point out the street in the picture. Elicit the word **street** from the students.

▸ Repeat for **park, doctor's office,** and **library**.

Phonemic Awareness

 Students practice identifying, differentiating, and producing the / b /, / p /, / n /, / d /, and / l / sounds.

Review of the / b /, / p /, / n /, / d /, and / l / Sounds

Materials
Blank cards

▸ Write the words **bandages, pond, nose, dictionary** and **librarian** on the board and say each word.

▸ Have students:

- Repeat each word with you.

▸ Underline the **b** in **bandages,** the **p** in **pond,** the **n** in **nose,** the **d** in **dictionary,** and the **l** in **librarian.**

▸ Have students:

- Identify each letter that you underlined.

- Pronounce each sound that the letter makes in each word.

▸ Review the gestures for each sound with the students as practiced throughout the week. Say "Box your buddy!" and turn to a nearby student to make the boxing motion when you make the / b / sound. Say "Point your pinky!" and point your pinky finger when you make the make the / p / sound. Say "Nod to your neighbor!" and turn to nod your head to a nearby student when you make the / n / sound. Say "Do a dance!" and do a dance when you make the / d / sound. Say "Lift your legs!" and lift your legs when you make the / l / sound.

▸ Say each word with the students.

▸ Have the students:

- Make the gesture associated with each sound in the word.

Try These Tongue Twisters

▸ Write the tongue twisters from the week on the board.

1. Bobby buys big books.
2. Paula paints pretty pictures.
3. Nancy needs nine new notebooks.
4. David's doctor dries the dishes.
5. Liliana likes late lunches.

▸ Choose one of the tongue twisters and say it aloud.

▸ Have students:

- Repeat the tongue twister.

- Make the correct motion while they are saying the tongue twister.

▸ Invite volunteers to:

  • Choose a tongue twister and say it aloud to the class.

  • Lead students in the motion that goes with the featured sound.

A Symphony of Sounds

▸ Assign each student one of the week's lessons.

▸ Write **periodicals** on the board. Underline the *p*, the *d*, and the *l*. Say the word out loud and make the motion for each sound as you say the word.

▸ Have students:

  • Repeat your example and make the correct gestures while pronouncing the word.

  • Prepare one card from their lesson that includes the week's sounds.

  • Take turns reading the word on their card to the class and leading the class in pronouncing the word and making the correct gesture.

STEP 2

Everyday Words

➡ Students review and seasons, feelings, and weather expressions for everyday conversation.

Review Everyday Words: Seasons and Weather

Materials

Student Text
p. 46–65

Copies of
prepared
chart

▸ Prepare and distribute copies of a table with five columns and two rows as shown:

Season	Weather	Feelings	Temperature	Activities
winter				
summer				

On Their Own

▸ Have students:

  • Complete the missing seasons in the chart.

  • Complete the table with the weather, their feelings, the temperature, and activities that they like to do.

  • Share their answers with a partner.

  • Write a paragraph with their partner in which they present their activities.

  • Use a range of pronouns, including **I, we, he,** and/or **she**.

  • Use pages 46–65 of the *Student Text* as a reference.

Vocabulary Development

Students work with the core content vocabulary related to the neighborhood for everyday conversation.

Review: Core Vocabulary

Materials
Student Text
p. 67

▸ Direct students to the activity on page 67 of the *Student Text*.

▸ Have students:

- Complete the crossword puzzle using the picture clues.
- Check answers.

Practice Vocabulary

Neighborhood Talk

▸ Review the names of neighborhood people learned during the week.

▸ Write the words on the board.

▸ Have students:

- Write the names of people on a piece of paper.
- Tell a partner where each person can be found.

  Example: The receptionist is at the doctor's office.

Describe Your Neighborhood

▸ Tell students to:

- Think about the people and places in their neighborhood.
- Brainstorm different questions that they can ask other people about their neighborhoods.

  Examples: Is your neighborhood big or small?
  Who is your doctor?

▸ Record the questions on the board.

▸ Have students:

- Choose five or six questions from the list on the board.
- Interview a partner about his or her neighborhood.
- Report to the class about their partner's neighborhood.

How English Works

 Students are introduced to the dialog. Students participate in the dialog. Students review and practice **pronouns**.

Introduce the Dialog

Picture Walk-Through

Materials

Student Text
p. 66

Students'
photos

Paper

Glue

Colored
markers

Poster board or
Chart paper

▸ Have students:

  • Look at pictures on page 66 of the *Student Text*.

▸ Ask students simple questions about the pictures to predict the main idea of the dialog.

▸ Point to the picture in each panel. Act out or point to vocabulary words as necessary. Ask:

  1. Panel 1: Where are the boys? at their houses

  2. Panel 2: What does the boy ask the other boy about? a playground

  3. Panel 3: What can the boys do at the park? ride their bikes and skateboard

  4. Panel 4: What does one boy think about? going to the doctor's office

  5. Panel 5: What other places do the boys talk about? the grocery store and the library

▸ Record student responses on the board.

Read the Dialog

▸ Read through the dialog in steps. Have students:

  • Track print with you as you read.

  • Listen for cognates, or English words that are similar in students' native language.

Trang:	Hi. My name is Trang. What's your name?
Charlie:	I'm Charlie. I'm thirteen. How old are you?
Trang:	I'm twelve. How do you like your new house?
Charlie:	I really like it. It's a lot bigger than our old house.

▸ Check students' comprehension by asking "How old is Charlie?" thirteen "How old is Trang? twelve

Trang:	I love our neighborhood. There's so much to do. And there are lots of other kids.
Charlie:	Where's the playground? My mom wants me to take my sister Melinda there.

Check students' comprehension by asking "Where does Charlie want to go?" to the playground

> | Trang: | It's at the park. |
> |---|---|
> | Charlie: | Can we ride our bicycles there? |
> | Trang: | Yes, but only on the paths. You can ride your skateboard there too. |

‣ Check students' comprehension by asking "What activities can the boys do on the way to the park?" ride bicycles, skateboard

> | Charlie: | Do you want to go bike riding? |
> |---|---|
> | Trang: | Sure, but my doctor says I have to go slow. I almost broke my arm once. |
> | Charlie: | Really? Did you go to the hospital in an ambulance? |
> | Trang: | No, my mom just took me to the doctor. |

‣ Check students' comprehension by asking "What does Trang think about?" when he fell off of his bicycle and had to go to the doctor

> | Charlie: | I have to go to the grocery store with my mom. When I come back, we can ride bikes, okay? |
> |---|---|
> | Trang: | Sure! We can go to the park. I'll show you the library on the way. |

‣ Check students' comprehension by asking "Why can't Charlie go to the park right now?" He has to go to the grocery store with his mom.

Practice the Dialog

‣ Assign the class the role of Charlie. You will read the role of Trang. Read through the dialog line by line.

‣ Have students:

- Read Charlie's part of the dialog aloud.

Variation:

‣ Divide the class in half.

‣ Assign one role to each half of students.

‣ Have students:

- Choral read each half of the dialog as a group.

‣ Check students' comprehension of the dialog by revisiting the questions from the Picture Walk-Through.

Pronoun Picture Dictionary

‣ Have students:

- Bring in pictures of important people and objects in their lives.

- Bring in pictures in which they appear alone and with other people.

‣ Review the pronouns with students. Write them on the board. Distribute paper and glue to students.

▸ Have students:

- Create a pronoun picture dictionary.
- Paste their pictures onto a piece of paper.
- Write sentences to using the pronouns to identify the people in the picture.
- Underline the pronoun in each sentence.

    Example: For a picture of the student: <u>I</u> am thirteen years old.
    For a picture of the student with his or her pet: <u>We</u> play in the park.

▸ Invite volunteers to share their pictures and descriptions with the class.

Revisit the Dialog

▸ Direct students' attention again to the dialog on page 66 of the *Student Text*.

▸ Have students:

- Read the dialog out loud with a partner.
- Practice intonation and natural conversational tone.

▸ Ask one pair of students to:

- Volunteer to perform the dialog in front of the class.

Your Turn

The Neighborhood of My Dreams

▸ Provide students with poster board or chart paper and colored markers.

Have students:

- Work in small groups to design their dream neighborhood.
- Draw a street plan overview of the neighborhood.
- Label the important people and places in the neighborhood.
- Share their posters with the class and point out what makes their neighborhood special.

▸ Display the posters around the room.

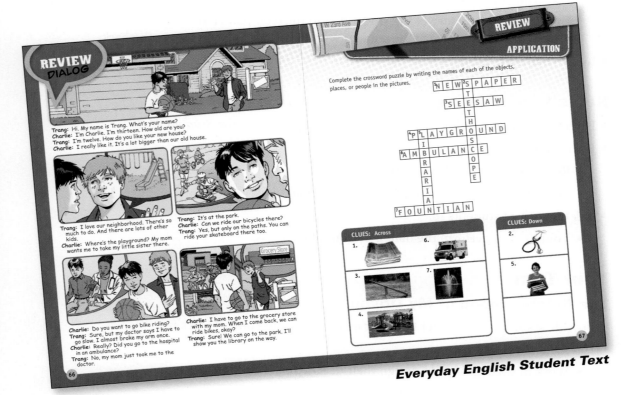

REVIEW
DIALOG

Trang: Hi. My name is Trang. What's your name?
Charlie: I'm Charlie. I'm thirteen. How old are you?
Trang: I'm twelve. How do you like your new house?
Charlie: I really like it. It's a lot bigger than our old house.

Trang: I love our neighborhood. There's so much to do. And there are lots of other kids.
Charlie: Where's the playground? My mom wants me to take my little sister there.

Trang: It's at the park.
Charlie: Can we ride our bicycles there?
Trang: Yes, but only on the paths. You can ride your skateboard there too.

Charlie: Do you want to go bike riding?
Trang: Sure, but my doctor says I have to go slow. I almost broke my arm once.
Charlie: Really? Did you go to the hospital in an ambulance?
Trang: No, my mom just took me to the doctor.

Charlie: I have to go to the grocery store with my mom. When I come back, we can ride bikes, okay?
Trang: Sure! We can go to the park. I'll show you the library on the way.

66

REVIEW
APPLICATION

Complete the crossword puzzle by writing the names of each of the objects, places, or people in the pictures.

Across:
¹NEWSPAPER
³SEESAW
⁴PLAYGROUND
⁶AMBULANCE
⁷FOUNTIAN

Down:
²TOOTHPASTE
⁵LIBRARIAN
STETHOSCOPE

CLUES: Across
1.
6.
3.
7.
4.

CLUES: Down
2.
5.

67

Everyday English Student Text

156   Unit 3 • Review

Everyday English Student Text

HOUSEHOLD ITEMS

In

DOG FOOD

CASHIER

Coins

Money

71

Everyday English Student Text

Introduction: Oral Fluency

 Students learn to use *where* and are introduced to the week's scenario. Then, students focus on one of the areas within the scenario.

Question Words: *Where*

Materials
Student Text
pp. 68–71

▸ Review the question words *what, which, who,* and *how* with the students by asking yes/no, embedded, and open-ended questions using the question words. For example, ask students "Who works in the library?" the librarian "What day is it today, Monday or Tuesday?"

▸ Have students:
- Respond to the questions.

▸ Place a book or another object that the students know in English and put it in a location where the students can see it. Ask "Where is the book?" Hold your hands up with your palms up as you shrug your shoulders and look around to suggest you do not know where it is.

▸ Have students:
- Point to the book.

▸ Write on the board:

Where is the book?

▸ Read it aloud, underline the word **where**.

▸ Have students:
- Chorally and individually repeat the question.

▸ Repeat with other items that the students know in English.

▸ Have students:
- Point to the items.
- Volunteer to ask where items are in the room.

Unit Overview: Grocery Store

▸ Direct students' attention to the picture on pages 68–69. Say "grocery store."

▸ Have students:
- Choral repeat the words.

▸ Have students:
- Identify any parts of the grocery store they may know in English by sharing the words with the class.

- ▸ Point to the **produce** section. Say "produce."
- ▸ Have students:
  - • Point to the produce section.
  - • Choral repeat the word.
- ▸ Turn to page 70 and repeat for **meats, household items,** and **cashier.**
- ▸ Direct students' attention to pages 70–71. Ask students "Where is the produce?"
- ▸ Have students:
  - • Point to the produce section picture and repeat the word **produce.**

Introduction to Produce

- ▸ Direct students' attention to the picture of the produce section on page 70.
- ▸ Elicit words that students know in English that are in the picture and share them with the class.
- ▸ Point out the words and pictures of **fruit** and **vegetables.**
- ▸ Have students:
  - • Choral repeat the words.

STEP 1

Phonemic Awareness

 Students practice identifying, differentiating, and producing the / ă / sound.

The / ă / Sound

Materials
Red cards
Green cards
Red and green chalk or markers for the board

- ▸ Draw on the board or point to a table in the room if there is one and elicit the word **table** from the students. Write the word on the board.
- ▸ Have students:
  - • Pronounce the word with you.
- ▸ Remind students that in this word, we use the / ā / sound. Underline the **a** in the word and pronounce the sound.
- ▸ Explain that the letter **a** in English sometimes makes the sound / ă /. Pronounce the sound for the students.
- ▸ Have students:
  - • Choral repeat the sound.
- ▸ Write the word **apple** on the board. Underline the **a** with red and pronounce the word.
- ▸ Have the students:
  - • Choral repeat the word.
- ▸ Point out the difference in the / ā / and / ă / sounds. Repeat each sound. Hold up a green card when you say the / ā / sound and a red card when you say the / ă / sound.

▸ Explain that the / ă / sound is shorter and we have to "stop" the pronunciation of the short vowel sound. Hold up the red card at the / ă / sound as you repeat the pronunciation of **apple**.

▸ Repeat with the words **taxi, backpack,** and **map**.

▸ Have the students:

  • Chorally and individually repeat the words.

Red Short, Green Long with / ă / and / ā /

▸ Prepare a set of red cards and a set of green cards for the students. There should be enough cards so that each student has both a red and green card.

▸ Point out the longer / ā / sound in the word **table**. Explain that we "go on" with our pronunciation of a long vowel sound. Hold up a green card when you say the / ā / sound as you say the word.

▸ Give each student a red and green card.

▸ Have students:

  • Listen to each word.

  • Hold up a red card each time they hear the / ă / sound.

  • Hold up a green card each time they hear the / ā / sound.

  • Repeat each word.

▸ Say the following words:

  plate   napkin   salad   paper   sand   banana

▸ Model an example with the students

Pair/Share

▸ Have students:

  • Work in pairs to come up with a list of words with the / ă / and / ā / sounds to call out to the class.

STEP 2 · Everyday Words

Students learn and practice vocabulary related to the senses as well as prepositions for everyday conversation.

Recognize Everyday Words: The Senses

Materials

Various items or pictures of items

▸ Gather items or pictures of items that can be described with the senses such as pictures of flowers, garbage, cotton, fruit, etc.

▸ Draw a chart on the board like the one below.

- Have students:
  - Identify the body parts they know.
- Explain that each body part corresponds to a sense. Write the words **look, taste, smell, sound,** and **feel** under the drawing that corresponds to each sense verb.
- Say each word for the students as you act out looking, tasting, smelling, listening, and touching.
- Have students:
  - Chorally and individually repeat each verb.
  - Act out each verb as they repeat.

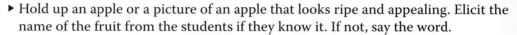

- Hold up an apple or a picture of an apple that looks ripe and appealing. Elicit the name of the fruit from the students if they know it. If not, say the word.
- Look at the apple and say "This apple looks good." Point to your eyes and point to the apple as you say the sentence.
- Act out smelling the apple and say "This apple smells good." Point to your nose and the apple as you say the sentence.
- Act out taking a bite of the apple, smile and say "This apple tastes good." Point to your mouth and the apple.
- Write the sentences on the board under the corresponding columns. Repeat each sentence.
- Have students:
  - Chorally and individually repeat the sentences.
  - Act out the verbs as they say the sentences.
- Repeat with other items and senses to teach the words **soft, hard, sweet, juicy** and **delicious**.

Recognize Everyday Words: Prepositions

- Put a book on a chair in the classroom so that the students can see. Ask the students "Where is the book?"
- Have the students:
  - Point to the book.
- Then say "The book is on the chair." Pick up the book and put it on the chair as you pat the chair to indicate **on**.
- Write the word **on** on the board and say the word. Then repeat the sentence "The book is on the chair."
- Have students:
  - Chorally and individually repeat the word and the sentence. The book is on the chair.
- Repeat for the prepositions **in** and **at** by modeling examples. For example, put a pen in a drawer to demonstrate **in**. Stand at the board to demonstrate **at**.

In, On, or At?

- Place an object that the students know in English on a desk. Ask the students "Is the (object) on the desk or in the desk?" The (object) is on the desk.

▸ Have students:

- Respond in complete sentences.

▸ Repeat with other items and other locations to practice **in, on,** and **at**.

▸ Have students:

- Respond in complete sentences.

- Volunteer to place items **in, on,** or **at** other locations for the class to say where the items are.

STEP 3

Vocabulary Development

Students work with the core content vocabulary related to produce for everyday conversation.

Introduce: Core Vocabulary

Materials

Student Text
pp. 72–73

Model

▸ Direct students' attention to the produce picture and list on pages 72–73 of the *Student Text*. Point out the **fruit** and **vegetables** in the picture. Tell students that fruit and vegetables are **produce**. Say each word as you point to them in the picture.

▸ Have students:

- Repeat the words and point to the pictures.

▸ Elicit the names of any fruits or vegetables that students know in English that are in the picture and share them with the class.

▸ Point to each item that appears on the items list on page 73. As you point, say each word out loud.

▸ Have students:

- Point to each item.

- Repeat each word.

Practice Vocabulary

Color Sort

▸ Elicit the names of the colors from the students.

▸ Have students:

- Point to an item in the classroom of each color named.

- Repeat the name of each color.

▸ Divide the students into pairs.

▸ Call out a color.

Pair/Share

▸ Have students:

- Write the names of produce items that are the color that is called out.

- Share their lists with the class as the others point to each item.

- Say if each item called out is a fruit or a vegetable.

▸ Repeat with other colors.

▸ More advanced students may share their items list by using complete sentences.

Back to the Board Beep

▸ Write the word **peach** on the board. Ask students "Is a peach big or small?" small Write on the board:

a _____ is small.

▸ Read the sentence aloud and say "beep" in the blank.

▸ Ask "What color is a peach?" orange Write on the board:

a _____ is orange.

▸ Read the sentence aloud and say "beep" in the blank.

▸ Repeat to ask about the shape, taste, smell, and feel of a peach. Write each sentence on the board with a blank space where "peach" would go. Read each sentence aloud with a "beep" in the space.

▸ Invite a volunteer to:

 • Stand with his or her back to the board.

 • Guess the produce item written on the board.

▸ Write the name of a produce item on the board so that the volunteer cannot see it.

▸ Have students:

 • Describe the item, substituting a "beep" for the name of the item for the volunteer to guess.

 • Take turns standing with their back to the board.

▸ Model an example for the class with a volunteer.

▸ Repeat with other produce items.

STEP

 How English Works

Students are introduced to the dialog. Students participate in the dialog. Students learn and practice verb conjugation.

Introduce the Dialog

Picture Walk-Through

Materials
Student Text
pp. 74–75

▸ Have students:

 • Look at the pictures on page 74 of the *Student Text*.

▸ Ask students simple questions about the pictures to predict the main idea of the dialog.

▸ Point to the picture in each panel. Act out or point to vocabulary words as necessary. Ask:

1. Panel 1: What are Dad and Isabel going to buy? fruit and vegetables
2. Panel 2: Are they looking at apples? yes
3. Panel 3: Does Dad like the bananas? no What is Isabel doing with the strawberries? She's smelling the strawberries.
4. Panel 4: What fruit does Isabel have? a watermelon
5. Panel 5: What is Dad putting in the bag? grapes
6. Panel 6: What do you think Isabel and Dad will make? Answers may vary.

▸ Record student responses on the board.

Read the Dialog

▸ Read through the dialog in steps. Have students:

- Track print with you as you read.
- Listen for cognates, or English words that are similar in students' native language.

Dad:	Let's buy all of the fruit we need for the fruit salad. Do you have the list?
Isabel:	Yes. We need a lot of fruit.

▸ Explain to students what a **list** is. Ask students "What do you think is on Isabel and Dad's list?" fruit

▸ Have students:

- Choral repeat the word **list**.
- Point to the list.

▸ Check students' comprehension by asking "What will Isabel and Dad make with the fruit?" a fruit salad

Dad:	How do the apples look?
Isabel:	They look good. We also need bananas.

▸ Check students' comprehension by asking "Do Isabel and Dad like the apples?" yes "How do the apples look?" good

Dad:	They feel too soft. What about the strawberries?
Isabel:	They smell fresh. They're big too. We also need oranges.

▸ Check students' comprehension by asking "What is the problem with the bananas?" The bananas are soft. "What is good about the strawberries?" The strawberries smell fresh. They are big.

▸ Have students:

- Point to the **bananas** and the **strawberries** in the picture and say the words.

Dad:	They feel hard. How does the watermelon sound?
Isabel:	It sounds perfect. It's probably very sweet.

▸ Have students:

- Point to the fruits in the picture.
- Say the names of the fruits.

▸ Check students' comprehension by asking "How will the watermelon taste?" good/sweet

Dad:	The grapes look juicy. Let's buy some of them.

▸ Check students' comprehension by asking "How do the grapes look?" juicy

Isabel:	Do we want to add cherries to the fruit salad?
Dad:	The cherries look a little too small. They might be difficult to eat because they have seeds.
Isabel:	This fruit salad is going to be delicious!

▸ Explain that many fruits and vegetables have **seeds**. Draw a picture of a cut apple with seeds to illustrate the word.

▸ Check students' comprehension by asking "Does Dad want cherries?" no "Why not?" They are small. They have seeds.

Practice the Dialog

▸ Assign the class the role of Isabel. You will read the role of Dad. Read through the dialog line by line.

▸ Have students:

- Read Isabel's part of the dialog aloud.

Variation:

▸ Divide the class in half.

▸ Assign one role to each half of students.

▸ Have students:

- Choral read each half of the dialog.

▸ Check students' comprehension of the dialog by revisiting the questions from the Picture Walk-Through.

Working with Verbs

▸ Point to Panel 1 on page 74 of the *Student Text*. Write the sentence on the board and say:

Isabel wants apples.

▸ Ask "Does Dad want apples?" yes Write on the board:

Dad wants apples.

- ▸ Underline *Isabel* and *Dad* in the sentences and ask students what pronoun we use to substitute each person. she and he Write the pronouns under each person.
- ▸ Circle *wants* in each sentence. Tell students that we add an *-s* at the end of the verb with *he* and *she*.
- ▸ Say "I want bananas." Write the sentence on the board. Underline *I* and circle *want*.
- ▸ Have students:
  - tell you the difference between the verbs in the first two sentences and the last sentence. There is no -s after want in the last sentence.
- ▸ Continue with other examples to demonstrate the conjugations of the affirmative of *want* with *you, we, they,* and *it.*
- ▸ Point out that we use the verb without *-s* for all people except *he, she,* and *it.*
- ▸ Have students:
  - Copy the sentences from the board.
  - Substitute the verb *want* with *need.*
  - Volunteer to write the new sentences on the board.
- ▸ Extend the activity by substituting the verbs with **eat** and **like**.

Revisit the Dialog

- ▸ Have students:
  - Read through the dialog on their own.
  - Identify words that are related to the senses.
  - Share and point out the words to the class.
- ▸ Write the words that the students identified on the board.
- ▸ Have students:
  - Complete Application A on page 75 of the *Student Text.*
  - Share their sentences with the class.

On Their Own

Your Turn

- ▸ Direct students to page 75 of the *Student Text.*
- ▸ Have students:
  - Complete Application B on page 75 of the *Student Text.*
  - Compare their answers with a partner.
- ▸ Check answers.

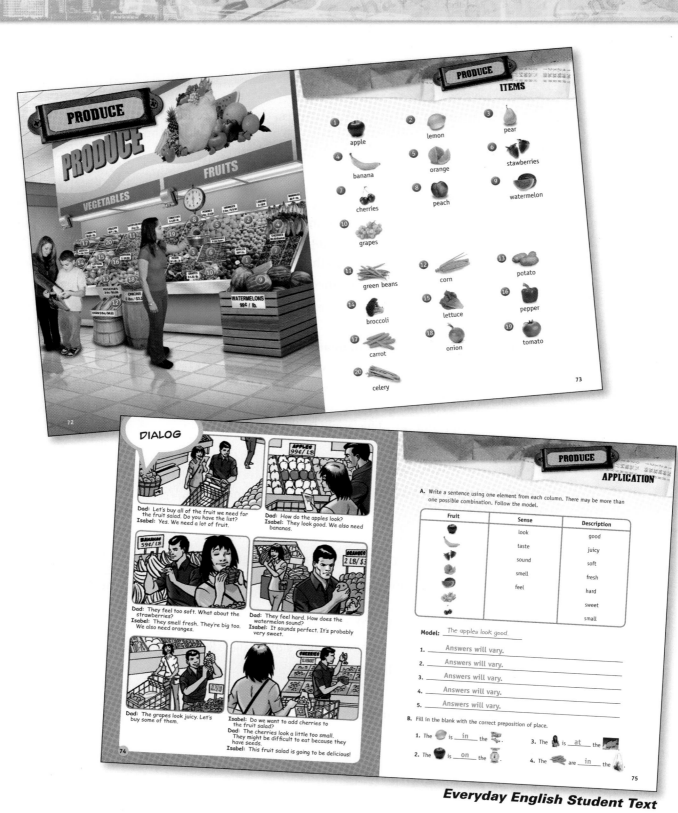

Everyday English Student Text

Introduction: Oral Fluency

 Students learn to talk about qualities and are reintroduced to the week's scenario. Then, students focus on one of the areas within the scenario.

Qualities

Materials

Student Text
pp. 68–71

Various
pictures

Model

▸ Begin the class by reminding students that they know many words to describe how things look, taste, feel, smell, and sound.

▸ Review some of the adjectives learned in previous lessons. For example, to review the word **round,** ask "What is something that is **round**?"

▸ Review other previously learned adjectives such as **delicious, red, square, big,** etc.

▸ Tell students that they are going to learn other words that can be used to describe people, places, or things.

▸ Write the adjectives **good, bad, beautiful,** and **ugly** on the board.

▸ Point to the word **good** and say the word. Make a "thumbs up" gesture and smile as you say the word to demonstrate the word **good**.

▸ Give an example of the use of the word. Act out taking a bite of an apple. Smile, give the "thumbs up," and say "This apple is good."

▸ Have students:

  • Repeat the word **good**.

▸ Repeat for the word **bad.** Give a "thumbs down" and frown.

▸ Have students:

  • Repeat the word **bad**.

  • Tell you things that they think are **good** or **bad**.

▸ Hold up a picture of something beautiful, like a picture of beautiful scenery. Say "This is beautiful."

▸ Write the word **beautiful** on the board.

▸ Hold up a picture of something ugly, like a dirty alley. Say "This is ugly."

▸ Write the word **ugly** on the board.

▸ Have students:

  • Repeat the words **beautiful** and **ugly**.

  • Tell you things or places that they think are **beautiful** or **ugly**.

Review: Grocery Store

▸ Direct students' attention to the picture on pages 70–71. Say "grocery store." Point to the produce section and elicit the word **produce** from the students.

▸ Point to the **meats** section and say the word **meats**.

▸ Have students:

  • Point to the **meats** section.

  • Repeat the word.

▸ Direct students' attention to pages 70–71. Ask students "Where are the meats?"

▸ Have students:

  • Point to the meats section picture and say the word **meats**.

Introduction to Meats

▸ Direct students' attention to the picture of the meats section on page 70.

▸ Elicit words that students know in English that are in the picture and share them with the class.

▸ Have students:

  • Choral repeat the words.

STEP 1

Phonemic Awareness

Students practice identifying, differentiating, and producing the / ĕ / sound.

The / ĕ / Sound

Materials
Red cards
Green cards
Red and green chalk or markers for the board

Model

▸ Point to your knee. Elicit the word **knee** from the students. Write the word on the board.

▸ Have students:

  • Pronounce the word with you.

▸ Remind students that in this word, we use the / ē / sound. Underline the **ee** with green in the word and pronounce the sound.

▸ Explain that the letter *e* in English sometimes makes the sound / ĕ /. Pronounce the sound for the students.

▸ Have students:

  • Choral repeat the sound.

▸ Write the word **lemon** on the board. Underline the *e* with red and pronounce the word.

▸ Have the students:

  • Choral repeat the word.

▸ Point out the difference in the / ē / and / ĕ / sounds. Repeat each sound. Hold up a green card when you say the / ē / sound and a red card when you say the / ĕ / sound.

- ▸ Explain that the / ĕ / sound is shorter and we have to "stop" the pronunciation of the short vowel sound. Hold up the red card at the / ĕ / sounds as you repeat the pronunciation of **lemon**.

- ▸ Repeat with the words **pepper, celery,** and **lettuce.**

- ▸ Have the students:

  - Chorally and individually repeat the words.

Red Short, Green Long with / ĕ / and / ē /

- ▸ Prepare a set of red cards and a set of green cards for the students. There should be enough cards so that each student has both a red and green card.

- ▸ Point out the longer / ē / sound in the word **knee**. Explain that we "go on" with our pronunciation of the long vowel sound. Hold up a green card when you say the / ē / sound as you say the word.

- ▸ Give each student a red and green card.

- ▸ Have students:

  - Listen to each word.

  - Hold up a red card each time they hear the / ĕ / sound.

  - Hold up a green card each time they hear the / ē / sound.

  - Repeat each word.

- ▸ Say the following words:

  ear   cherry   beans   celery   pepper   knee   lemon

- ▸ Model an example with the students.

Pair/Share

- ▸ Have students:

  - Work in pairs to come up with a list of words with the / ĕ / and / ē / sound sounds to call out to the class.

STEP 2

Everyday Words

➡ Students learn and practice talking about prices and vocabulary related to the sense of taste for everyday conversation.

Recognize Everyday Words: Prices

Materials
Student Text
p. 72

- ▸ Review the numbers from 1–100 with the students.

- ▸ Lead the students in counting from 1–20.

- ▸ Have students:

  - Each say the next consecutive number from 1–20 as you randomly point to a student.

  - Count from 20–100 by tens as you randomly point to a student.

- ▸ After reviewing the numbers write a dollar sign ($) on the board. Say **dollar** as you point to the sign.

- ▸ Repeat with the **cent** sign (¢).
- ▸ Have students:
  - • Choral repeat the words **dollar** and **cent**.
- ▸ Direct students to page 72 to look back at the produce section.
- ▸ Point to the corn. Say "How much does corn cost?" Write **$4.00** on the board. Point to the price and say "four dollars."
- ▸ Point to the lemons. Say "How much do the watermelons cost?" Write **99¢** on the board. Point the price and say "ninety-nine cents."
- ▸ Have students:
  - • Chorally and individually repeat both prices after you ask the price again.
- ▸ Point to the onions. Say "How much do the onions cost?" Write **$3.50** on the board. Point to the price and say "three dollars and fifty cents."
- ▸ Have students:
  - • Chorally and individually repeat the price after you ask the price again.
- ▸ Point out other produce items in the picture. Ask students the price of each item.
- ▸ Have students:
  - • Chorally and individually say the price of each item.

Recognize Everyday Words: Taste

- ▸ Gather food items or pictures of food items that can be described by taste.
- ▸ Draw a picture of a mouth on the board and elicit the word **taste** from the students.

- ▸ Have students:
  - • Tell you some words they know that can describe how something tastes. delicious, good, bad, sweet
  - • Describe a food using the words. For example, Watermelon is sweet.
- ▸ Write the adjectives on the board under the drawing of the mouth.
- ▸ Hold up a lemon or picture of a lemon. Act like you are eating a lemon and grimace as though eating something sour. Say "A lemon is **sour**."
- ▸ Write the word on the board.
- ▸ Have students:
  - • Repeat the word.
  - • Volunteer to share another food that is sour.
  - • Provide the word in English if the students do not know it.
- ▸ Repeat for the words **salty** and **bitter**. Examples of salty items might include potato chips, pretzels, and popcorn. Examples of bitter items might include coffee, bitter melon, and olives.

STEP 3

Vocabulary Development

 Students work with the core content vocabulary related to meats for everyday conversation.

Introduce: Core Vocabulary

Materials
Student Text
p. 77

▸ Tell students that they already know some words for things that we eat. Tell them they are going to learn more food words.

▸ Point to each item that appears on the items list on page 77. As you point, say each word out loud.

▸ Have students:

  • Point to each item and repeat each word.

Practice Vocabulary

I Went to the Grocery Store, and I Bought...

▸ Point to the **beef** in the picture and say "I went to the grocery store and I bought some **beef**."

▸ Have students:

  • Repeat the sentence.

  • Each add a meat item to the sentence and repeat the sentence with all of the previous items.

    Example: Start the class with the sentence: I went to the grocery store, and I bought beef. **The next student says:** I went to the grocery store, and I bought beef and sausages. **The next student says:** I went to the grocery store, and I bought beef, sausages, and chicken, etc.

STEP 4

How English Works

 Students are introduced to the dialog. Students participate in the dialog. Students learn and practice verb conjugations.

Introduce the Dialog

Picture Walk-Through

Materials
Student Text
pp. 78–79
Dice

▸ Have students:

  • Look at pictures on page 78 of the *Student Text*.

▸ Ask students simple questions about the pictures to predict the main idea of the dialog.

▸ Point to the picture in each panel. Act out or point to vocabulary words as necessary. Ask:

1. Panel 1: Are Dad and Isabel going to buy produce now? no
2. Panel 2: Does Isabel want steak or chicken? chicken
3. Panel 3: What does Dad want? pork chops
4. Panel 4: Does Isabel want hot dogs or hamburgers? hamburgers
5. Panel 5: Do Isabel and Dad want liver or ham? no
6. Panel 6: Does Isabel like what she sees? yes

▸ Record student responses on the board.

Read the Dialog

▸ Read through the dialog in steps.

▸ Have students:

- Track print with you as you read.
- Listen for cognates, or English words that are similar in students' native language.

Dad:	What do you want to make for dinner?
Isabel:	Let's see what they have today. What do you want to eat?

▸ Check students' comprehension by asking "What do Isabel and Dad need to buy?" something to make for dinner, meat

Dad:	Do you want steak?
Isabel:	Steak tastes delicious, but we ate that last night. Do you want to eat chicken?

▸ Check students' comprehension by asking "What does Dad want to eat?" steak "What does Isabel want to eat?" chicken "Why?" They had chicken last night.

▸ Have students:

- Point to the steak and chicken in the picture.
- Say each word as they point to the picture.

Dad:	Your mom had chicken for lunch. She said to buy anything but chicken. What about pork chops?
Isabel:	The pork chops look too small, don't you think?

▸ Check students' comprehension by asking "Why doesn't Dad want to buy chicken?" Isabel's mom doesn't want chicken. "What is the problem with the pork chops?" They are too small.

Dad:	You're right. Do you want me to make a roast?
Isabel:	That looks too big! Do you feel like eating hamburgers?

▸ Explain to students that we use **feel like** as a way to say **want**. Provide other examples for the students.

► Check students' comprehension by asking "Is the roast big or small?" big

> Dad: Hamburgers are okay. I don't want liver or ham.
>
> Isabel: I don't like liver either. And ham is too salty.

► Check students' comprehension by asking "Why doesn't Isabel want ham?" It's too salty.

> Dad: Mom doesn't like liver or ham either. How about lamb?
>
> Isabel: I love lamb. It's my favorite!

► Check students' comprehension by asking "What do Isabel and Dad buy?" lamb

Practice the Dialog

► Assign the class the role of Isabel. You will read the role of Dad. Read through the dialog line by line.

► Have students:
   • Read Isabel's part of the dialog aloud.

Variation:

► Divide the class in half.

► Assign one role to each half of students.

► Have students:
   • Choral read each half of the dialog.

► Check students' comprehension of the dialog by revisiting the questions from the Picture Walk-Through.

Making It Negative

► Review the affirmative conjugation of the verbs in the present tense. Draw a table on the board.

I		we	
you		you	
he she it		they	

► Have students:
   • Help you fill in the chart with the correct form of the verb **like** in the present tense.
   • Use each subject and verb in a sentence.

   Example: Students will tell you to put **like** next to *I, you, we,* and *they,* and **likes** next to *he, she,* and *it.*

Model

▸ Say "I like oranges." Smile and make a "thumbs up" gesture to demonstrate **like**. Then say, "I don't like lemons." Frown and make a "thumbs down" gesture.

▸ In the table, next to the *I*, write **don't like**.

▸ Remind students that **don't** is the contraction of **do not**.

▸ Ask students "Do you like lemons?"

▸ Find a student who does not like lemons. Point to that student and say "You don't like lemons."

▸ Write **don't like** next to *you*.

▸ Remind students that **doesn't** is the contraction of **does not**.

▸ Say "Jessica likes lamb. She doesn't like liver." Write **doesn't like** on the board next to *she*.

▸ Continue in a similar many to complete the *we, you,* and *they* spaces in the chart by finding examples from the dialog or people in the class.

▸ Point out the differences between **don't** and **doesn't**. Point out that the verb **like** does not have an *-s* at the end when it is used with **doesn't**.

▸ Have students:

  • Repeat the words **don't** and **doesn't**.

  • Complete the chart with a different verb in the negative.

Practice Verb Forms

▸ Direct students' attention to page 79 of the *Student Text*.

▸ Have students:

On Their Own

  • Complete Application A by writing sentences to say whether or not the people like the item pictured.

  • Complete Application B to write about what they like or do not like.

  • Share what they like and do not like with the class.

Who Does or Doesn't Do It? Dice Roll

▸ Write the following information on the board:

1 = I	4 = we
2 = you	5 = you
3 = he, she, it	6 = they

▸ Have students:

  • Name some activities that people do such as **eat, drink, buy, play,** etc.

▸ Record the activities on the board.

▸ Choose one of the verbs from the board.

▸ Roll one die. Hold up the number and show it to the class.

▸ Have students:

  • Tell you the number on the die.

▸ Point to the corresponding number and the subject pronoun on the chart.

▶ Have students:

- Say the subject pronoun and the correct form of the verb for that pronoun.
- Use the subject and verb in a sentence.
- Volunteer to write the sentence on the board.

    Example: You chose the verb eat. You roll a 1. Point to the 1 and pronoun *I* on the chart. Students will say: I don't eat. Then they will use these words to make a sentence.

▶ Break students into groups or pairs, give each group or pair one die to play the game.

Variation:

▶ Alternate between negative and affirmative verb forms.

Revisit the Dialog

▶ Direct students' attention again to the dialog on page 78 of the *Student Text*.

▶ Have students:

- Read the dialog aloud with a partner.
- Write a list of what each person in the dialog wants or doesn't want.
- Write sentences to say what the people in the dialog want or don't want.

Your Turn

▶ Have students:

- Create a dialog for role play between Isabel and Dad, in which the two are deciding what meat to buy for a picnic on Saturday. (Isabel wants: **hamburgers** and **chicken**. Dad wants **hot dogs** and **sausages**.)
- Take turns playing the two roles.
- Use the affirmative and negative forms of the verbs to explain why they like/dislike, want/don't want, etc. a certain item.
- Use words to describe how items look, taste, feel, etc.

    Example:

Isabel:	I like hamburgers. They are good for a picnic.
Dad:	I don't want the hamburgers. They don't look good. I like hot dogs.

▶ Invite volunteers to:

- Perform their dialog in front of the class.

Everyday English Student Text

HOUSEHOLD ITEMS

LESSON 3

Introduction: Oral Fluency

 Students learn to use words to ask for and give directions and are reintroduced to the week's scenario. Then, students focus on one of the areas within the scenario.

Directions: *Left, Right* and *Straight*

Materials
Student Text
pp. 68–71
A blindfold

▶ Review the question word *where* with the students by pointing to something in the classroom and asking where it is.

▶ Tell students they are going to learn some words to give simple directions.

▶ Turn your back to the students so that you are facing the same direction they are. Hold up your **left** hand. Say "left." Write the word on the left side of the board.

▶ Have students:

- Hold up their left hand.

- Repeat the word.

▶ Repeat to demonstrate the word **right**.

▶ Stand again in front of the students and walk in a straight line as you indicate with your hand moving in a **straight** motion. Say "straight" and write the word on the board.

▶ Have students:

- Repeat the word.

▶ Tell students we can use the verb **go** with the words **left, right,** and **straight** to give directions.

How do I Get There?

▶ Blindfold a volunteer at the front of the class.

▶ Have students:

- Call out directions for the volunteer to direct the students to different places in the classroom, such as the door, the window, the bulletin board, etc.

- Take turns to be blindfolded and follow directions.

Variation:

▶ If possible, have students:

- Work in pairs in an open area such as the school yard or hall.

- Lead their partner around by calling out directions.

- Take turns to follow the directions with a blindfold or closed eyes.

Review: Grocery Store

▸ Direct students' attention to the picture on pages 70–71. Say "grocery store." Point to the produce section and elicit the word **produce** from the students. Then, point to the **meats** section and elicit the word **meats**.

▸ Point to the household items aisle and say **household items**.

▸ Have students:

  • Point to the **household items** aisle.

  • Repeat the words.

Introduction to Household Items

▸ Direct students' attention to the picture of the household items picture on page 71.

▸ Elicit words that students know in English that are in the picture and share them with the class.

▸ Have students:

  • Choral repeat the words.

STEP 1

Phonemic Awareness

 Students practice identifying, differentiating, and producing the / ĭ / sound.

The / ĭ / Sound

Materials
Red cards
Green cards
Red and green chalk or markers for the board

Model

▸ Draw on the board or point to a picture of a slide. Elicit the word **slide** from the students. Write the word on the board.

▸ Have students:

  • Pronounce the word with you.

▸ Remind students that in this word, we use the / ī / sound. Underline the *i* with green in the word and pronounce the sound.

▸ Explain that the letter *i* in English sometimes makes the sound / ī /. Pronounce the sound for the students.

▸ Have students:

  • Choral repeat the sound.

▸ Write the word **sister** on the board. Underline the *i* with red and pronounce the word.

▸ Have the students:

  • Choral repeat the word.

▸ Point out the difference in the / ī / and / ĭ / sounds. Repeat each sound. Hold up a green card when you say the / ī / sound and a red card when you say the / ĭ / sound.

▸ Explain that the / ĭ / sound is shorter and we have to "stop" the pronunciation of the short vowel sound. Hold up the red card at the / ĭ / sound as you repeat the pronunciation of **sister**.

▸ Repeat with the words **liver, chicken, ribs,** and **dish**.

▸ Have the students:

  • Chorally and individually repeat the words.

Red Short, Green Long with / ĭ / and / ī /

▸ Prepare a set of red cards and a set of green cards for the students. There should be enough cards so that each student has both a red and green card.

▸ Point out the longer / ī / sound in the word **slide**. Explain that we "go on" with our pronunciation of the long vowel sound. Hold up a green card when you say the / ī / sound as you say the word **slide**.

▸ Give each student a red and green card.

▸ Have students:

  • Listen to each word.

  • Hold up a red card each time they hear the / ĭ / sound.

  • Hold up a green card each time they hear the / ī / sound.

  • Repeat each word.

▸ Say the following words:

bicycle   chicken   liver   line   tissue   picnic   kite

▸ Model an example with the students.

Pair/Share

▸ Have students:

  • Work in pairs to come up with a list of words with the / ĭ / and / ī / sound sounds to call out to the class.

STEP 2

Everyday Words

➡ Students learn and practice the months of the year and prepositions.

Recognize Everyday Words: Months

Materials

Student Text
pp. 70–71

Year-calendar

Various food items or pictures of food items

▸ Review the days of the week with the students. Ask them "What day is today?"

▸ Have students:

  • Respond with the day of the week. Today is (day of the week).

  • Recite the rest of the days of the week in order.

▸ Point to today's date on the year calendar. Say "Today is (day)." Point to the month and say "It is (month)."

▸ Have students:

  • Choral repeat the month.

▸ Write each month on the board for the students to see. Say each month aloud as you point to it.

▸ Have students:
- Choral repeat each month.
- Copy the months in their notebooks.

▸ Say "My birthday is in (month)." Draw a picture of a birthday cake on the board next to the month. Ask students "When is your birthday?"

Model

▸ Have students:
- Come to the board and write their name next to the month of their birthday.
- Say: My birthday is in (month).
- Choral repeat each month as each student says when their birthday is.

Round Robin of the Months

▸ Tell students they are going to play a game to help them remember the months.

▸ Have students:
- Stand or arrange their chairs in a circle.
- Volunteer to say what month their birthday is in.
- Go around the circle and recite the months in order starting from the first student's birthday month until they reach the original month again.
- Repeat until all the students have had a chance to start a round by telling when their birthday is.

  Example: One student says: My birthday is in May. The student next to him or her says: June. The next student says July, etc.

Recognize Everyday Words: In, On, At

▸ Review the prepositions **in, on,** and **at** with the students by asking where various items or people are in the classroom that demonstrate these prepositions.

▸ Direct students' attention to pages 70–71 in the *Student Text*.

▸ Point to the called out preposition **on** in the produce scenario picture.

▸ Ask "Where are the apples?" as you point to the apples on the scale. Then answer by saying "The apples are **on** the scale."

▸ Have students:
- Point to the apples.
- Repeat the sentence.
- Point to the called out prepositions **at** and **in** in the meats and household items scenarios.
- Tell you where the woman in the meats section is (at the meats section) and where the grocery items are (in the shopping cart).
- Find other items or people in the pictures to describe where they are with **in, on**, and **at**.

  Example: Students can point to the carrots in the plastic bag and say: The carrots are in the bag.

STEP 3

Vocabulary Development

 Students work with the core content vocabulary related to household items in everyday conversation.

Introduce: Core Vocabulary

Materials
Student Text
pp. 80–81, p. 83

▸ Anchor students' knowledge of home vocabulary by eliciting rooms in the house from previous lessons.

▸ Have students:

• Name some items that belong in each room.

▸ Tell students that some items for the home can be bought in a grocery store even though they are not food items.

▸ Point to each item that appears on the items list on page 81. As you point, say each word out loud.

▸ Have students:

• Point to each item.

• Repeat each word.

Practice Vocabulary

Cooking or Cleaning?

▸ Write the words **cook** and **clean** in two columns on the board. Act out the meaning of both words. Then, point to the sponge and elicit the word from the students. Say "I use a sponge to clean."

▸ Write **sponge** under the column for **clean**.

▸ Write the sentence frame:

I use _____ to _____.

▸ Have students:

• Repeat the sentence: I use a sponge to clean.

• Tell you other items that are used for cooking and cleaning.

• Use the sentence frames to say a complete sentence.

• Write the item on the board under the correct column.

In the Kitchen, In the Bathroom

On Their Own

▸ Direct students' attention to page 83 of the *Student Text*.

▸ Have students:

• Complete Application A by drawing a line from the item to the room.

• Share their answers.

• Choose other items from the household items scenario and say what room of the house they might go in.

How English Works

 Students are introduced to the dialog. Students participate in the dialog. Students learn and practice distinguishing **countable** and **non-countable nouns**.

Introduce the Dialog

Picture Walk-Through

Materials

Student Text pp. 70–71, pp. 82–83

Non-countable items or pictures of non-countable items.

▸ Have students:

• Look at pictures on page 82 of the *Student Text*.

▸ Ask students simple questions about the pictures to predict the main idea of the dialog.

▸ Point to the picture in each panel. Act out or point to vocabulary words as necessary. Ask:

1. Panel 1: What do you think Isabel and Dad need to buy? Answers may vary.

2. Panel 2: What is Dad getting? paper towels

3. Panel 3: What does Dad need? light bulbs

4. Panel 4: Does Isabel need a mop? no

▸ Record student responses on the board.

Read the Dialog

▸ Read through the dialog in steps. Have students:

• Track print with you as you read.

• Listen for cognates, or English words that are similar in students' native language.

> Dad: We still have a few more things to buy. Do we need cat litter?
>
> Isabel: Yes. We also need dog food. Mom said we don't need cat food.

▸ Have students:

• Volunteer to point out and name items in the picture.

▸ Check students' comprehension by asking: "What do Isabel and Dad need to buy?" cat litter and dog food

> Dad: How are we on paper towels?
>
> Isabel: Well, they're on the list. The list says two rolls of paper towels.

▸ Explain the word **rolls** to the students.

► Have students:

- Name other household items that come in rolls. toilet paper, garbage bags

Dad:	I also need two light bulbs. The lamps in the bedroom need bulbs.	
Isabel:	Oh, don't forget. Mom needs batteries for the flashlight.	

► Check students' comprehension by asking "What will Dad do with the light bulbs?" put them in the lamps in the bedroom "What does Mom need the batteries for?" the flashlight

► Have students:

- Tell you other items they know that need batteries.

Dad:	Oh yeah, I almost forgot. Is detergent on the list?
Isabel:	Yes. We need detergent for the dishwasher. We also need sponges.
Dad:	Okay. Let's get the sponges and then we'll go pay. Did I forget anything?
Isabel:	No. We're ready to go!

► Check students' comprehension by asking "Does Dad need detergent for clothes or dishes?" dishes "What does Isabel need?" sponges

► Have students:

- Point out the detergent and sponges and say the name of each item.

Practice the Dialog

► Assign the class the role of Isabel. You will read the role of Dad. Read through the dialog line by line.

► Have students:

- Read Isabel's part of the dialog aloud.

Variation:

► Divide the class in half.

► Assign one role to each half of students.

► Have students:

- Choral read each half of the dialog.

► Check students' comprehension of the dialog by revisiting the questions from the Picture Walk-Through.

Countable and Non-countable Nouns

► Point to an item in the classroom of which there are at least two, for example, two chairs. Ask "How many (items) are there?" two

► Explain to student that there are some items that can be counted, like chairs. Point to other countable items in the room.

▸ Have students:

　• Count the items and tell you how many of each item there are.

▸ Hold up a non-countable item or picture of a non-countable item such as a picture of water. Ask the students to count the water.

▸ When they are unable to count the water, say "Some things, like water, cannot be counted."

▸ Hold up other non-countable items like salt, coffee, milk, soda, sand, etc.

▸ Tell students that non-countable items are substances. Draw a picture of a glass of liquid on the board.

▸ Point to the liquid and say "We can count the cup. There is one cup. But, we cannot count what is inside."

▸ Explain to students that with non-countable nouns we do not use a number or *a/an* in front of it. Explain that we do not use non-countable nouns in the plural.

▸ Write the word **water** on the board. Write *1* in front of it and make an X through it. Do the same with *a* and *an*.

▸ Write the word **chair** on the board. Write *3* in front of it. Write *a chair* underneath.

▸ Point to the boxes of detergent on page 80 of the *Student Text* and explain again that we can count the containers, but we cannot count what is inside.

Can You Count It?

▸ Direct students' attention to pages 70–71 of the *Student Text*.

▸ Have students:

　• Look for non-countable items in the produce, meats, and household items scenarios.

　• Make a list of the non-countable items

　• Share their words with the class.

▸ Write the list of words on the board for the class.

Revisit the Dialog

▸ Direct students' attention to Application A on page 82 of the *Student Text*.

▸ Have students:

　• Read the dialog.

　• Pick out the countable and non-countable items in the dialog.

　• Write out the countable and non-countable items.

▸ Review the students' items.

Your Turn

▸ Direct the students' attention to page 83 of the *Student Text.*

▸ Have students:

- Complete Application B.

- Share their answers.

▸ To extend the activity, have students:

- Illustrate their sentences.

- Volunteer to show their illustrations to the class for them to describe.

    Example: A student has drawn a tube of toothpaste on the sink. The class will say: The toothpaste is on the sink.

Unit 4

CASHIER

LESSON 4

Introduction: Oral Fluency

 Students learn to use adjectives to describe qualities and are reintroduced to the week's scenario. Then, students focus on one of the areas within the scenario.

Cheap and *Expensive*

Materials

Student Text
p. 68–71

Various pictures or items

▸ Gather items or pictures of items that can be described as cheap or expensive.

▸ Review some of the adjectives learned in previous lessons by pointing to various items or pictures of items.

▸ Have students:

• Describe the item using some of the adjectives they have learned

Example: Point to a picture of a flower. Students might say: It is beautiful. It smells good. It is small.

▸ Write the adjectives **cheap** and **expensive** on the board.

▸ Draw two cameras on the board.

Draw a price tag hanging from each camera. Write $20 on one price tag and $300 on the other.

▸ Point to the cheap camera and say "This camera is cheap." Point to the word **cheap** and say the word.

▸ Repeat for the word **expensive**.

▸ Have students:

• Repeat the words **cheap** and **expensive**.

▸ Hold up an item or a picture of something cheap and ask "Is this expensive?" yes

▸ Hold up another item or picture of something expensive and ask "Is this cheap or expensive?" expensive

▸ Repeat with all the items.

▸ Have students:

• Sort the items or pictures of items into the categories of **cheap** or **expensive**.

• Describe each item with a full sentence.

Review: Grocery Store

▸ Direct students' attention to the pictures on pages 70–71. Say "grocery store." Point to the produce section, the meats section, and the household items aisle. Elicit the words **produce, meats,** and **household items** from the students.

▸ Point to the checkout aisles and say **cashier**.

▶ Have students:

- Point to the checkout aisles.
- Repeat the word **cashier**.

▶ Direct students' attention to pages 70–71. Ask students "Where is the cashier?"

▶ Have students:

- Point to the checkout aisles say the words **cashier**.

Introduction to Cashier

▶ Direct students' attention to the picture of the cashier picture on page 71.

▶ Elicit words that students know in English that are in the picture and share them with the class.

▶ Point out the words and pictures of **coins** and **money**.

▶ Have students:

- Choral repeat the words.

STEP 1

Phonemic Awareness

 Students practice identifying, differentiating, and producing the / ŏ / and / ŭ / sounds.

The / ŏ / and / ŭ / Sounds

Materials
Red cards
Green cards
Red and green chalk or markers for the board
Prepared word cards

 Model

▶ Wrote the word **grocery** on the board.

▶ Have students:

- Pronounce the word with you.

▶ Remind students that in this word, we use the / ō / sound. Underline the **o** with green in the word grocery and pronounce the sound.

▶ Explain that the letter **o** in English sometimes makes the sound / ŏ /. Pronounce the sound for the students.

▶ Have students:

- Choral repeat the sound.

▶ Write the word **clock** on the board. Underline the **o** with red and pronounce the word.

▶ Have the students:

- Choral repeat the word.

▶ Point out the difference in the / ō / and / ŏ / sounds. Repeat each sound. Hold up a green card when you say the / ō / sound and a red card when you say the / ŏ / sound.

▶ Explain that the / ŏ / sound, like the / ă /, / ĕ /, and / ĭ / sounds, is shorter and we have to "stop" the pronunciation of the short vowel sound. Hold up the red card at the / ŏ / sounds as you repeat the pronunciation of **clock**.

▶ Repeat with the words **hot dog, doctor,** and **sock**.

▸ Walk through the / ū / and / ŭ / sounds in the same way. Use the words **duck, bus, truck,** and **rug** for the / ŭ / sound and **spatula, vacuum,** and **computer** for the / ū / sound.

Red Short, Green Long with / ŏ /, / ō /, / ŭ /, and / ū /

▸ Prepare a set of word cards. Write a word that the students know in English that include the / ŏ /, / ō /, / ŭ /, and / ū / sounds. Make sure each word only includes one of the target sounds. Make sure you have enough cards for each student.

▸ Draw a green square on one half of the board and a red square on the other half of the board.

▸ Pick out one of the word cards and read the word aloud. Position yourself underneath the green or red square in front of the board according to the long or short vowel sound in the word.

Example: The word card has the word **closet** on it. Read the word aloud. Then, stand under the red square in front of the blackboard.

▸ Give each student a word card.

▸ Have students:

  • Stand under the red or green square.

  • Say their word out loud.

▸ To extend the activity, have students:

  • Write their words on the board.

  • Underline the letters that produce the / ŏ /, / ō /, / ŭ /, and / ū / sounds.

  • Choose other words to categorize.

STEP

2

Everyday Words

 Students learn and practice money words for everyday conversation.

Recognize Everyday Words: Money

Materials
Student Text
p. 71, 81
Real or play
money

▸ Anchor students' knowledge of money by reviewing how to talk about prices. Write **$2.75** on the board.

▸ Have students:

  • Tell you the price.

▸ Direct students' attention to the cashier picture on page 71 of the *Student Text.* Point out the **money.** Say "Dollars and cents are money." Repeat the word **money.** Have students:

  • Point to the **money** and repeat the word aloud.

▸ Point to the coins in the picture and say **coins.** If you have real coins available, show them to the class. Say "Coins are money." Repeat the word **coins** and write it on the board.

► Have students:

  • Point to the picture of the **coins** and repeat the word aloud.

► Hold up a dollar bill. Say "a dollar" and write **one dollar** = **$1.00** on the board.

► Show a quarter to the class. Say "quarters" and write the phrase **one quarter** = **25¢**.

► Repeat with a **dime, nickel,** and **penny**.

Model

► Hold up the dollar bill and ask "Is this a dollar or a penny?" a dollar

► Show the class a dime and ask "Is this a nickel?" no "What coin is it?" a dime

► Repeat with other money items and ask similar questions.

Variation for more advanced students:

► Write **$2.91** on the board.

► Have students:

  • Tell you how many dollars and coins of each type are needed for this amount.

► If possible, have students use real or play money to come up with various combinations.

► Model an example with the students. Write on the board:

dollars: 2, quarters: 3, dimes: 1, nickels: 1, pennies: 1

► Repeat with other quantities.

Everyday Words Practice: Dollars and Coins

On Their Own

► Direct students' attention to page 87 in the *Student Text*.

► Have students:

  • Complete Application A to identify the coins each person has.

► Check answers.

► Have students:

  • Complete Application B.

  • Volunteer to share their answers.

STEP

3

Vocabulary Development

Students work with the core content vocabulary related to the cashier for everyday conversation.

Introduce: Core Vocabulary

Materials

Student Text
pp. 70–71,
pp. 84–85

Blank cards

► Direct students' attention to pages 70–71 of the *Student Text*. Say "I have everything I need to buy. Where do I pay?"

► Have students:

  • Point to the cashier area in the picture.

  • Repeat the sentence I pay at the cashier.

- ▶ Point out the use of the preposition **at**.
- ▶ Point to each item that appears on the items list on page 85. As you point, say each word out loud.
- ▶ Have students:
  - Point to each item.
  - Repeat each word.

Practice Vocabulary

Picture This

- ▶ Draw a picture of a milk carton on the board.
- ▶ Point to the picture and ask "What is it?" milk
- ▶ Explain to students that they are going to play a guessing game.
- ▶ Give students blank cards.
- ▶ Have students:
  - Write one cashier related word on each card.
- ▶ Collect all the cards and shuffle them.
- ▶ Have students:
  - Volunteer to choose a card from the stack.
  - Draw the item for the class to guess.

Define That

- ▶ Distribute the word cards from the previous activity to the students. Make sure each student has at least one card.
- ▶ Tell students that they are going to write a definition for each word that they have chosen.
- ▶ Choose one word card to model with the students.
- ▶ Example: For example, you have the word **coupon**. Write: This is a paper. You give it to the cashier. You pay less money.
- ▶ Have students:
  - Follow the model and write definitions.
  - Share their definitions with the class.
  - Guess what each defined item is.

STEP 4

How English Works

Students are introduced to the dialog. Students participate in the dialog. Students practice identifying **non-countable nouns**.

Introduce the Dialog

Picture Walk-Through

Materials

Student Text pp. 86–87

Picture of countable and non-countable items

▸ Have students:

 • Look at pictures on page 86 of the *Student Text*.

▸ Ask students simple questions about the pictures to predict the main idea of the dialog.

▸ Point to the picture in each panel. Act out or point to vocabulary words as necessary. Ask:

 1. Panel 1: Where are Isabel and Dad in the grocery store? at the cashier

 2. Panel 2: Do Isabel and Dad have a lot of things in their shopping cart? yes

 3. Panel 3: Does Dad pay with dollars and coins or a credit card? a credit card.

▸ Record student responses on the board.

Read the Dialog

▸ Read through the dialog in steps. Have students:

 • Track print with you as you read.

 • Listen for cognates, or English words that are similar in students' native language.

Isabel:	I hope we remembered everything on the list.
Dad:	If not, I can always come back later.
Isabel:	Dad, I think we have more than fifteen items. We should not be in the express checkout.
Dad:	Oh you're right.
Cashier:	It's okay. The line isn't too long. You can stay in this line.

▸ Check students' comprehension by asking "Are Dad and Isabel in the correct checkout?" no "Do Dad and Isabel have to go to a different line?" no

Dad:	Thanks. Sorry about that. I'll look more closely next time.
Isabel:	Our shopping cart is full. It's definitely more than fifteen items!
Cashier:	Paper or plastic?
Dad:	Plastic.

▸ Explain the difference between **paper** and **plastic** by pointing to items in the room that are paper or plastic.

▸ Have students:

  • Repeat the words.

▸ Check students' comprehension by asking "Which bag does Dad want, paper or plastic?" plastic

> | Cashier: | That will be eighty-nine dollars and thirty-nine cents. |
> | --- | --- |
> | Dad: | Hmm, I don't have enough money in my wallet. I'll have to pay with a credit card. |

▸ Check students' comprehension by asking "How much does everything cost?" $89.39 "How does Dad pay?" with a credit card

▸ Have students:

  • Point to the credit card in the picture.

Practice the Dialog

▸ Assign the class the role of Isabel. You will read the roles of Dad and the cashier. Read through the dialog line by line.

▸ Have students:

  • Read Isabel's part of the dialog aloud.

Variation:

▸ Divide the class in half.

▸ Assign one role to each half of students.

▸ Have students:

  • Choral read each half of the dialog.

▸ Check students' comprehension of the dialog by revisiting the questions from the Picture Walk-Through.

Non-Countable Noun Shout-Out and Slap Down

▸ Gather pictures of countable and non-countable items, preferably items that the students know in English.

▸ Divide the class into two teams.

▸ Have each team line up on either side of a desk or table.

▸ Put a picture face up on the table. Put another picture, face up, on top of the first picture. Continue until you reach a picture of a non-countable noun.

▸ Have students:

  • Stand with their hands behind their back.

  • Slap the picture of the non-countable noun when it appears and shout out "Non-count!"

  • Take turns within their teams slap down and shout out.

▸ Give each team a point every time they correctly identify a non-countable noun before the other team.

Example: You flip a picture of pencils (countable). Next, you flip over a picture of a book (countable). The next picture is of milk. The two students from the teams compete to be the first to slap the picture and call out "Non-count!"

▸ If using items that students know in English, have students:

- Say the name of the non-countable noun for an extra point.

Variation:

▸ Give each team a stack of pictures.

▸ Have students:

- Flip over pictures at the same time to identify the non-countable nouns.

Revisit the Dialog

▸ Direct students' attention again to the dialog on page 86 of the *Student Text*

▸ Divide the class into groups of three. If there is a group that does not have three students, have one person read both the role of Isabel and the cashier.

▸ Have students:

- Read the dialog out loud with their group.
- Point out each item in the picture that their character says.

Your Turn

Pair/Share

▸ Have students:

- Create a dialog between Isabel and Dad in which Isabel remembers that they need to buy peppers. Isabel asks Dad where the peppers are. Dad gives Isabel directions to get to the peppers.
- Refer to the Unit Overview picture if necessary.
- Take turns playing the two roles.

Example:

Isabel:	Dad, we need to buy peppers. We don't have peppers at home.
Dad:	Okay. Can you go get some nice, red peppers?

▸ Invite volunteers to:

- Perform their dialog in front of the class.

CASHIER ITEMS

1. quarter
2. dollars
3. coupons
4. nickel
5. check
6. receipt
7. dime
8. credit card
9. wallet
10. penny
11. shopping cart
12. milk
13. bag
14. cash register
15. eggs
16. bagger
17. scanner
18. bread
19. cashier

85

84

DIALOG

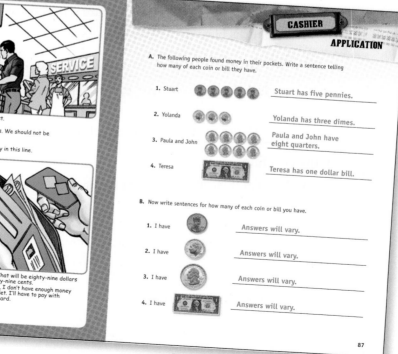

Isabel: I hope we remembered everything on the list.
Dad: If not, I can always come back later.
Isabel: Dad, I think we have more than fifteen items. We should not be in the express checkout.
Dad: Oh, you're right.
Cashier: It's okay. The line isn't too long. You can stay in this line.

Dad: Thanks. Sorry about that. I'll look more closely next time.
Isabel: Our shopping cart is full. It's definitely more than fifteen items!
Cashier: Paper or plastic?
Dad: Plastic.

Cashier: That will be eighty-nine dollars and thirty-nine cents.
Dad: Hmm, I don't have enough money in my wallet. I'll have to pay with a credit card.

86

CASHIER APPLICATION

A. The following people found money in their pockets. Write a sentence telling how many of each coin or bill they have.

1. Stuart — Stuart has five pennies.

2. Yolanda — Yolanda has three dimes.

3. Paula and John — Paula and John have eight quarters.

4. Teresa — Teresa has one dollar bill.

B. Now write sentences for how many of each coin or bill you have.

1. I have — Answers will vary.

2. I have — Answers will vary.

3. I have — Answers will vary.

4. I have — Answers will vary.

87

Everyday English Student Text

Introduction: Oral Fluency

 Students review the use of *where*, adjectives to describe qualities, and how to give and understand directions. Students revisit the Unit Overview.

Qualities Cards

Materials

Student Text
pp. 70–71

Blank cards

▸ Give each student at least two blank cards.

▸ Have students:

- Write one adjective on each card.

▸ Collect the cards from the students.

▸ Give each student two cards.

▸ Have students:

- Read each of their adjectives.

- Think of an item that fits the description of both adjectives.

- Write one or two sentences to describe the item using both adjectives.

  Example: A student picks the words **cheap** and **good**. The student might write: An apple is cheap. It tastes good.

Which Way?

▸ Review the directions **left, right,** and **straight** with the students by pointing to each direction and saying the words.

Pair/Share

▸ Have students:

- Get into pairs.

- Draw a supermarket with their partners and label sections that they have been studying.

- Each choose one location in the supermarket.

- Ask their partners where the location is.

- Give directions for their partner to the location from the other location chosen, which will be used as the starting point.

  Example: One partner chose the meats section. The other partner chose the produce section. The first partner asks: Where is the meats section? The other partner gives directions to the meats section from the produce section.

Unit Review: Grocery Store

▸ Direct students' attention to the pictures on pages 70–71. Elicit the word **grocery store** from the students.

▸ Point out the produce section in the picture. Elicit the word **produce** from the students.

▸ Repeat for **meats, household items,** and **cashier**.

▸ Have students:

  • Chorally and individually repeat the words.

STEP 1

Phonemic Awareness

Students practice identifying, differentiating, and producing the / ă /, / ĕ /, / ĭ /, / ŏ /, and / ŭ / sounds.

Review of the / ă /, / ĕ /, / ĭ /, / ŏ /, and / ŭ / Sounds

Materials
Red cards
Green cards
Red and green chalk or markers for the board,
Red and green pencils

▸ Review the long and short vowel sounds with the students. Say the word **apple**.

▸ Have students:

  • Hold up the correct color card for the vowel sound / ă /.

▸ Repeat with the words **apple, grapes, check, beef, milk, dime, mop, police, cup,** and **tissue** or other words that students know.

▸ Write the words on the board. Underline the **a** in apple with red.

▸ Tell students that the colors can help them remember the pronunciation of words. Go through the other words with them to underline the vowel sounds with red or green.

▸ Have students:

  • Volunteer to underline the vowel sounds on the board.

  • Write down the words **salami, magazine, tomato, watermelon,** and **spatula**.

  • Underline the vowel sounds with red or green pencil.

▸ Model an example with a longer word with the students.

  Example: Write the word **salami** on the board. Underline the two **a**'s with red and the **i** with green. Say the word aloud.

▸ Check answers.

▸ Have students:

  • Volunteer to write their answers on the board.

  • Say each word aloud.

  • Extend the activity by having students look for more words to write out with the colors.

Everyday Words

 Students review and practice the prepositions *in, on,* and *at,* months, money, and the senses for everyday conversation.

Review Everyday Words: Prepositions

Materials

Student Text pp. 72, 76

Twelve blank pieces of poster board or cardboard

Pair/Share

▸ Review the prepositions with the students by pointing out items or people that demonstrate the prepositions **in, on,** or **at.**

▸ Have students:

• Work with a partner and describe the location of a person or item for their partner to draw.

• Draw the item in the location as described by their partners.

• Share their pictures with the class to describe what they see.

Example: One student tells his or her partner: The milk is in the shopping cart. The partner will draw a picture of milk on the scanner.

Review Everyday Words: Money

▸ Have students:

• Look at pages 72 and 76 of the *Student Text.*

• Tell you the price of five items that they see in the pictures.

▸ Write the five prices on the board.

▸ Have students:

• Work in pairs to come up with a combination of dollars and coins that they need to make the amounts written on the board.

• Share their answers with the class.

Review Everyday Words: Senses

▸ Write the five senses: **look, taste, feel, smell,** and **sound** on the board in five columns.

▸ Elicit adjectives from the students that can be used to describe each sense.

▸ Have students:

• Come up with items for each sense and an adjective that fits the description.

• Describe the item using a complete sentence.

• Volunteer to write the sentences on the board.

Example: Under the column **look,** the students have suggested the word **juicy.** Students will say: The orange looks juicy.

Review Everyday Words: Months

▸ Review the months of the year with the students by asking them what month it is.

▸ Have students:

- Recite the rest of the months.

▸ Assign each student a month of the year. If there are more than twelve students, have students work together. If there are fewer than twelve students, assign students two months of the year.

▸ Give each student one poster board or cardboard for their month.

▸ Have students:

- Write their assigned month in large letters on the cardboard.

- Each tell the class what month their birthdays are in.

- Listen to the names of the students whose birthdays fall in that month and write their names on the poster.

- Write or draw information that they know about their month. This could be the season that the month is in, the weather in that month, and sports or holidays in that month.

- Share their month posters with the class and explain what they included.

STEP 3

Vocabulary Development

Students work with the core content vocabulary related to the grocery store for everyday conversation.

Review: Core Vocabulary

▸ Divide the class into teams of 3 or 4 students.

▸ Assign each team a space at the board.

▸ Call out a category.

▸ Have students:

- Line up in front of their space at the board.

- Do a relay race to write items that fit each category.

- Check the lists of the other teams to see if the items fit the category

  Example: Say the category, "Things that are sweet." The first person goes to the board and writes **strawberries**. That person then returns to the line and passes the chalk to the next person in line who writes **apples**.

▸ Give students a time limit for each relay.

Possible categories might include: things that need batteries, things that are for the bedroom, things that are juicy, vegetables, things that are red.

How English Works

Students are introduced to the dialog. Students participate in the dialog. Students review and practice verb conjugations and **countable** and **non-countable nouns**.

Introduce the Dialog

Picture Walk-Through

Materials

Student Text
p. 88–89

Prepared cards

Pictures of
countable and
non-countable
nouns

▸ Have students:

   • Look at pictures on page 88 of the *Student Text*.

▸ Ask students simple questions about the pictures to predict the main idea of the dialog.

▸ Point to the picture in each panel. Act out or point to vocabulary words as necessary. Ask:

   1. Panel 1: What are Isabel and Dad doing? putting the bags in the car

   2. Panel 2: Does Isabel think her mom will like the fruit salad? yes

   3. Panel 3: Is the family going to eat hamburgers for dinner? no

   4. Panel 4: Is Isabel happy or sad? happy

▸ Record student responses on the board.

Read the Dialog

▸ Read through the dialog in steps. Have students:

   • Track print with you as you read.

   • Listen for cognates, or English words that are similar in students' native language.

Dad:	I'm glad I used the coupons.	
Isabel:	Tonight's dinner is going to be great!	
Dad:	Yes, and it will be fun to cook!	

▸ Check students' comprehension by asking "Did Dad use coupons at the cashier?" yes

▸ Have students:

   • Tell you if they have used coupons.

   • Explain why people use coupons.

Isabel:	I think Mom is really going to love the fruit salad.
Dad:	I have to ask her for her special recipe for the lamb.

▸ Check students' comprehension by asking "What will Isabel and Dad make for dinner?" fruit salad and lamb

> Isabel: I love mom's recipe for lamb. Where did she get it?
>
> Dad: I think she got it from your Aunt Victoria.
>
> Isabel: Well, it tastes so delicious!

▸ Explain the meaning of **recipe** to the students. Ask students if they have a favorite recipe.

> Dad: Your mom is coming home a little late tonight. Let's prepare everything. This way, the food will be ready when she gets home.
>
> Isabel: Yes, we need to start chopping the fruit!

▸ Have students:

- Predict where Isabel and Dad are going next and what they will do.

Practice the Dialog

▸ Assign the class the role of Isabel. You will read the role of Dad. Read through the dialog line by line.

▸ Have students:

- Read Isabel's part of the dialog aloud.

Variation:

▸ Divide the class in half.

▸ Assign one role to each half of students.

▸ Have students:

- Choral read each half of the dialog.

▸ Check students' comprehension of the dialog by revisiting the questions from the Picture Walk-Through.

What Do They Do?

▸ Prepare cards with either the subject pronouns or the name of a person or people. There should be enough cards so that each pair has at least four cards.

▸ Elicit action verbs from the students and write them on the board. Focus on verbs that are regular in the present tense.

▸ Divide the class into pairs and give each pair four prepared cards.

Pair/Share

▸ Have students:

- Choose four verbs from the list on the board.

- Write one sentence for each card, using the word on the card as the subject and one of the verbs they chose from the list.

- Write two affirmative sentences and two negatives.

- Share their sentences with the class.

What's What on Your List?

‣ Direct students' attention to Application A on page 89 of the *Student Text.*

‣ Have students:

On Their Own

- Complete the activity by circling all of the non-countable nouns on the list.
- Compare answers with a partner.

‣ Check answers.

Revisit the Dialog

‣ Direct students' attention again to the dialog on page 88 of the *Student Text.*

‣ Have students:

- Read the dialog out loud with a partner.
- Practice intonation and natural conversational tone.

‣ Ask one pair of students to:

- Volunteer to perform the dialog in front of the class.

Your Turn

‣ Direct students' attention to Application B on page 89 of the *Student Text.*

‣ Have students:

- Complete the activity about their favorite meal.
- Share their favorite meal with a partner and describe what it tastes like.
- Identify any items that are non-countable nouns.

‣ Invite volunteers to:

- Share their meal with the class.

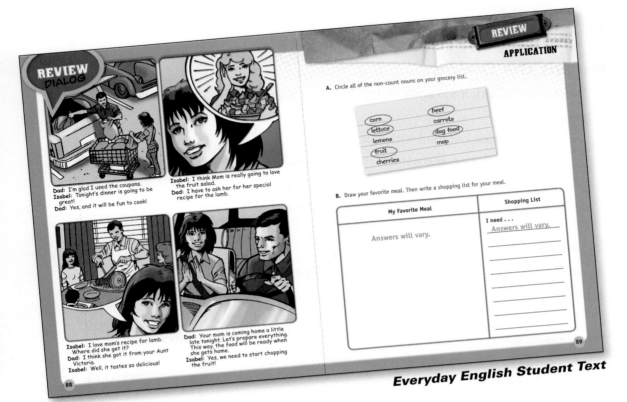

Dad: I'm glad I used the coupons.
Isabel: Tonight's dinner is going to be great!
Dad: Yes, and it will be fun to cook!

Isabel: I think Mom is really going to love the fruit salad.
Dad: I have to ask her for her special recipe for the lamb.

Isabel: I love mom's recipe for lamb. Where did she get it?
Dad: I think she got it from your Aunt Victoria.
Isabel: Well, it tastes so delicious!

Dad: Your mom is coming home a little late tonight. Let's prepare everything. This way, the food will be ready when she gets home.
Isabel: Yes, we need to start chopping the fruit!

88

A. Circle all of the non-count nouns on your grocery list.

corn	beef
lettuce	carrots
lemons	dog food
fruit	mop
cherries	

B. Draw your favorite meal. Then write a shopping list for your meal.

My Favorite Meal	Shopping List
Answers will vary.	I need . . . Answers will vary.

89

Everyday English Student Text

Everyday English Student Text

CLOTHING STORE

Behind

Salesperson

3 for $19.

ENTERTAINMENT STORE

CUSTOMER SERVICE

Service Technician

Customer

ACCESSORIES

JAZZ

NEW AGE

POP/ROCK

in front of

92

93

Everyday English Student Text

CLOTHING STORE

LESSON 1

Introduction: Oral Fluency

Students review *where* and learn *here* and *there* and are introduced to the week's scenario. Then, students focus on one of the areas within the scenario.

Question Words: *Where*

Materials

Student Text pp. 90–93

Folder

▸ Review the question words **what, which, who**, and **how** with the students by asking yes/no, embedded, and open-ended questions using the question words. For example, ask students the following questions to review:

1. How are you today?
2. Who works at the grocery store?
3. What day is it today? Monday or Tuesday?
4. Which fruit do you like better, apples or oranges?

▸ Have students:

- Respond to the questions.

▸ Place a book or another object that the students know in English and put it in a location where the students can see it. Ask "Where is the folder?" Hold your hands up with your palms up as you shrug your shoulders and look around to suggest you do not know where it is.

▸ Have students:

- Point to the folder.

▸ Write on the board:

Where is the folder?

▸ Read it aloud. Underline the word **where**.

▸ Put the folder close to you. Point to it and say "The folder is here." Write the sentence on the board and underline the word **here**.

▸ Have students:

- Chorally and individually repeat the sentence.

▸ Place the folder far away from you and return to where you were standing before. Point to the folder and say "The folder is there." Write the sentence on the board and underline the word **there**.

▸ Have students:

- Chorally and individually repeat the sentence.

▸ Repeat with other classroom items.

► Have students:
  • Point to the items.
  • Volunteer to ask where items are in the room.
  • Answer the questions with the sentence frames:
    The _____ is here.
    The _____ is there.

Unit Overview: The Mall

► Direct students' attention to the pictures on pages 92–93. Say "the mall."
► Have students:
  • Choral repeat the words.
  • Identify any parts of the mall they may know in English by sharing the words with the class.
► Point to the **clothing store** section. Say "clothing store."
► Have students:
  • Point to the clothing store.
  • Choral repeat the word.
► Repeat for **entertainment store, movies,** and **food court**.
► Direct students' attention to pages 92–93. Ask students "Where is the clothing store?"
► Have students:
  • Point to the clothing store picture and repeat the word **clothing store**.

Introduction to Clothing Store

► Direct students' attention to the picture of the clothing store on page 92.
► Elicit words that students know in English that are in the picture and share them with the class.
► Point out the words and picture of the **salesperson**.
► Point to the salesperson and say "The salesperson is behind the counter." Write the word **behind** on the board. Stand behind your desk and say "I am behind the desk."
► Have students:
  • Choral repeat the word.

STEP 1

Phonemic Awareness

 Students practice identifying, differentiating, and producing the / *j* / sound.

The / *j* / Sound

Materials
Chart paper

► Prepare a piece of chart paper by writing / *j* / the top of the paper. Post the paper on the wall in the classroom.

- ▸ Find someone in the classroom who is wearing jeans. Point to the jeans and say "jeans." Write the word **jeans** on the chart paper.
- ▸ Have students:
  - Pronounce the word with you.
- ▸ Tell students that in this word, we use the / j / sound. Underline the **j** in the word and pronounce the sound.
- ▸ Point to something in the classroom that is the color orange. Say "This is orange." Write the word **orange** on the chart paper.
- ▸ Have students:
  - Pronounce the word with you.
- ▸ Tell students that in this word, we also use the / j / sound. Underline the **g** in the word and pronounce the sound.
- ▸ Explain that the letter **j** and **g** in English sometimes makes the sound / j /. Pronounce the sound for the students.
- ▸ Have students:
  - Choral repeat the sound.
- ▸ Tell students that they will learn more words with the / j / sound spelled with the letters **g** and **j** throughout the week. Throughout the week, record vocabulary words with the sound on the chart paper. Underline the letter that makes the sound.
- ▸ Have students:
  - Repeat the words with the / j / sound throughout the week.
  - Indicate to you throughout the week when a word needs to be recorded on the chart.
- ▸ Add the following words to the chart. Point to, act out, or draw the items to clarify meaning. As you say each word aloud, underline the letter **j** or **g** that makes the / j / sound in each word.

  jacket   jump   Jacob   garage
- ▸ Have students:
  - Repeat the words after you.
- ▸ Keep the charts posted throughout the week and add words to it.

STEP 2

Everyday Words

 Students learn and practice vocabulary related to sequence for everyday conversation.

Recognize Everyday Words: Sequence

Materials
Student Text
pp. 90–91
Prepared
sentence strips

- ▸ Direct students' attention to the pages 90–91 of the *Student Text*.
- ▸ Point to the clothing store. Say "Today I want to go to the mall. I want to buy a shirt."
- ▸ Say "Before I buy a shirt, I want to eat." Point to the food court.
- ▸ Point to the entertainment store. Say "After I eat, I am going to meet my friend."

▶ Point to the clothing store and say "Then, we are going to go to the clothing store to buy my shirt."

▶ Point to the movies and say "After I buy my shirt, we are going to the movies."

▶ Write the following sentences on the board in the following order:

_____ *I go to the mall.*

_____ *I eat.*

_____ *I buy my shirt.*

_____ *We go to the movies.*

_____ *I meet a friend.*

Answers: 1, 2, 4, 5, 3

▶ Have students:

• Number the sentences in the order that you mentioned them.

Model

▶ Walk through the sentences using the sequence words. Point to each sentence as you go.

I go to the mall. I want to eat before I buy my shirt. Then, I meet my friend. After I meet my friend, I buy my shirt. Last, we go to the movies.

▶ Write the words **before, then, after,** and **last** on the board. Say each word aloud.

▶ Have students:

• Repeat the words.

▶ Point to each of the sentences in the correct order. After each sentence, prompt students to:

• Say **before, then, after,** or **last** to indicate the sequence in which you mentioned each activity.

Fruit Salad Sequence

▶ Prepare and cut sets of sentence strips with the following text. Write one sentence per strip.

I want to make a fruit salad.

I need to go to the grocery store to buy some fruit.

I buy the fruit.

I wash the fruit.

I cut the fruit.

I put all of the fruit into a bowl.

I eat a fruit salad.

▶ Divide students into pairs or small groups and give each group one set of sentence strips.

Pair/Share

▶ Have students:

• Put the sentences in order.

- Write a brief paragraph using the sequence words **before, after, then,** and **last** to describe the order of how to make a fruit salad.
- Volunteer to share their paragraphs with the class.

Vocabulary Development

 Students work with the core content vocabulary related to the clothing store for everyday conversation.

Introduce: Core Vocabulary

Materials
Student Text pp. 94–95
Old clothing catalogs to cut out
Scissors

▸ Direct students' attention to the clothing store and list on pages 94–95 of the *Student Text*. Point out the **jacket** and **jeans** in the picture. Tell students that jeans and jacket are **clothing**. Say each word as you point to them in the picture.

▸ Have students:
- Repeat the words and point to the pictures.

▸ Elicit the names of any clothing items that students know in English that are in the picture and share them with the class.

▸ Point to each item that appears on the items list on page 93. As you point, say each word out loud.

▸ Have students:
- Point to each item and repeat each word.

Practice Vocabulary

Clothes Hamper

▸ Bring enough clothing catalogs and scissors for each pair of students. Make sure catalogs have different types of clothing for different occasions and weather.

▸ Divide the class into pairs. Give each pair of students a catalog and a pair of scissors.

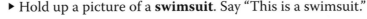 ▸ Hold up a picture of a **swimsuit**. Say "This is a swimsuit."

▸ Have students:
- Repeat the word.

▸ Draw a swimming pool or a beach scene on the board. Act out swimming. Point to your pictures and say "beach" and "pool." Ask "Where do we wear a swimsuit?" to the beach, to the pool

▸ Ask "When do we wear a swimsuit?" in the summer

▸ Repeat with **sunglasses** and **sandals**.

▸ Say "It is summer. These are clothes for the beach. We have a swimsuit, sunglasses, and sandals in our clothes hamper."

▸ Have students:
- Look through the pictures in their catalogs.
- Cut out pictures of twenty different clothing items from the catalog.

- Sort the clothing according to their own criteria.

▸ Make suggestions for different categories, such as colors, weather, event, similarities, etc.

▸ Have students:

- Follow your model and sort the clothing items.

- Present their categories to the class, acting and drawing scenes as necessary.

- Identify some of the clothing items in each category.

Dress Your Classmate

▸ Have students:

- Use the clothes from their cutouts to put together an outfit for their partner.

- Choose an occasion and piece together the outfit.

- Have a conversation in which they ask where they are going and what they are wearing.

  Example: **Where am I going?** to the beach
  What am I wearing? a swimsuit, sandals, and sunglasses

▸ Extend the activity by having students:

- Ask what color the clothing item is and answering.

STEP 4

How English Works

Students are introduced to the dialog. Students participate in the dialog. Students learn and practice more with **prepositions**.

Introduce the Dialog

Picture Walk-Through

Materials
Student Text
pp. 96–97

▸ Have students:

- Look at the pictures on page 96 of the *Student Text*.

▸ Ask students simple questions about the pictures to predict the main idea of the dialog.

▸ Point to the picture in each panel. Act out or point to vocabulary words as necessary. Ask:

1. Panel 1: What clothing item is Maya looking at? sweaters Who is Maya talking to? the salesperson

2. Panel 2: What clothing item is Maya looking at? jeans What color sweater does the salesperson bring? light blue

3. Panel 3: Where is Maya coming from? the fitting room Do you think she will buy the sweater? yes

▸ Record student responses on the board.

Read the Dialog

▸ Read through the dialog in steps. Have students:

- Track print with you as you read.

- Listen for cognates, or English words that are similar in students' native language.

Maya:	Excuse me. Does this sweater come in other colors?
Salesperson:	Let's see. It comes in red, pink, black, cream, and light blue.
Maya:	Do you have any more in light blue?
Salesperson:	Sure. What size do you need: small, medium, large, or extra large?
Maya:	Medium.
Salesperson:	I can go check for you.

▸ Check students' comprehension by pointing to the sweater and asking "What colors does the sweater come in?" red, pink, black, cream, and light blue

▸ Act out the sizes by putting your hands close together for **small**. Say "small."

▸ Have students:

- Repeat the word.

▸ Repeat by acting out for **medium, large,** and **extra large**.

▸ Check students' comprehension by asking "What size sweater does Maya want?' medium

Salesperson:	We had one left. Would you like to try it on?
Maya:	Yes. And are these jeans on sale?
Salesperson:	These jeans are part of the new fall collection, so they are not on sale. But we have some summer pants on sale.
Maya:	That's okay. Thank you. Where are the fitting rooms?
Salesperson:	They are behind you.

▸ Check students' comprehension by asking "Are the jeans on sale?" no "What is on sale?" the pants "Where are the fitting rooms?" behind Maya

Salesperson:	How did the sweater fit?
Maya:	Perfectly. I love it. I'll take it.
Salesperson:	Is there anything else I can help you with today? Are you interested in t-shirts? All of our t-shirts are fifty percent off, as part of our summer sale.
Maya:	No, I'm just going to buy the sweater.
Salesperson:	Great. You have a nice day, now.
Maya:	Thank you, you too.

▸ Check students' comprehension by asking "How does Maya feel about the sweater?" She loves it. "What other clothes are on sale?" the t-shirts "What does Maya decide to buy?" the sweater

▶ Have students:

- Point to the **t-shirt** and the **sweater** in the picture and say the words.

Practice the Dialog

▶ Divide the class into pairs.

▶ Have students:

- Assign the speaking roles within each pair.
- Read the roles out loud in pairs.
- Volunteer to perform the dialog in front of the class.

▶ Check students' comprehension of the dialog by revisiting the questions from the Picture Walk-Through.

Prepositions

▶ Review the prepositions **in, on,** and **at** by asking simple questions about the classroom.

   Example: The stapler is **on** the desk.

▶ Have students:

- Describe where things are in the classroom using **in, on,** or **at**.

To and *From*

▶ Write the words **to** and **from** on the board.

▶ Walk to the window and say "I am walking **to** the window." Say "to."

▶ Have students:

- Repeat the word **to**.

▶ Walk back to where you were standing and say "I am walking away **from** the window." Say "from."

▶ Have students:

- Repeat the word **from**.

▶ Invite a student volunteer to:

- Choose a place to walk to in the classroom.

▶ Ask students "Where is (student's name) going?"

▶ Have students:

- Answer in a complete sentence using **to** or **from**.

   Example: Tasha is going to the desk.
      Tasha is walking away from the chalkboard.

▶ Continue for several rounds until all students have had a chance to speak.

Revisit the Dialog

In What Order?

On Their Own

▸ Direct students' attention to Application A on page 97 of the *Student Text*.

▸ Have students:

- Number each sentence in the order that Maya did things in the clothing store.

- Share their answers with the class.

- Write sentences using sequence words to tell about Maya's experience in the clothing store.

Your Turn

▸ Direct students to page 97 of the *Student Text*.

▸ Have students:

- Work with a partner to categorize the clothes into clothing for winter, spring, summer, and fall.

- Compare their answers with the class.

- Choose one of the seasons and the clothing for that season to role play a dialog between Maya and the salesperson. Maya should ask about the items of clothing, and the salesperson should answer questions about the clothing and describe other items of clothing available at the store for that season.

Example:

Salesperson:	Hello, how may I help you?
Maya:	I am looking for a winter jacket.
Salesperson:	What color jacket would you like?
Maya:	Red. Do you have hats and gloves?
Salesperson:	Yes, they do. Would you like to see them?
Maya:	Yes, thank you.

▸ Have students:

- Volunteer to perform their dialog in front of the class.

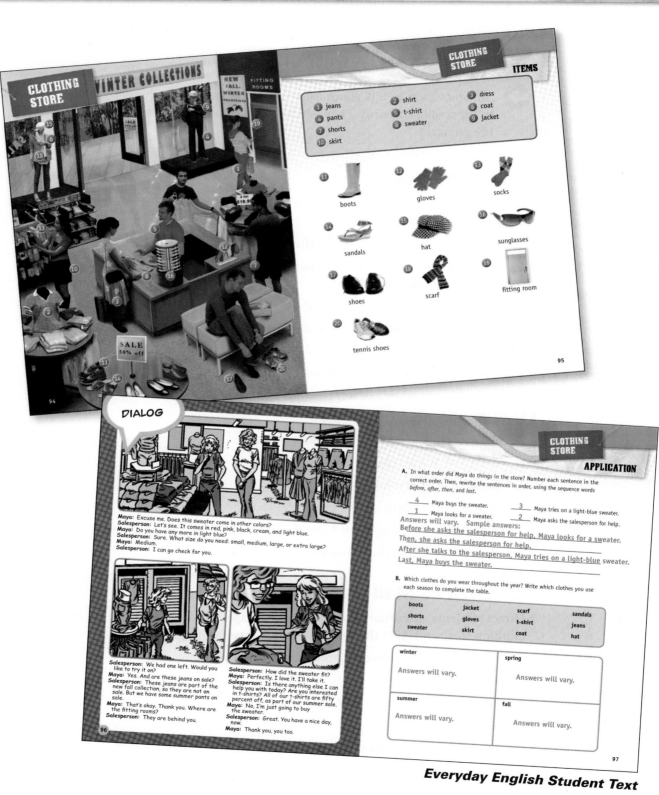

ENTERTAINMENT
STORE

Introduction: Oral Fluency

Students learn to talk about *where, here,* and *there,* and are reintroduced to the week's scenario. Then, students focus on one of the areas within the scenario.

Where? Here and *There*

Materials

Student Text
pp. 90–93
Vocabulary
cards
Copies
of list of items

▶ Begin the class by reminding students that they know how to ask where things are and describe their location.

▶ Write the words **where, here,** and **there** on the board.

▶ Prepare vocabulary cards with the names of items that students have learned throughout the program.

▶ Write the name of one item per card.

▶ Prepare and copy a list of all the items that you have listed on the cards.

▶ Give each student a vocabulary card and a copy of the items list.

▶ Choose an item from the list and ask the class where it is.

Example: Where is the sweater?

▶ Have the student who has the item:

• Answer the question. The sweater is here.

▶ Have the rest of the class:

• Point to the person who has the item.

• Say where the item is. The sweater is there.

• Take turns choosing items from the list and asking where they are.

• Repeat until all of the items have been located.

Review: The Mall

▶ Direct students' attention to the pictures on pages 92–93. Say "the mall." Point to the clothing store and elicit the word **clothing store** from the students.

▶ Point to the **entertainment store** and say "entertainment store."

▶ Have students:

• Point to the entertainment store.

• Repeat the word.

▶ Direct students' attention to pages 92–93.

▶ Ask students "Where is the entertainment store?"

▸ Have students:
- • Point to the entertainment store picture and say **entertainment store**.

Introduction to the Entertainment Store

▸ Direct students' attention to the picture of the entertainment store on page 92.

▸ Elicit words that students know in English that are in the picture and share them with the class.

▸ Have students:
- • Choral repeat the words.

STEP 1

Phonemic Awareness

➡ Students practice identifying, differentiating, and producing the / j / and / v / sounds.

The / v / Sound

Materials
Chart paper
/ j / chart from previous day
Student Text p. 92

▸ Prepare a piece of chart paper by writing *the* / v / at the top of the paper.

▸ Post the paper on the wall in the classroom next to the / j / chart.

▸ Review the / j / sound by writing the word **digital** and underlining the letter *g* on the / j / chart. Say "digital."

▸ Have students:
- • Pronounce the word with you.
- • Pronounce the other / j / words on the chart.

▸ Direct students' attention to the / v / chart.

▸ Explain to students that the / v / sound is made by putting the upper teeth on the lower lip and pushing air through your mouth and vocalizing.

▸ Demonstrate how to make the sound.

▸ Have students:
- • Make the sound with you.

▸ Direct students' attention to the picture of the entertainment store on page 92 of the *Student Text*.

▸ Point to the video game. Say "video game."

▸ Write the word **video** on the / v / chart.

▸ Underline the letter *v*.

▸ Have students:
- • Pronounce the word with you.

▸ Repeat for the word **veal**.

▸ Tell students that they will learn more words with the / j / and / v / sounds throughout the week.

- With each new lesson, record vocabulary words with the sounds on their respective pieces of chart paper.
- Underline the letter that makes the sound.
- Have students:
  - Repeat the words with the / j / and / v / sounds throughout the week.
  - Indicate to you throughout the week when a word needs to be recorded on the chart.
- Add the following words to the / v / chart.

  <u>v</u>ideo   ele<u>v</u>ator   ser<u>v</u>ice

- Point to, act out, or draw the items to clarify meaning.
- Underline the letter *v* in each word as you say each word aloud.
- Have students:
  - Repeat the words after you.
- Keep the charts posted throughout the week and add words to them.

STEP 2

Everyday Words

 Students learn and practice talking about sequence and placement of objects for everyday conversation.

Recognize Everyday Words: *Before* and *After*

Materials
Student Text
pp. 92–93

Model

- Copy the graphic organizer on the board.

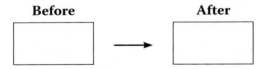

Before   **After**

- In the **Before** box of the graphic organizer, write:

  I went to the clothing store.

- In the **After** box of the graphic organizer, write:

  I ate after I went to the clothing store.

- Say "This morning I went to the clothing store. I ate after I went to the clothing store."
- Point to the corresponding box in the graphic organizer as you say each sentence.
- Explain to students that **before** is what you did first, and **after** is what you did next.
- Have students:
  - Copy the graphic organizer onto a piece of paper.
  - Think of two things that they did in a sequence.
  - Illustrate the situation in the corresponding box of the graphic organizer.

- Use the following sentence frames to describe their sequence of activities.

  Before _____.   After _____.

- Share their sentences with the class.

Recognize Everyday Words: *First, Then,* and *Last*

▸ Tell students that they already know how to talk about what happens **before** and **after** in a sequence.

▸ Write the words **first, then,** and **last** on the board.

▸ Point to each word and say it aloud.

▸ Have students:

- Chorally and individually repeat each word.

▸ Explain that **first, then,** and **last** are also words that help identify a sequence of actions.

▸ Draw the following graphic organizer on the board.

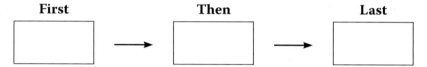

▸ Leave the classroom and reenter.

▸ As you enter the classroom, say "I go into the classroom."

▸ Walk to the desk.

▸ As you are walking, say "I walk to the desk."

▸ Sit down at the desk.

▸ As you are sitting, say "I sit at the desk."

▸ Point to the **First** box of the graphic organizer.

▸ Say "First, I go into the classroom."

▸ Point to the **Then** box of the graphic organizer.

▸ Say "Then, I walk to the desk."

▸ Point to the **Last** box of the graphic organizer.

▸ Say "Last, I sit at the desk."

▸ Have students:

- Repeat the words **first, then** and **last**.

▸ Ask "What do I do first?" go into the classroom

▸ Write **go into the classroom** in the **First** box of the graphic organizer.

▸ Ask "Then, what do I do?" walk to the desk

▸ Write **walk to the desk** in the **Then** box of the graphic organizer.

▸ Ask "What do I do last?" sit at the desk

▸ Write **sit at the desk** in the **Last** box of the graphic organizer.

▸ Point to each box of the graphic organizer as you summarize the sequence of events with the following talk-through:

First, I go into the classroom. Then, I walk to the desk. Last, I sit at the desk.

On Their Own

▸ Have students:

- Copy the graphic organizer onto a piece of paper.
- Think of a sequence of events.
- Illustrate the story sequence in each of the boxes of the graphic organizer.
- Write sentences about their sequence using the sequence words.
- Share their sentences and pictures with a partner.

Recognize Everyday Words: Placement

▸ Direct students' attention to the pictures on pages 92–93 of the *Student Text*.

▸ Point to the salesperson behind the counter in the clothing store picture.

▸ Say "The salesperson is behind the counter."

▸ Go behind a desk.

▸ Say "I am behind the desk."

▸ Repeat "behind."

▸ Have students:

- Repeat the word **behind**.

▸ Ask students "Where am I?" behind the desk

▸ Go in front of the desk.

▸ Sat "I am in front of the desk."

▸ Repeat "in front of."

▸ Have students:

- Repeat the phrase **in front of**.

▸ Ask students "Where am I?" in front of the desk

▸ Have individual students:

- Stand behind or in front of different places in the room.
- Ask each other "Where are you?"
- Respond to the question using the word **behind**.

  Example: Where are you?
  I am behind the door.

STEP 3 Vocabulary Development

Students work with the core content vocabulary related to the entertainment store for everyday conversation.

Introduce: Core Vocabulary

Materials
Student Text
pp. 98–99, p. 101

▸ Direct students' attention to pages 98–99 of the *Student Text*.

▸ Point to the customer and say "customer."

- ▸ Have students:
  - • Repeat the word **customer**.
- ▸ Repeat for **service technician**.
- ▸ Point to the boys playing video games.
- ▸ Say "The boys are in front of the TV."
- ▸ Motion that you are standing **in front of** the class.
- ▸ Say "I am in front of the class."
- ▸ Have students:
  - • Repeat the phrase **in front of**.
- ▸ Point to each item that appears on the items list on page 99.
- ▸ As you point, say each word out loud.
- ▸ Have students:
  - • Point to each item and repeat each word.

Practice Vocabulary

What Is It For?

- ▸ Direct students' attention to Application A on page 101 of the *Student Text*.
- ▸ Have students:
  - • Match each item on the right to its description on the left.
  - • Check answers with the class.
- ▸ To extend the activity, have students:
  - • Write two more descriptions and share them with a partner.
  - • Identify the object that their partner describes.

STEP

How English Works

Students are introduced to the dialog. Students participate in the dialog. Students learn and practice **prepositions**.

Introduce the Dialog

Picture Walk-Through

Materials
Student Text
pp. 100–101

- ▸ Have students:
  - • Look at pictures on page 100 of the *Student Text*.
- ▸ Ask students simple questions about the pictures to predict the main idea of the dialog.
- ▸ Point to the picture in each panel. Act out or point to vocabulary words as necessary. Ask:
  1. Panel 1: What are the two boys doing? playing a video game
  2. Panel 2: What are the two boys looking at? CDs

3. Panel 3: What section of the store are the boys in? cameras
4. Panel 4: Do the boys stay in the store? no

▸ Record student responses on the board.

Read the Dialog

▸ Read through the dialog in steps.

▸ Have students:

- Track print with you as you read.

- Listen for cognates, or English words that are similar in students' native language.

Carlos:	This video game is so fun.
Justin:	Yeah. I want this for my birthday. But, my mom says I play too many video games.
Carlos:	Let's go look at the CDs.

▸ Check students' comprehension by asking "What does Justin want for his birthday?" a video game "What does Carlos want to go look at?" CDs

Justin:	I want to find a CD for my sister.
Carlos:	What kind of music does she like?
Justin:	She likes country music a lot.
Carlos:	I don't know much about country music.
Justin:	I think this CD will be good. I need a memory card for my camera while we're here.

▸ Check students' comprehension by asking "What does Justin want to buy for his sister?" a CD "What kind of music does Justin's sister like?" country

Carlos:	I wish I had a digital camera.
Justin:	I like mine a lot. It connects to my laptop. It's really easy to use.
Carlos:	Do you want to look at the DVDs?

▸ Check students' comprehension by asking "What does Justin think about his digital camera?" He likes it. It is easy to use.

Justin:	No, we better go.
Carlos:	When are we meeting your family?
Justin:	At 1:30.

▸ Check students' comprehension by asking "What time are the boys meeting Justin's family?" at 1:30

Practice the Dialog

▶ Divide the class into pairs.

▶ Have students:

- Assign the speaking roles within each pair.
- Read the roles out loud in pairs.
- Volunteer to perform the dialog in front of the class.

▶ Check students' comprehension of the dialog by revisiting the questions from the Picture Walk-Through.

Prepositions

▶ Tell students that they already know how to describe the position of things.

▶ Write the words **in, on, at, behind, in front of, to** and **from** on the board.

▶ Explain to students that these words are called **prepositions**. They give information about nouns in a sentence. They connect the nouns to other information in the sentence.

▶ Explain to students that a prepositional phrase is made up of a preposition and a noun, or object of the preposition.

▶ Write the sentence on the board "We are in the classroom."

▶ Underline the prepositional phrase "in the classroom."

▶ Identify the preposition **in** in the sentence.

▶ Identify the noun phrase "the classroom" in the sentence.

▶ Draw an arrow between "in the classroom" and "We are."

▶ Say "The phrase *in the classroom* connects one idea to the other. It tells us where we are."

▶ Write the following sentence on the board:

The student walks to the window.

▶ Have students:

- Identify the preposition. to
- Identify the noun phrase, or object of the preposition. the window

▶ Write the following sentences on the board:

1. The entertainment store is in front of the clothing store.

2. I found the DVDs behind the television.

3. We returned from the mall.

4. I pay for my jeans at the counter.

On Their Own

▶ Have students:

- Work in pairs to identify the prepositions and objects of prepositions in each sentence.
- Share answers with the class.

Revisit the Dialog

▶ Direct students' attention again to the dialog on page 100 of the *Student Text*.

▶ Have students:

- Reread the dialog individually.
- Write five true or false statements about information in the dialog on a piece of paper.

  Example: Carlos wants a video game for his birthday. False

- Exchange their paper with a partner and decide whether the statements are true or false.
- Check their answers.
- Correct the false statements to be true.

  Example: Carlos wants a video game for his birthday. False

  Justin

  ~~Carlos~~ wants a video game for his birthday.

Your Turn

▶ Direct students' attention to Application B on page 101 of the *Student Text*.

▶ Have students:

- Write Justin's half of the dialog in the blanks provided.
- Make sure their dialog makes sense.
- Take turns sharing their dialog with a partner to share their answers.

▶ Invite volunteers to:

- Perform Justin's role with a partner in front of the class.

Unit 5

LESSON 3

MOVIES

Introduction: Oral Fluency

Students practice the words *where, here,* and *there*. Students learn to order food and other items. Then, students focus on one of the areas within the scenario.

Where? Here and *There*

Materials

Student Text pp. 92–93

Prepared word cards

▸ Write the words **here** and **there** on the board.

▸ Review the question word **where** with the students by pointing to something in the classroom and asking where it is.

▸ Prompt individual students to:

• Answer using the words **here** or **there** in their answers.

• Ask another student where a different object in the classroom is.

Placing Orders

▸ Direct students' attention to the picture of the movies on page 93 of the *Student Text*.

▸ Ask students "Where can I buy something to eat at the movies?"

▸ Have students:

• Point to the concession stand.

▸ Say "concession stand."

▸ Have students:

• Chorally and individually repeat the words **concession stand**.

▸ Tell students that in English, we use certain phrases to order food and other things. Say "At the movies, we can order food and drinks at the concession stand."

▸ Write the following phrases on the board:

1. How may I help you?

2. I would like _____ please.

▸ Say each phrase aloud.

▸ Have students:

• Chorally and individually repeat the phrases.

I Would Like...

▸ Prepare word cards with food items and other items from previous lessons. Write one item per card.

• Give each student a word card.

▸ Approach a student and say "How may I help you?" Prompt the student to:

• Show you his or her vocabulary word card.

Example: fruit salad

▸ Point to the sentence frame on the board.

▸ Say "I would like a fruit salad, please."

▸ Have students:

• Chorally and individually repeat the phrases.

▸ Divide the class in half. If there is an odd number of students, include yourself in the group.

▸ Have students:

• Form two concentric circles, with students in the inner circle facing students in the outer circle.

• Ask "How may I help you?" if they are in the outer circle.

• Answer using their vocabulary card and sentence frame "I would like _____." if they are in the inner circle.

▸ After students have asked and answered a question, have students:

• In the inner circle move one place to the left to face a new partner.

• In the inner circle ask a new partner who is in the outer circle "How may I help you?"

• In the outer circle answer using their vocabulary card and sentence frame "I would like _____."

• Trade cards with their partner to get a new vocabulary card.

• Repeat the rotation until the students have made one full rotation with the class and have spoken with all their classmates.

Review: The Mall

▸ Direct students' attention to the pictures on pages 92–93. Say "mall." Point to the clothing store and elicit **clothing store** from the students. Then, point to the **entertainment store** and elicit **entertainment store**.

▸ Point to the **movies** and say "movies."

▸ Have students:

• Point to the movies and repeat the words.

▸ Direct students' attention to pages 93. Ask students "Where can we see movies?"

▸ Have students:

• Point to the movie theater and say the word **movies**.

Introduction to Movies

▸ Direct students' attention to the picture of the movies on page 93.

▸ Elicit words that students know in English that are in the picture and share them with the class.

▸ Have students:

• Choral repeat the words.

Phonemic Awareness

Students practice identifying, differentiating, and producing the / j /. / v /, / h /, and / r / sounds.

The / h / and / r / Sounds

Materials

Chart paper, / j / and / v / charts from previous days

Student Text p. 102

▸ Prepare two more pieces of chart paper by writing the / h / at the top of one and / r / at the top of the other.

▸ Post the papers on the wall in the classroom next to the / j / and / v / charts.

▸ Review the / j / sound by writing the word **projector.**

▸ Underline the letter *j* on the letter / j / chart. Say "projector."

▸ Have students:

• Pronounce the word with you.

• Pronounce the other / j / words on on the chart.

▸ Review the / v / sound by writing the word **movies** and underlining the letter *v* on the letter / v / chart. Say "movies."

▸ Have students:

• Pronounce the word with you.

• Pronounce the other / v / words on the chart.

The / h / sound

▸ Direct students' attention to the / h / chart.

▸ Explain to students that the / h / sound is made by pushing air from the back of your throat through your mouth.

▸ Demonstrate how to make the sound.

▸ Have students:

• Make the sound with you.

▸ Say "Hello. How are you?"

▸ Write the words **hello** and **how** on the chart, and underline the letter *h*.

▸ Have students:

• Pronounce the words with you.

▸ Add the following words to the / h / chart.

<u>h</u>orror   <u>h</u>ere   <u>h</u>at   <u>h</u>eadphones

▸ Act out, or draw the items clarify meaning.

▸ As you say each word aloud, underline the letter *h* in each word.

The / r / sound

▸ Direct students' attention to the / r / chart.

▸ Explain to students that the / r / sound is made by curving the tongue toward the roof of the mouth, but not touching the teeth or roof of the mouth and vocalizing.

- ▸ Demonstrate how to make the sound.
- ▸ Have students:
  - • Make the sound with you.
- ▸ Say "room." Write the word **room** on the chart, and underline the letter *r*.
- ▸ Have students:
  - • Pronounce the word with you.
- ▸ Add the following words to the / *r* / chart.

<u>r</u>ows   <u>r</u>omance   popco<u>r</u>n   custome<u>r</u>

- ▸ Point to pictures on page 102, act out, or draw the items clarify meaning.
- ▸ As you say each word aloud, underline the letter *r* in each word.
- ▸ Tell students that they will learn more words with the / *j* /, / *v* /, / *h* /, and / *r* / sounds throughout the rest of the week.
- ▸ With each new lesson, record vocabulary words with the sounds on their respective pieces of chart paper.
- ▸ Underline the letter that makes the sound.
- ▸ Have students:
  - • Repeat the words with the / *j* /, / *v* /, / *h* /, and / *r* / sounds throughout the week.
  - • Indicate to you throughout the week when a word needs to be recorded on the chart.
- ▸ Keep the charts posted throughout the week and add words to them.

STEP 2 — Everyday Words

Students learn and practice prepositions of placement and sequence for everyday conversation.

Recognize Everyday Words: Placement

Materials
Copies of graphic organizer worksheet

- ▸ Write the prepositions of place **in, on, at, in front of,** and **behind** on the board.
- ▸ Point to an object in the classroom that is over another object. Use the preposition **over** in a sentence.

  Example: The map is over the bulletin board.
- ▸ Have students:
  - • Repeat the word **over**.
- ▸ Add the word **over** to the list on the board.
- ▸ Point to an object in the classroom that is under another object. Use the preposition **under** in a sentence.

  Example: The desk is under the window.

▸ Have students:

• Repeat the word **under**.

▸ Add the word **under** to the list on the board.

▸ Have students:

• Find objects in the classroom and describe their position.

Variation:

▸ Divide the class into pairs.

▸ Have students:

• Think of an object in the classroom without revealing it to their partners.

• Ask each other where the object is.

• Answer the question with the position of the object.

• Identify the object.

Example: Where is the object?
It is under the window.
Is it a desk?

Recognize Everyday Words: Sequence

▸ Write the title of your favorite movie on the board.

▸ Read the title aloud and ask students if they have seen or heard of the movie.

▸ Prepare a worksheet with the graphic organizer.

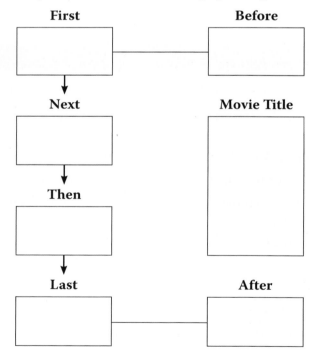

▸ Write the title of the movie in the box.

▸ Point to each box and give an example of the sequence of events from the movie. Act out or draw vocabulary as needed.

Example: **Movie Title:** *Jaws*

First: A shark attacks people on the beach.
Next: The town closes the beach.
Then: The police chief tries to find the shark and kill it.
Last: They find the shark and kill it.
Before: There were many shark attacks.
After: They killed the shark, so the beach is safe.

On Their Own

▸ Have students:

- Work with a partner to choose a movie.

- Write sentences in the graphic organizer to describe the sequence of events in the movie.

- Present their sentences to the class.

STEP 3

Vocabulary Development

 Students work with the core content vocabulary related to the movies for everyday conversation.

Introduce: Core Vocabulary

Materials
Student Text
pp. 102–103
Prepared cards

▸ Anchor students' knowledge of mall vocabulary by eliciting stores and objects in the mall from previous lessons.

▸ Have students:

- Name some items they can buy at the mall.

▸ Direct students' attention to the movies picture on page 102 of the *Student Text*.

▸ Point to the **usher**. Say "usher."

▸ Act out the motion of taking tickets from moviegoers and say "The usher takes the tickets from the customers."

▸ Have students:

- Repeat the word **usher**.

▸ Review the word **behind**. Stand behind the desk. Point to the employee behind the cash register in the picture.

▸ Say "He is behind the cash register. Behind. I am behind the desk."

▸ Have students:

- Repeat the word **behind**.

▸ Review the word **over**. Point to the marquee on the picture. Say "over."

▸ Point to something that is over you and the students in the classroom. Repeat "over."

▸ Have students:

- Repeat the word **over**.

▸ Point to each item that appears on the items list on page 103 and say each word aloud.

Practice Vocabulary

What Kind of Movie Is It?

Pair/Share

▸ Prepare cards with the different movie genres. Write one movie genre per card.

▸ Divide students into pairs or small groups.

▸ Give each pair or small group a movie genre card.

▸ Have students:

- Invent a movie title for the genre on their card.

- Share their movie title with the class for the class to identify which genre it is.

  Example: Thunder at Midnight action

STEP 4

How English Works

 Students are introduced to the dialog. Students participate in the dialog. Students learn and practice more **prepositions**.

Introduce the Dialog

Picture Walk-Through

Materials

Student Text
pp. 104–105

Poster board
and markers

▸ Have students:

- Look at pictures on page 104 of the *Student Text*.

▸ Ask students simple questions about the pictures to predict the main idea of the dialog.

▸ Point to the picture in each panel. Act out or point to vocabulary words as necessary. Ask:

1. Panel 1: Does the girl want to see a horror movie? no Does she want to see a drama? no

2. Panel 2: What kind of movie does the boy want to see? action

3. Panel 3: What kind of movie does the girl talk about? comedy

4. Panel 4: Do they buy tickets for the movies? yes

5. Panel 5: Where do you think the boy and the girl will sit? Answers will vary.

6. Panel 6: Do the boy and the girl sit in the front row? no

▸ Record student responses on the board.

Read the Dialog

▸ Read through the dialog in steps. Have students:

- Track print with you as you read.

- Listen for cognates, or English words that are similar in students' native language.

| Thomas: | So, which movie do you want to see? |
| Shanice: | Well, I don't want to see the horror movie. I'm not really in the mood for drama. What do you want to see? |

▶ Explain to students that the question word **why** is used to ask people for a reason, and the word **because** is used to explain the reason. Write the words on the board and say them aloud.

Example: Why do you want to eat?
I want to eat because I am hungry.

▶ Have students:

• Chorally and individually repeat the words.

▶ Check students' comprehension by asking: "Why doesn't Shanice want to see the drama?" because she is not in the mood

Thomas:	How about an action film? I want to see this one.
Shanice:	Sorry, I already saw that with my dad.
Thomas:	Was it good?

▶ Check students' comprehension by asking "What movie does Thomas suggest?" action "Why doesn't Isabella want to see the action film?" because she saw it with her dad

Shanice:	Yes. Well, that leaves only one movie: a comedy.

▶ Check students' comprehension by asking "What movie will Shanice and Thomas see?" a comedy

Thomas:	Two, please.

▶ Remind students that when ordering at the movie theater, they do not necessarily have to speak in complete sentences.

▶ Point out that Thomas just tells how many tickets he wants. We know that he wants two tickets because of the context. He is at the ticket booth. The context tells us he wants two tickets.

Thomas:	Where do you want to sit?
Shanice:	How about in the middle?

▶ Check students' comprehension by asking "Where does Shanice want to sit?" in the middle

▶ Have students:

• Point out the middle in the picture.

Thomas:	I hope no one sits in front of us.
Shanice:	I hope the people behind us aren't noisy.
Thomas:	Oops. I'll be right back. I forgot to buy the candy!

▶ Check students' comprehension by asking "Why does Thomas hope no one sits in front of them?" so he and Shanice can see the movie "Why does Shanice hope the people behind them aren't noisy?" so she and Thomas can hear the movie "Where does Thomas go?" to buy candy

Practice the Dialog

▸ Divide the class into pairs.

▸ Have students:

- Assign the speaking roles within each pair.
- Read the roles out loud in pairs.
- Volunteer to perform the dialog in front of the class.

▸ Check students' comprehension of the dialog by revisiting the questions from the Picture Walk-Through.

Preposition Practice

▸ Review prepositions that students have learned: **behind, in front of, over, under, in, on, at, to,** and **from**.

▸ Direct students' attention to Application A on page 105 of the *Student Text*.

▸ Have students:

- Look at the picture and select the correct preposition to complete each sentence.

Revisit the Dialog

▸ Redirect students' attention to the dialog on page 104 of the *Student Text*.

▸ Have students:

- Reread the dialog and summarize Thomas and Shanice's trip to the movies, using the sequence words **before, after, first, next, then,** and **last**.
- Share their sequences with the class.

Your Turn

▸ Direct the students' attention to Application B on page 105 of the *Student Text*.

▸ Have students:

On Their Own

- Create their own movie posters.
- Share their posters with the class.

▸ To extend the activity, have students:

- Present the sequence of events in the movie using the sequence words **before, after, first, next, then,** and **last**.

MOVIES

ITEMS

1. lobby
2. theater
3. marquee
4. balcony
5. projector
6. ticket booth
7. wheelchair ramp
8. screen
9. concession stand
10. rows
11. seats

12. tickets
13. horror
14. action
15. candy
16. comedy
17. romance
18. popcorn
19. soda
20. drama

103

102

DIALOG

Thomas: So, which movie do you want to see?
Shanice: Well, I don't want to see the horror movie. I'm not really in the mood for drama. What do you want to see?

Thomas: How about an action film? I want to see this one.
Shanice: Sorry, I already saw that with my dad.
Thomas: Was it good?

Shanice: Yes. Well, that leaves only one movie: a comedy.

Thomas: Two, please.

Thomas: Where do you want to sit?
Shanice: How about in the middle?

Thomas: I hope no one sits in front of us.
Shanice: I hope the people behind us aren't noisy.
Thomas: Oops. I'll be right back. I forgot to buy the candy!

104

MOVIES

APPLICATION

A. Look at the picture. Then circle the correct word that completes each sentence.

1. The ticket booth is _____ under _____ the marquee.
2. The family buys food _____ at _____ the concession stand.
3. The man is _____ behind _____ the cash register.
4. The balcony is _____ over _____ the seats.
5. People are waiting in line _____ in front of _____ the ticket booth.

B. Choose a type of movie. Then create a movie poster for it. Make up a title and draw a picture of an important scene.

105

Everyday English Student Text

Introduction: Oral Fluency

 Students learn to order food and other items and are reintroduced to the week's scenario. Then, students focus on one of the areas within the scenario.

May I Take Your Order?

Materials

Student Text pp. 92–93

Pictures of food items

▸ Start class by telling students that you are opening a new restaurant in the mall.

▸ Have students:

- Brainstorm what kind of foods they would like to sell.

- Identify some dishes that they would like to serve.

  Example: We could open a fresh fruit smoothie stand.

▸ Draw a blender on the board and some fruits inside the blender.

▸ Act out and explain to students that a smoothie is a drink made from fresh fruit.

▸ Records students' ideas on the board.

▸ Divide the class into pairs and small groups.

▸ Have students:

- Decide what food they will sell at their restaurant.

- Prepare a role play in which one student is the customer ordering food, and the other student is the employee behind the counter taking the order.

- Volunteer to perform their role play in front of the class.

Review: The Mall

▸ Direct students' attention to the pictures on pages 92–93. Say "the mall." Point to the clothing store, the entertainment store, and the movies. Elicit the words **clothing store, entertainment store,** and **movies** from the students.

▸ Point to the **food court** and say "food court."

▸ Have students:

- Point to the food court.

- Repeat the word **food court**.

▸ Direct students' attention to pages 93. Ask students "Where is the food court?"

▸ Have students:

- Point to the food court and say the words **food court**.

Introduction to the Food Court

▸ Direct students' attention to the picture of the food court picture on page 93.

▸ Elicit words that students know in English that are in the picture and share them with the class.

▸ Point out the words and pictures of **fast food** places and the **salad bar**.

▸ Point to the pizzas **under** the heat lamps. Say "under." Put a piece of paper underneath a book on the desk. Repeat "under."

▸ Have students:

- Choral repeat the words.

STEP 1

Phonemic Awareness

Students practice identifying, differentiating, and producing the / j /, / v /, / h /, / r /, and / f / sounds.

The / f / sound

Materials

Chart paper, / j /, / v /, / h /, and / r / charts from previous days

Student Text p. 106

▸ Prepare a piece of chart paper by writing the letter *f* at the top of it. Post the paper on the wall in the classroom next to the / j /, / v /, / h /, and / r / charts.

▸ Review the / j / sound by writing the word **juice** and underlining the letter *j* on the / j / chart. Say "juice."

▸ Have students:

- Pronounce the word with you.
- Pronounce the other / j / words on the chart.

▸ Review the / v / sound by writing the word **vinegar** and underlining the letter *v* on the / v / chart. Say "vinegar."

▸ Have students:

- Pronounce the word with you.
- Pronounce the other / v / words on the chart.

▸ Review the / h / sound by writing the word **hamburger** and underlining the letter *h* on the / h / chart. Say "hamburger."

▸ Have students:

- Pronounce the word with you.
- Pronounce the other / h / words on the chart.

▸ Review the / r / sound by writing the word **return** and underlining the letter *r* on the / r / chart. Say "return."

▸ Have students:

- Pronounce the word with you.
- Pronounce the other / r / words on the chart.

▸ Direct students' attention to the / f / chart. Explain to students that the / f / sound is made the same way the / v / sound is made but without voice. Place your upper teeth on the lower lip and push air out without vocalizing. Demonstrate how to make the sound. Alternate making the / v / sound and the / f / sound.

▸ Have students:

- Put their hands on their throat to feel their vocal chords vibrating when they pronounce the / v / sound, and feel their vocal chords stop vibrating when they pronounce the / f / sound.

▸ Have students:

- Make the sounds with you.

▸ Say "food." Write the words **food** and **Friday** on the chart, and underline the letter *f*.

▸ Have students:

- Pronounce the words with you.

▸ Add the following words to the / f / chart. Point to pictures on page 106 of the *Student Text*, act out, or draw the items clarify meaning. As you say each word aloud, underline the letter *f* in each word.

<u>f</u>ast   **<u>f</u>rench**   **<u>f</u>ries**

▸ Have students:

- Repeat the words with the / j /, / v /, / h /, / r /, and / f / sounds throughout the rest of the week.

- Indicate to you throughout the week when a word needs to be recorded on the chart.

▸ Keep the charts posted throughout the week and add words to them.

<h2>STEP 2   Everyday Words</h2>

 Students learn and practice prepositions of placement and sequence for everyday conversation.

Recognize Everyday Words: Placement

▸ Review the prepositions of place with students.

▸ Have students:

- Name the prepositions **in, on, at, to, from, behind, in front of, under,** and **over**.

▸ Write the prepositions on the board.

Where Is It? What Is It?

▸ Look around the room for an object. Do not reveal what the object is to students.

▸ Tell students that you are thinking of an object in the room.

▸ Have students:

- Ask yes/no questions about the object until they can identify it.

  Example: Is it behind the desk?

- Give students clues as to whether they are getting closer to discovering the object or not by saying "You are getting closer" or "You are getting farther."
- After students have identified the object, have them:
  - State where the object is, using an appropriate preposition of place.
    Example: The globe is on the table.

Recognize Everyday Words: Sequence

Order of Ordering

- Write the following sentences on the board. Write a blank in front of each sentence.

  _____ I pay for my food.

  _____ I am full.

  _____ I go to the food court.

  ___1___ I am hungry.

  _____ I say "I would like…" when I place my order.

  _____ I sit down and eat.

  _____ I decide what food I want to eat.

- Read the sentences aloud.
- Act out or draw any vocabulary that students do not know.
- Have students:
  - Put the sentence in order by numbering each step in order.
  - Use sequence words to share their answers with the class.
    Answers: 5, 7, 2, 1, 4, 6, 3
    Example: After I go to the food court, I decide what food I want to eat.
- Do the first one with the students.

STEP 3

Vocabulary Development

 Students work with the core content vocabulary related to the food court for everyday conversation.

Introduce: Core Vocabulary

Materials

Student Text
pp. 106–107
Blank Cards

- Direct students' attention to pages 106–107 of the *Student Text*. Say "I am hungry. Where can we eat?"
- Have students:
  - Point to different food stalls at the food court.
- Ask students "What can we eat at the mall?"
- Have students:
  - Look at the pictures to see what food items they recognize.

- Say what we can eat at the mall using the sentence frame.

  We can eat _____ at the mall.

▸ Point to each item that appears on the items list on page 107. As you point, say each word out loud.

▸ Have students:

  • Point to each item.

  • Repeat each word.

Practice Vocabulary

Picture This

▸ Draw a picture of a hamburger and fries on the board.

  Point to the picture and ask "What are these?" a hamburger and fries

▸ Explain to students that they are going to play a guessing game.

▸ Give students blank cards.

▸ Have students:

  • Write one food court related item on the card.

▸ Collect all the cards and shuffle them.

▸ Have students:

  • Volunteer to choose a card from the stack.

  • Draw the item for the class to guess.

  • Point to the food court picture on page 106 of the *Student Text* and use the sentence frames to talk about the food item.

    You can buy _____ here. You can buy _____ there.

STEP 4

How English Works

Students are introduced to the dialog. Students participate in the dialog. Students practice **prepositions**.

Introduce the Dialog

Picture Walk-Through

Materials

Student Text pp. 108–109

Copies of prepositions worksheet

▸ Have students:

  • Look at pictures on page 108 of the *Student Text*.

▸ Ask students simple questions about the pictures to predict the main idea of the dialog.

▸ Point to the picture in each panel. Act out or point to vocabulary words as necessary. Ask:

  1. Panel 1: Does Maya want pizza or ice cream? pizza

  2. Panel 2: Who is Maya with? her mother and the baby

3. Panel 3: Does Mom want a hamburger and fries? no
4. Panel 4: Does Maya ask for ketchup and mustard? yes
5. Panel 5: Who meets Maya and Mom at the food court? Justin and Carlos

▸ Record student responses on the board.

Read the Dialog

▸ Read through the dialog in steps. Have students:

- Track print with you as you read.
- Listen for cognates, or English words that are similar in students' native language.

Mom:	Maya, what do you want to eat?
Maya:	Maybe pizza.
Mom:	Do you know what your brother wants to eat?
Maya:	I'm not sure. What time is it?
Mom:	Almost 1:30. They should be here any minute.

▸ Check students' comprehension by asking "What does Maya want to eat?" pizza

Maya:	Should I get a high chair for the baby?
Mom:	Yes. Thank you.

▸ Check students' comprehension by asking "What will Maya get for the baby?" a high chair

Mom:	I think I'm going to have a sandwich and salad.
Maya:	I changed my mind. I want a hamburger and fries.

▸ Check students' comprehension by asking "What does Mom want to eat?" a sandwich and salad "Does Maya still want to eat pizza?" no "What does Maya want to eat now?" a hamburger and fries

▸ Explain to students that **fries** is a short way of saying **french fries**.

Mom:	Why don't you get a table, and I'll go buy the food. Take the baby.
Maya:	Okay. Could you bring some ketchup and mustard please?

▸ Check students' comprehension by asking "What does Maya ask her mother to bring?" ketchup and mustard

Mom:	Sure. Do you want a soda?
Maya:	Yes, please.
Mom:	Oh, there are Justin and Carlos now. I wonder where your Dad is. Justin, can you go find Dad?

▸ Check students' comprehension by asking "What will Maya have to drink?" a soda

Practice the Dialog

▸ Divide the class into pairs.

▸ Have students:

- Assign the speaking roles within each pair.
- Read the roles out loud in pairs.
- Volunteer to perform the dialog in front of the class.

▸ Check students' comprehension of the dialog by revisiting the questions from the Picture Walk-Through.

Of, By, and *With*

▸ Write the word **of** on the board. Say "of."

▸ Have students:

- Repeat the word.

▸ Repeat with **by** and **with**.

▸ Point to the word **of**.

▸ Explain to students that **of** can refer to the material that things are made of, or to the owner of an object.

    Examples: The book is made **of** paper.
                  The owner **of** the movie theater is my neighbor.

▸ Point to the word **by**.

▸ Explain to students that **by** has several different meanings. It can refer to the physical position of an object next to another object. It can also refer to the creation of someone else.

    Examples: The desk is **by** the window.
                  That story is **by** a famous author.

▸ Point to the word **with**.

▸ Explain to students that **with** can refer to company.

    Example: We went to the party **with** our friends.

▸ Have students:

- Choral repeat each preposition.
- Write a complete sentence for each preposition.
- Read their sentences aloud.

Revisit the Dialog

▸ Direct students' attention again to the dialog on page 108 of the *Student Text*.

▸ Have students:

- Reread the dialog.
- Complete Application A on page 109 of the *Student Text*.

That's Using Your Prepositions

▸ Write the prepositions **in, on, at, by, with, to,** and **from** on the board.

▸ Prepare and copy a worksheet with the following sentences on it:

  1. The pizzas are made _____ only natural ingredients. from, with
  2. My favorite book is _____ Mark Twain. by
  3. Did you go _____ your friend to the mall? with
  4. We went _____ the mall on Saturday. to
  5. There is a lot to eat _____ the food court. at
  6. So many stores _____ the mall have sales. in, at
  7. My new cell phone is _____ the entertainment store. from

▸ Distribute copies of the worksheet to students and have them fill in the correct preposition to complete each sentence in a logical way.

▸ Remind students that there may be more than one possible answer to each sentence.

Your Turn

On Their Own

▸ Have students:

  • Look at the graphic organizer in Application B on page 109 of the *Student Text.*

  • Complete the graphic organizer about what to do in the food court.

  • Share and compare their answers with the class.

    Example: Before I eat, I go to the food court.

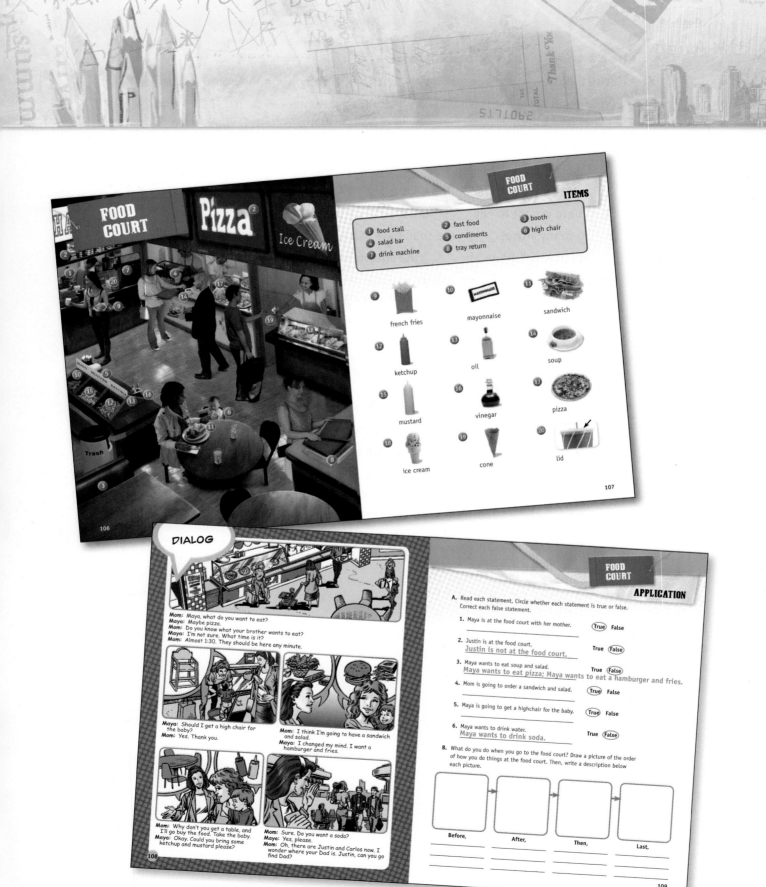

Introduction: Oral Fluency

 Students review the use of *where, here,* and *there,* and ordering food and other items. Students revisit the Unit Overview.

Where can I Find It?

Materials

Student Text
pp. 92–93

Blank cards

▸ Give each student at least two blank cards.

▸ Have students:

• Write one item they can buy at the mall on each card.

▸ Collect the cards from the students and shuffle them. Distribute two cards to each student.

▸ Have students:

• Work with a partner to have a role play in which they ask a mall employee where to find the item.

Example: How may I help you?

I would like to buy a DVD. Where can I find it?

You can find DVDs in the entertainment store.

Thank you very much.

Unit Review: Mall

▸ Direct students' attention to the pictures on pages 92–93. Elicit the word **mall** from the students.

▸ Point out the clothing store in the picture. Elicit the word **clothing store** from the students.

▸ Repeat for **entertainment store, movies,** and **food court**.

▸ Have students:

• Chorally and individually repeat the words.

STEP 1

Phonemic Awareness

Students practice identifying, differentiating, and producing the / j /, / v /, / h /, / r /, and / f / sounds.

Review of the / j /, / v /, / h /, / r /, and / f / Sounds

Materials:

Student Text
pp. 90–109

Phoneme charts
from the week

Chart paper

Rocks or marbles

▸ Post the week's phoneme charts at the front of the room for easy viewing.

▸ Review the week's sounds.

▸ Have students:

- Pronounce each sound.

- Look through pages 90–108 in the *Student Text* and add new words to the chart.

- Underline the corresponding letter for each new word.

- Present the new words to the class.

- Choral repeat the new words.

Phoneme Hopscotch

▸ Make hopscotch boards from chart paper. Make enough boards for groups of four students. Tape the charts to the floor.

- Write one phoneme from the week in each of the squares, in any order.

  Example:

  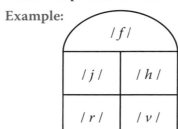

▸ Throw a rock down onto the board. Jump on each square except the square that has a rock on it. As you jump on each square, say a word from the week's charts that has the phoneme that is in the square. Go forward once and then return, as if playing hopscotch.

▸ Give each group a rock or marble.

▸ Have students:

- Take turns in their groups playing phoneme hopscotch on their board to practice the week's sounds.

- Repeat until everyone has had a few turns to play.

- Adapt the game to suit different physical needs.

STEP 2 Everyday Words

Students review and practice the prepositions of place and sequence words for everyday conversation.

Review Everyday Words: Placement

Mall Designs

Materials

Paper to draw on board

Newspaper comic strips

On Their Own

▸ Give students two blank pieces of paper to draw on.

▸ Write the following on the board:

1. Clothing store
2. Entertainment store
3. Movies
4. Food court

▸ Have students:

- Count off from 1 to 4.
- Determine which area of the mall they have, according to their number and the list on the board.
- Design that area of the mall and draw a sketch of the area on one piece of paper.

▸ After students have finished their sketches, divide the class into pairs.

▸ Have students:

- Sit back to back with their partner without showing their partner their design.
- Describe their picture to their partner using the prepositions so that their partner can sketch the design.

  Example: I designed a clothing store. **In** the store there are many clothes. There are a lot of sweaters and t-shirts **on** the shelves. The fitting room is **behind** the jeans.

- Compare their drawings to their partner's original drawing.

Review Everyday Words: Sequence

▸ Cut out different comic strips from the newspaper.

▸ Cut the comic strip panels apart and put them into an envelope. Each envelope should contain one comic strip.

▸ Have students:

- Work with a partner to put the comic strip in order.
- Read the comic strip and describe what happens.
- Write sentences using the sequence words **before, after, first, next, then,** and **last.**
- Present their comic strip to the class.

Variation:

▸ Use correction fluid to remove the dialog from a comic strip.

► Have students:
- Piece together the comic strip using the pictures.
- Write a dialog based on the sequence of events in the pictures.
- Share their comic strips with the class.

STEP 3

Vocabulary Development

 Students work with the core content vocabulary related to the mall for everyday conversation.

Review: Core Vocabulary

Mall Memory

Materials
Student Text
pp. 92–93, p. 111

► Direct students' attention to the picture of the mall scenes on pages 92–93 of the student text.

► Give students thirty seconds to:
- Study the pictures carefully.

► After thirty seconds have passed, divide the class into four teams.

► Assign each team a space at the board.

► Call out an area of the mall. (**clothing store, entertainment store, movies,** and **food court**)

► Have students:
- Line up in front of their space at the board.
- Do a relay race to write items that fit the area of the mall.
- Check the lists of the other teams to see if the items fit the category

  Example: Say "entertainment store." The first person goes to the board and writes **CDs.** That person then returns to the line and passes the chalk to the next person in line who writes **DVDs.**

► Give students a time limit for each relay.

► See how many different items each group can come up with.

Where Can I Buy It?

► Direct students' attention to Application A on page 111 in the *Student Text.*

► Have students:
- Look at each item and write where they can find each item in the mall.
- Check answers with a partner.

STEP 4

How English Works

Students are introduced to the dialog. Students participate in the dialog. Students review and practice **prepositions**.

Introduce the Dialog

Picture Walk-Through

Materials

Student Text
p. 110–111

Blank T-shirt
cutouts

Colored markers

▸ Have students:

- Look at the pictures on page 110 of the *Student Text*.

▸ Ask students simple questions about the pictures to predict the main idea of the dialog.

▸ Point to the picture in each panel. Act out or point to vocabulary words as necessary. Ask:

1. Panel 1: Where is Dad? in the clothing store
2. Panel 2: What are Dad and Justin looking at? scarves
3. Panel 3: What store is Dad talking about? entertainment store
4. Panel 4: What does Dad look at in the entertainment store? DVDs
5. Panel 5: Are Justin and Maya going to watch the baby? yes

▸ Record student responses on the board.

Read the Dialog

▸ Read through the dialog in steps. Have students:

- Track print with you as you read.
- Listen for cognates, or English words that are similar in students' native language.

Justin:	Hey, Dad. We're all waiting for you at the food court.
Dad:	Oh, is it 1:30 already?
Justin:	Yeah. Mom told me to look for you. Did you find a gift for her yet?

▸ Check students' comprehension by asking "Did Dad find a gift for Mom?" no

Dad:	Well, I saw a nice scarf, but they didn't have it in gray.
Justin:	She already has a gray scarf, doesn't she?

▸ Check students' comprehension by asking "What color scarf does Dad want to buy for Mom?" gray

Dad:	After, I went to look for a new cell phone. She wants a cell phone with a camera in it.
Justin:	Yeah, she needs a new cell phone.

► Check students' comprehension by asking "What kind of cell phone does Mom want?" a cell phone with a camera

> | | |
> |---|---|
> | Dad: | I wanted to buy her some DVDs. Her favorite movies are all out on DVD already. |
> | Justin: | You guys should go out to the movies. |

► Check students' comprehension by asking "What else did Dad look at in the entertainment store?" DVDs "What does Justin suggest?" going out to the movies

> | | |
> |---|---|
> | Dad: | Justin, that's a great idea! I'll get her a gift card for the movies! |
> | Justin: | Yeah. We can watch the baby. |
> | Dad: | Let's go eat! We'll stop by the movie theater on the way to the food court. |
> | Justin: | Yeah, let's go. I'm hungry! |

► Check students' comprehension by asking "What does Dad decide to get Mom?" a gift card for the movies "What does Justin say he will do?" watch the baby with Maya

► Ask students if they have ever given or received a gift card before.

Practice the Dialog

► Divide the class into pairs.

► Have students:

  • Assign the speaking roles within each pair.

  • Read the roles out loud in pairs.

  • Volunteer to perform the dialog in front of the class.

► Check students' comprehension of the dialog by revisiting the questions from the Picture Walk-Through.

Preposition Pictograms

► Review the prepositions **in front of, behind, over, under, at, on, in, to, from, by,** and **with**.

► Tell students that you are opening a new t-shirt store in the mall.

► Divide the class into pairs and assign each pair a preposition.

► Give each pair a blank paper t-shirt cutout.

Pair/Share

► Have students:

  • Come up with a t-shirt design that could represent their preposition.

  • Draw the design on the paper t-shirt cut out.

- Share their design with the class to see if the class can identify the preposition.

Example:

▸ Post t-shirt designs around the room.

Revisit the Dialog

▸ Direct students' attention again to the dialog on page 110 of the *Student Text*.

▸ Draw the graphic organizer on the board.

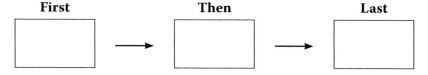

▸ Have students:

- Copy the graphic organizer in their notebooks.
- Reread the dialog.
- Work with a partner to complete the sequence graphic organizer.
- Share their answers with the class.

Your Turn

▸ Direct students' attention to Application B on page 111 of the *Student Text*.

▸ Have students:

- Draw items that they bought at the mall in their shopping bag.
- Share their items with a partner in a dialog.

    Example: Where did you go? I went to the entertainment store.
    What did you buy there? I bought a digital camera.

REVIEW DIALOG

Justin: Hey, Dad. We're all waiting for you at the food court.
Dad: Oh, is it 1:30 already?
Justin: Yeah. Mom told me to look for you. Did you find a gift for her yet?

Dad: Well, I saw a nice scarf, but they didn't have it in gray.
Justin: She already has a gray scarf, doesn't she?

Dad: After, I went to look for a new cell phone. She wants a cell phone with a camera in it.
Justin: Yeah, she needs a new cell phone.

Dad: I wanted to buy her some DVDs. Her favorite movies are all out on DVD already.
Justin: You guys should go out to the movies.

Dad: Justin, that's a great idea! I'll get her a gift card for the movies!
Justin: Yeah. We can watch the baby.
Dad: Let's go eat! We'll stop by the movie theater on the way to the food court.
Justin: Yeah, let's go. I'm hungry!

110

REVIEW APPLICATION

A. Write where you can go to buy each item.

1. movie theater
2. entertainment store
3. clothing store
4. entertainment store
5. food court
6. movie theater, food court

B. You just came home from the shopping mall. In the shopping bag, draw the things you bought and label them.

111

Everyday English Student Text

MY DAY

Unit 6

Thursday October 11th

MORNING
- help mom with breakfast
- 7:45 Walk to school with Mai

Afternoon
4:00
- Soccer - don't forget gym bag
- Go to grocery store with dad

EVENING
6:00 - Dance class
Study for math test

VERY IMPORTANT

112

Friday October 12th

Morning

8:15 - Take bus to school
9:00 - Math Test

AFTERNOON

:30 - Homework help with Mr. Suárez
:00 - Mall with Mai after Soccer?

Night

- Call Mai about town festival
- dishes clear table

Town Festival Tomorrow!!

Everyday English Student Text

114

EVENING

6:30 PM

9:30 PM

MON   AM
NIGHT

115

Everyday English Student Text

Unit 6
LESSON 1

Introduction: Oral Fluency

Students learn to tell the time and are introduced to the week's scenario. Then, students focus on one of the areas within the scenario.

Telling Time

Materials

Student Text
pp. 112–115

Paper plates

Round-head
fasteners

Long and short
cut-out arrows

▸ Draw a round clock face on the board without the hands.

▸ Have students:

  • Recite the numbers as you write them on the clock face.

▸ Say "What time is it?" and write the question above the clock. Point to the clock.

▸ Draw the hands on the board to show 9:00.

▸ Say "It's nine o'clock." Point to the short hand pointing to 9 as you say "**nine**", and point to the long hand pointing to 12 as you say "**o'clock**."

▸ Have students:

  • Repeat the sentence.

▸ Write "o'clock" above the 12 on the clock face. Give students further examples of o'clock with other hours. For example, erase the short hand and re-draw it, pointing it to 5 for five o'clock.

▸ Have students:

  • Tell you what time it is.

▸ Explain to students that each number on the clock represents five minutes. On the outside of the clock face, next to each number, write the number of minutes that each number represents. For example, next to the 1, write "5 minutes," and next to the 2, write "10 minutes," etc.

▸ Draw hands on the clock to show "one thirty." Ask "What time is it?" Then say "It's one thirty." Point to the short hand and 1 as you say "one" and the long hand and 6 as you say "thirty."

▸ Have students:

  • Repeat the time.

▸ Go through other examples with students to show other times. For example, 4:20, 11:45, 8:10, 6:05. For 6:05, point out that we usually say "oh five" instead of just "five."

▸ Have students:

  • Tell you the times shown on the board.

▸ To extend the activity, teach students to tell the time using "till / to" and "after." Use the examples It's **five** till / to eight and "It's ten after six."

Show Me the Time

- ▶ Distribute the paper plates, long and short arrows, and fasteners to the students.
- ▶ Have students:
  - Make their own clock faces with the paper plate, fasteners, and arrows.
- ▶ Ask: What time is it?
  - Position the arrows on their clock faces to show the times you call out.
  - Say the time shown on their clock faces.
- ▶ Call out different times for the students to show on their clock faces.
- ▶ Model an example with the students.
- ▶ Have students:
  - Work with a partner to ask and tell the time.
  - Show the time on their clock faces.
  - Repeat the time shown on their clock faces.
  - Volunteer to call out times for the class to show on their clock faces.

Unit Overview: My Day

- ▶ Direct students' attention to the picture on pages 112–113. Say "my day." Have students:
  - Choral repeat the words.
- ▶ Have students:
  - Identify any words that they may know by sharing the definitions with the class.
- ▶ Point to the **morning** section of the planner. Ask "What time of day is it?"
- ▶ Have students:
  - Point to the morning section.
  - Tell you what time of day it is.
- ▶ Repeat for **afternoon, evening,** and **night**.
- ▶ Direct students' attention to pages 114–115. Ask students "Which pictures show morning activities?"
- ▶ Have students:
  - Point to the morning scenario and repeat the word **morning**.

Introduction to Morning

- ▶ Direct students' attention to the picture of the morning scenario on page 114.
- ▶ Have students:
  - Describe the picture.
- ▶ Point out the times on the alarm clock (7:30 A.M.) and the kitchen clock (8:00 A.M.). Explain to students that A.M. means "morning."
- ▶ Have students:
  - Tell you what time it is.

Phonemic Awareness

➡️ Students practice identifying and producing the / *ch* / sound.

The / *ch* / Sound

▸ Draw on the board or point to a chair in the room and elicit the word **chair** from the students. Write the word on the board.

▸ Have students:

  • Pronounce the word with you.

▸ Underline the ***ch*** in the word and pronounce the sound.

Model

▸ Explain that the letter ***ch*** in English makes the sound / *ch* /.

▸ Pronounce the sound for the students.

▸ Have students:

  • Choral repeat the sound.

▸ Repeat with the words **teacher, chalk,** and **children**.

▸ Elicit other words with the / *ch* / sound.

/ *ch* / Cha-Cha-Cha

▸ Tell students that they are going to learn a dance to help them remember the / *ch* / sound.

▸ Demonstrate the basic moves for the cha-cha-cha. Stand with your feet next to each other. Step back with your right foot. Then step in place with your left foot. Bring your right foot slightly forward of the left foot by taking a small step. Step in place with your left foot, and again with your right foot.

▸ Say the word **chicken**.

▸ Do the first step of the cha-cha-cha. Step back with your right foot and say "chicken."

▸ Repeat the word on the second step as you step in place with your left foot.

▸ Take the last three steps (the cha-cha-cha) and say / *ch* / as you take each step.

  Example: As you take each step, say "Chicken! Chicken! / *ch* /. / *ch* /. / *ch* /!"

▸ Have students:

  • Follow your dance steps.

  • Repeat the words and the sounds as they do the dance steps.

  • Call out another word with the / *ch* / sound for the class to dance to and say.

STEP

2 Everyday Words

➡️ Students review and practice vocabulary related to the days of the week and the calendar for everyday conversation.

Review Everyday Words: Days and Months

Materials
A ball
Poster board

‣ Review the days of the week with students. Ask them to say what day it is.

‣ Have students:

• Tell you what day it is and recite the rest of the days of the week in order.

‣ Review the months of the year with the students. Ask them what month it is.

‣ Have students:

• Tell you what month it is and recite the rest of the months in order.

Month-and-Day Ball

‣ Have students:

• Stand in a circle.

‣ Hold the ball and say the name of a month. Throw the ball to student.

‣ Have students:

• Catch the ball and say the month that follows the month stated.

• Throw the ball to a new student who will say the next month.

‣ Repeat until all students have had at least one turn to say a month.

‣ Repeat with the days of the week.

Example: Hold the ball and say "March." Throw the ball to a student. The student will say **April**. The student throws the ball to a different student, who says **May**.

Review Everyday Words: Seasons, Weather, and Temperature

‣ Review the seasons with the students.

‣ Have the students:

• Tell you the names of the season.

• Tell you what months are in each season.

‣ Write the seasons with the corresponding months on the board.

‣ Remind students that in many places, the weather and the temperature in each season changes.

‣ Elicit weather words from the students for each season.

‣ Write them down on the board next to the corresponding season.

‣ Divide the class into four groups.

‣ Assign each group one of the four seasons.

▸ Have students:

- Make a poster for their season that shows the weather associated with it.
- Show activities that they do in that season.
- Label the different parts of the poster.
- Present their posters to the class and explain what is in their poster.

Variation: Advanced students can write sentences to go with their poster.

3

Vocabulary Development

➡ Students work with the core content vocabulary related to the home, family and morning for everyday conversation.

Review and Introduce: Core Vocabulary

Materials
Student Text
pp. 116–117

▸ Review the words for family members that the students learned in previous lessons.

▸ Write the names of the family members in one column on one side of the board.

▸ If any family members are short forms, such as **mom** and **mother**, have students:

- Match the short forms to the long forms.

▸ Draw two columns on the board. Draw a stick figure of a man at the top of one column and a stick figure of a woman at the top of the other column.

On Their Own

▸ Have students:

- Copy the chart in their notebooks.
- Sort the family members into males and females.

▸ Check answers.

▸ Direct students' attention to the morning scenario and list on pages 116–117 of the *Student Text*.

▸ Tell students that they already know some words for things people do in the morning.

▸ Tell students that they are going to review and learn more words related to the morning.

▸ Point out the times on the alarm clock and the kitchen clock.

▸ Have students:

- Tell you the time on each clock.
- Tell you each room in the house that appears in each picture.

▸ Point to each item that appears on the items list on page 117. As you point, say each word out loud.

▶ Have students:

- Point to each item and repeat each word.
- Volunteer to act out the action words.

Practice Vocabulary

Who Does What?

▶ Direct students' attention to the morning scenario on page 116.

▶ Point to Panel 1. Ask "What family member is in the picture?" the sister "Where is she?" in the bedroom.

▶ Focus on the sister. Ask "What does she do in the morning?" She wakes up. "What time is it?" It's 7:30.

▶ Encourage students to answer in complete sentences.

▶ Divide the class into pairs.

Pair/Share

▶ Have students:

- Work in pairs to name each family member in each panel.
- Say what each family member is doing.
- Give more information about each family member, if they can.
- Share responses with the class.

STEP

4

How English Works

Students are introduced to the dialog. Students participate in the dialog. Students learn and practice **sentence structure**.

Introduce the Dialog

Picture Walk-Through

Materials

Student Text
pp. 118–119

Prepared
sentence strips

▶ Have students:

- Look at the pictures on page 118 of the *Student Text*.

▶ Ask students simple questions about the pictures to predict the main idea of the dialog.

▶ Point to the picture in each panel. Act out or point to vocabulary words as necessary.

▶ Ask:

1. Panel 1: What food do you think the sister is eating? Answers may vary. Are they eating breakfast, lunch, or dinner? breakfast

2. Panel 2: Which family members do you see? mother, father, brother, sister

3. Panel 3: What sport does Jessica play? soccer

4. Panel 4: Where does Jessica want to go? to the mall

5. Panel 5: What does Jacob want to eat? toast and cereal

6. Panel 6: Where do you think Dad is going? to work

▶ Record student responses on the board.

Read the Dialog

▸ Read through the dialog in steps. Have students:

- Track print with you as you read.
- Listen for cognates, or English words that are similar in students' native language.

> **Mom:** Jessica, you don't have much time. The school bus will be here in ten minutes.
>
> **Jessica:** Okay. I can eat quickly. I have to meet Mai. We have a math test today.
>
> **Mom:** Are you ready for the test?
>
> **Jessica:** Yes. We just want to meet this morning. We want to be ready.

▸ Explain to students what a **test** is. Ask them how they feel about tests..

▸ Check students' comprehension by asking "How is Jessica going to school?" on the school bus

▸ Have students:

- Point to the school bus.

> **Dad:** Honey, can you get Jacob ready for school? I have to go to work early before my meeting.
>
> **Mom:** Sure. What time is your meeting?
>
> **Dad:** It's at 9:00.

▸ Say "Jacob has to get ready for school." Check students' comprehension by asking "What does he need to do to get ready for school?" Answers will vary.

> **Jessica:** Are you coming to watch soccer practice today?
>
> **Mom:** I'll try. What time should I pick you up?
>
> **Jessica:** 5:00.

▸ Check students' comprehension by asking "What time is Jessica finished with soccer practice?" five o'clock

▸ Have students:

- Show 5:00 on the clock faces that they made.

> **Jessica:** Mom, can I go to the mall with Mai this afternoon?
>
> **Mom:** If you do your homework before dinner, you can.

▸ Check students' comprehension by asking "Where does Jessica want to go?" to the mall "When does Jessica have to do her homework?" before dinner

▸ Have students:

  • Tell you when they do their homework.

> | Mom: | Jacob, drink your milk. What do you want to eat? |
> | Jacob: | I want toast. Can I have cereal? |

▸ Check students' comprehension by asking "What is Jacob going to have for breakfast?" milk, toast, and cereal

▸ Have students:

  • Point to and say each item.

> | Dad: | Bye, everyone. Have a good day! |
> | Jessica: | Bye, Dad! See you later! |
> | Jacob: | Bye-bye! |

▸ Explain that we often use the expression **Have a good day!** as a way to say goodbye. Tell students we can also use the words **morning, afternoon, evening,** and **night** with **Have a good _____!**

▸ Have students:

  • Repeat the expression with **morning, afternoon, evening,** and **night.**

  • Tell you other ways the characters say goodbye in the dialog. Bye. See you later. Bye-bye.

Practice the Dialog

▸ Divide the class into groups of four. If there are not enough students, assign some students two roles.

▸ Have students:

  • Assign the speaking roles within each group.

  • Read the roles out loud in groups.

  • Volunteer to perform the dialog in front of the class.

▸ Check students' comprehension of the dialog by revisiting the questions from the Picture Walk-Through.

A Study of Sentence Structure

▸ Point to panel 1 on page 118 of the *Student Text.* Ask "How does Jessica go to school?" Jessica takes the bus.

▸ Write the sentence on the board.

▸ Tell students that statements start with a capital letter and end with a period. Point them out to the students in the model sentence.

▸ Explain that in English, a statement usually begins with a subject. Explain that a subject is who or what the sentence is about. Ask students "Who is this sentence about?" Jessica

▸ Circle **Jessica** in the sentence. Tell students that **Jessica** is the subject of the sentence.

▸ Explain that in a statement, the predicate follows the subject. Explain that a predicate tells about the subject. It might be information about the subject or what the subject does. Ask students "What does Jessica do?" takes the bus

▸ Underline **takes the bus** in the sentence. Tell students that *takes the bus* tells us what Jessica does.

▸ Point out the position of each part of the sentence. The subject is before the predicate.

▸ Repeat with the following sentences:

1. Jacob wants cereal and toast.

2. Jessica and Jacob say goodbye to Dad.

3. The family is in the kitchen.

Sorting Out Sentence Structure

▸ Prepare sentence strips for the students using words from the items list on page 117. Cut the sentence strips to separate the subject and the predicate. Do not repeat subjects.

Example: Write the sentence "The family eats breakfast." Cut the sentence strip after *family*.

▸ Divide the class into pairs. Give each pair a set of five cut sentence strips.

Pair/Share

▸ Have students:

• Work in pairs to match the parts to make logical and grammatically correct sentences.

• Write the completed sentences in their notebooks.

▸ Check answers.

Revisit the Dialog

On Their Own

▸ Have students:

• Choose one of the four characters to focus on.

• Read through the dialog on their own.

• Identify the activities that their characters are doing or plan to do.

• Share the activities that their characters are doing or plan to do with the class.

▸ Write the activities for each character on the board.

Your Turn

▸ Direct students to page 119 of the *Student Text*.

▸ Have students:

• Complete the dialog in Application A.

• Share their dialogs with a partner.

• Do a role play with a partner to perform their dialogs from Application A.

• Volunteer to perform their dialogs for the class.

Introduction: Oral Fluency

 Students learn to talk about the time that something occurs and are reintroduced to the week's scenario. Then, students focus on one of the areas within the scenario.

Talk about Schedules

Materials

Student Text
pp. 112–115

▸ Begin the class by asking "What time is it?"

▸ Have students:

- Tell you the time.

▸ Tell students that we use **It's (time).** to tell about the time at the moment, but that sometimes we use expressions of time to refer to things that are not happening now.

▸ Direct students' attention to pages 112–113 in the *Student Text.* Have them look at Jessica's planner. Point to the handwritten note that says "7:45 Walk to school with Mai"

▸ Ask students "Is it 7:45 now?" no Tell students that when we talk about time, we can use the preposition **at**. Say: "Jessica has to walk to school with Mai at 7:45." Write the sentence on the board. Underline the word **at**.

▸ Ask students to look at Jessica's planner and ask "At what time does Jessica have soccer practice?"

▸ Have students:

- Respond in a complete sentence.

▸ Repeat with other activities listed in Jessica's planner on pages 112–113.

▸ Tell students that we can also add the time of day to the sentence. Use the examples "Jessica has to walk to school with Mai at 7:45 in the morning." and "Jessica has soccer practice at 4:00 in the afternoon."

▸ Have students:

- Tell you what time and what time of day Jessica's activities take place.

▸ To extend the activity, show students how to add the day of the week. Use the examples "Jessica has to walk to school with Mai on Thursday at 7:45 in the morning." and "Jessica has soccer practice on Thursday at 4:00 in the afternoon."

Review: My Day

▸ Direct students' attention to the pictures on pages 114–115. Say "my day." Point to the picture of morning and elicit the word **morning** from the students.

▸ Point to the **afternoon** picture and say "afternoon."

► Have students:
  • Point to the afternoon picture.
  • Repeat the word.

Introduction to Afternoon

► Choral repeat the words. Direct students' attention to the picture of the afternoon scenario on page 114.
► Have students:
  • Describe the picture.
► Point out the time on the school clock (3:30 P.M.). Explain to students that P.M. means "after 11:59 A.M."
► Have students:
  • Tell you what time it is.

STEP

1

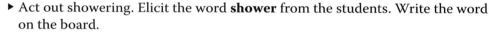

Phonemic Awareness

Students practice identifying, differentiating, and producing the / *sh* / sound.

The / *sh* / Sound

Materials
Prepared slips of paper
A large paper cup

Model

► Act out showering. Elicit the word **shower** from the students. Write the word on the board.
► Have students:
  • Pronounce the word with you.
► Underline the *sh* in the word and pronounce the sound.
► Explain that the letters *sh* in English usually make the sound / *sh* /. Pronounce the sound for the students.
► Have students:
  • Choral repeat the sound.
► Point out the difference between the / *ch* / sound and the / *sh* / sounds. Use the words **chip** and **ship** as examples.
► Repeat with the words **shave, shampoo,** and **wash**.
► Elicit other words with the / *sh* / sound.

/ *sh* / Shake

► Prepare slips of paper with words with the / *sh* / sound. Leave a blank space where the *sh* goes. The words do not necessarily have to be words that the students know in English, but they should be simple enough for the students to read and pronounce.

  Example: For the word **shampoo,** write ___ampoo on the slip of paper.

► Prepare at least three papers per student.
► Place the papers in the paper cup. Shake the paper cup to mix the papers.

- ▸ Explain to students that they are going to shake the cup to practice / *sh* /.

- ▸ Give the cup to one student.

- ▸ Have the student:

  - • Shake the cup and say **shake, shake, shake**.

  - • Take out a slip of paper.

  - • Fill in the *sh* to complete the word and say the word aloud.

  - • Pass the cup to the next student.

- ▸ Continue until all of the papers have been read.

STEP 2

Everyday Words

 Students review and practice talking about numbers, letters, and money for everyday conversation.

Review Everyday Words: Numbers and Letters

Materials

Pictures of various items

Real or play money

- ▸ Review the numbers from 1–100 with the students.

- ▸ Lead the students in counting from 1–20.

- ▸ Have students:

  - • Say the next consecutive number from 1–20 as you randomly point to a student.

  - • Count from 20–100 by tens as you randomly point to each student.

- ▸ After reviewing the numbers, point to one student and assign him or her the letter *a*. Assign the next student the letter *b*, and so on until all of the students have a letter. If there are more letters than students, continue assigning the rest of the letters in the alphabet to the students so that students have more than one letter.

- ▸ Have students:

  - • Write their assigned letter or letters on a piece of paper large enough for the rest of the class to see.

- ▸ Call out a letter and a number between 1–99.

- ▸ Have students:

  - • Listen for their letter.

  - • Say the next consecutive number if their letter is called out.

  - • Call out a new letter and number for the rest of the class.

    Example: You call out the letter *g* and the number **47**. The student assigned letter *g* says 48. That student then calls out a letter, for example *p,* and a number between 1–99 that has not yet been called, for example, 82 The student with the letter *p* calls out 83.

Review Everyday Words: Money

▸ Gather pictures of various items that students know in English. There should be enough so that each student has three pictures.

▸ Review the names of for different units of money by holding up the different coins and bills and eliciting the names in English.

▸ Review how to talk about prices. Write "$7.50" and "89¢" on the board.

▸ Have students:

- Tell you each amount.

▸ Show students each of the pictures of the items and elicit the names of each item.

▸ Write the names on the board.

▸ Give each student 3 pictures.

▸ Have students:

- Write a price for each of their three items between $.01 and $100.

- Write down the name of three items from the list that are not in one of their pictures.

- Search for the students in their class that have the three items on their list.

- Ask for the price of each item and write it down next to the item on their list.

- Use the sentence frames How much is _____? or How much are _____?

▸ Check the prices the students found with the prices that the students wrote in their pictures.

STEP 3

Vocabulary Development

Students work with the core content vocabulary related to school, the neighborhood, and the afternoon for everyday conversation.

Review and Introduce: Core Vocabulary

Materials
Student Text
pp. 120–121
Prepared cards

▸ Review words for places in the school and in the neighborhood the students learned in previous lessons.

▸ Write the names of the places on the board.

▸ Divide the class into the same number of groups that there are place names.

▸ Assign each group a place name.

▸ Have students:

- Create a list of ten items that they would find in that place, without using the *Student Text* for reference.

- Write their lists on the board under each place name.

- Call out each item in their list for the rest of the class to either find a picture of it in the *Student Text* or point out the item in the classroom, if it is there.

▸ Direct students' attention to the afternoon scenario and list on pages 120–121 of the *Student Text*.

- ▶ Tell students that they already know some words for things we do in the afternoon.
- ▶ Tell students they are going to review and learn more words related to the afternoon.
- ▶ Point out the times on the clock in the picture.
- ▶ Have students:
  - Tell you the time on the clock.
- ▶ Point to each item that appears on the items list on page 121. As you point, say each word out loud.
- ▶ Have students:
  - Point to each item and repeat each word.
  - Volunteer to act out the action words.

Practice Vocabulary

Guess Where and What

- ▶ Prepare one set of cards with the activities listed on page 121 of the *Student Text*. Prepare another set of cards with the names of places in the school and neighborhood.
- ▶ Have a student volunteer:
  - Choose one card from each set.
  - Draw a person on the board doing the activity written on the first card in the place written on the second card.

    Example: The student chooses the cards **play chess** and **library**. The student draws a picture of someone playing chess in the library.
- ▶ Have students:
  - Guess what the student volunteer has drawn.
  - Say what is happening and where it is happening in a complete sentence.

    Example: The boy is playing chess in the library.
- ▶ Continue until all students have had a chance to draw on the board.

Variation:

- ▶ Have students:
  - Work in pairs to prepare the cards.
  - Draw the activities for their partner to guess.
  - Take turns drawing and guessing.
  - Share one of their illustrations with the class.

STEP 4

How English Works

 Students are introduced to the dialog. Students participate in the dialog. Students learn and practice **interrogative** structures with *be*.

Introduce the Dialog

Picture Walk-Through

Materials
Student Text
pp. 122–123

▸ Have students:

  • Look at pictures on page 122 of the *Student Text*.

▸ Ask students simple questions about the pictures to predict the main idea of the dialog.

▸ Point to the picture in each panel. Act out or point to vocabulary words as necessary. Ask:

  1. Panel 1: Where are Jessica and Mai? at school What are they doing? studying and talking

  2. Panel 2: What does Jessica have to do later? play soccer

  3. Panel 3: Where does Mai want to go later? to the mall What does Jessica want to buy? a skirt

  4. Panel 4: Who will take Jessica and Mai to the mall? Jessica's mom

  5. Panel 5: Where are Jessica and Mai? in class

▸ Record student responses on the board.

Read the Dialog

▸ Read through the dialog in steps.

▸ Have students:

  • Track print with you as you read.

  • Listen for cognates, or English words that are similar in students' native language.

Mai:	What are you doing after school today?
Jessica:	I have to get extra help from Mr. Suárez in math.
Mai:	I hope the math test isn't too hard.

▸ Check students' comprehension by asking "What does Jessica have to do after school?" get extra help from Mr. Suárez

Jessica:	We studied a lot, so hopefully we'll do well.
Mai:	Do you want to come to my house after school?
Jessica:	I can't. I have soccer practice.

▸ Check students' comprehension by asking "What does Mai want Jessica to do after school?" go to her house "Can Jessica go?" no "Why not?" She has soccer practice.

> Mai: Do you want to go to the mall after soccer practice?
>
> Jessica: Maybe. My mom said I could go. I want to find a skirt for the town festival this weekend.

▸ Explain what a town **festival** is. Ask students about festivals that they celebrate.

▸ Check students' comprehension by asking "When can Jessica go to the mall?" after soccer practice "What does she want to buy?" a skirt "Why does she want a new skirt?" for the town festival

> Mai: Me too! What time do you finish soccer practice?
>
> Jessica: 5:00. Maybe my mom can take us to the mall.

▸ Check students' comprehension by asking "Does Mai want a new skirt?" yes "How will the girls get to the mall?" Jessica's mom can take them.

> Mai: Good luck on the math test, Jessica.
>
> Jessica: Thanks. You too, Mai.

▸ Explain the expression **Good luck** to the students.

▸ Have students:

- Give examples of situations when they might wish someone good luck.

Practice the Dialog

Divide the class into pairs.

Pair/Share

▸ Have students:

- Assign the speaking roles within each pair.

- Read the roles out loud in pairs.

- Volunteer to perform the dialog in front of the class.

▸ Check students' comprehension of the dialog by revisiting the questions from the Picture Walk-Through.

Interrogative Structures with *Be*

▸ Review the sentence structure of a statement. Write the sentence on the board:

Jessica is at school.

▸ Have students:

- Identify the subject. Jessica

- Identify the predicate. is at school

- Identify the position of each. The subject is first. The predicate follows the subject.

- ▶ Circle **Jessica** in the sentence and underline **is**. Tell students that **Jessica** is the subject and **is** is the verb.
- ▶ Tell students that in English, the structure of a question is different than the structure of a statement.
- ▶ Write the question "Is Jessica at school?" on the board above the statement.
- ▶ Have students:
  - Compare the statement to the questions.
  - Tell you what is different. the position of the subject and the verb and the punctuation.
- ▶ Draw an arrow from **Jessica** in the question to **Jessica** in the statement.
- ▶ Do the same for **is**.
- ▶ Point out the use of the question mark at the end of the question and the period at the end of the statement.
- ▶ Model another example with the sentence "Jessica and Mai are students." and the question "Are Jessica and Mai students?"
- ▶ Write the sentence "Jessica and Mai are in class."
- ▶ Have students:
  - Transform the sentence into a question. Are Jessica and Mai in class?
- ▶ Write the question on the board and underline it.
- ▶ Explain to students that we can make other questions with this base question by adding question words.
- ▶ Write the question word **why** at the start of the question. Change the *A* to *a* in the word *are*.
- ▶ Tell the students that the question is new, but the base of the question is the same. Point to the underlined part of the sentence.
- ▶ Repeat with the question word **when**.

Practice Interrogative Structure

- ▶ Write five simple, affirmative sentences with the verb *be* on the board. For example, "Mr. Suárez is a teacher."

On Their Own

- ▶ Have students:
  - Transform each sentence into a question.
  - Use correct capitalization and punctuation.
  - Compare their answers with a partner.
  - Volunteer to write the questions on the board.
- ▶ Check answers.
- ▶ Write the question words **what, when, where, why** and **how** on the board.
- ▶ Have students:
  - Add a question word to a question to make a logical and grammatically correct question.
  - Answer the new questions with a complete sentence.

Combine Columns

▶ Draw three columns on the board.

▶ Elicit words that can be used as subjects from the students. Write the words in the left column.

▶ Write the verbs **am, is, are** in the middle column.

▶ Elicit adjectives, locations, and people words from the students. Write them in the left column.

Pair/Share

▶ Have students:

- Work in pairs to choose one word or phrase from each column.

- Write a statement using the words.

- Transform the statement into a question.

- Choose three more sets of words or phrases to write three more statements and questions.

- Share their statements and questions with the class.

  Example: Students have chosen **man / is / police officer** from the three columns. They will write the statement The man is a police officer. They will write the question Is the man a police officer?

Revisit the Dialog

▶ Direct students' attention again to the dialog on page 122 of the *Student Text.*

▶ Have students:

- Read the dialog on their own.

- Complete Application A on page 123 of the *Student Text.*

- Compare the activities they wrote to the activities mentioned in the dialog.

Your Turn

▶ Direct students' attention again to the dialog on page 123 of the *Student Text.*

▶ Have students:

- Complete Application B.

- Share their paragraphs with a partner.

Unit 6 — LESSON 3

Introduction: Oral Fluency

 Students learn to tell a story and are reintroduced to the week's scenario. Then, students focus on one of the areas within the scenario.

Telling a Story

Materials
Student Text
pp. 112–115
Copies of graphic organizer

▸ Prepare a graphic organizer like the one shown and make enough copies for the students.

▸ Tell students that we often tell stories to other people. Explain that sometimes the stories are about what we did over the weekend or something that happened to us.

▸ Tell students that when we tell stories, it is important to give information to make the story clear and more interesting.

▸ Review with the question words **who, what, when, where, why** and **how** with the students.

▸ Tell students that a story is better and more interesting if we include these six ideas.

▸ Tell student they are going to help you tell a story. Say "Yesterday, I saw a movie."

▸ Explain that the sentence does not give much information about what happened.

▸ Draw a five-point star on the board as in the graphic organizer above. Write "saw a movie" in the center of the star.

▸ Tell students this answers the **what** question. Say "What did I do?" I saw a movie.

▸ Have students:

• Suggest information to fill in for the **who, where, when, why,** and **how** sections.

Example: Students suggest mall for the **where** section, with my friend for the **who** section, on the bus for the **how** section, birthday for the **why** section.

▸ Tell the story with the new information. As you reach each piece of information that the students suggested, point to the appropriate area on the completed graphic organizer on the board.

Example: Yesterday, I went to the mall with my friend. We went on the bus. It was her birthday, so we saw a movie.

Tell Me a Story

▸ Distribute a copy of the graphic organizer worksheet to the students.

▸ Have students:

- Complete their graphic organizer with their own information to tell a story.
- Tell the class their story using the information in their graphic organizers.

Review: My Day

▸ Direct students' attention to the pictures on pages 114–115. Say "my day." Point to the morning and afternoon pictures and elicit the words **morning** and **afternoon** from the students.

▸ Point to the **evening** picture and say, "evening."

▸ Have students:

- Point to the **evening sections** of the planner.
- Repeat the word.

Introduction to Evening

▸ Direct students' attention to the evening scenario on page 115.

▸ Have students:

- Describe the picture.

▸ Point out the time on the kitchen clock (6:30 P.M.)

▸ Have students:

- Tell you what time it is.

STEP 1

Phonemic Awareness

Students practice identifying, differentiating, and producing the / *g* / and / *ng* / sounds.

The / *g* / and / *ng* / Sounds

Materials
A bell
A buzzer, or other noisemaker

Model

▸ Write the word **bag** on the board.

▸ Have students:

- Pronounce the word with you.

▸ Underline the *g* with in the word and pronounce the sound.

▸ Explain that the letter *g* in English often makes the sound / *g* /. Pronounce the sound for the students.

▸ Have students:

- Choral repeat the sound.

▸ Repeat with the words **globe, dog, grass,** and **magazine**.

▶ Have students:

- Find other words with the / g / sound.
- Write the words on the board.

▶ Write the word **morning** on the board.

▶ Have students:

- Pronounce the word with you.

▶ Underline the *ng* in the word and pronounce the sound.

▶ Explain that the / ng / sound is similar to the / g / sound, except it is more nasal and the back of our tongue touches the roof of the mouth.

▶ Repeat with the words **evening, shopping,** and **sing**.

▶ Have students:

- Find other words with the / ng / sound.
- Write the words on the board.
- Repeat the words.

Minimal Pairs Sound Off

▶ Prepare a list of minimal pairs words with the final / g / and / ng / sounds.

   Examples: wig—wing, rag—rang, bag—bang, dig—ding, etc.

▶ Divide the class into two teams. Have each team line up on either side of a desk or table on which there is a bell, buzzer, or other noisemaker.

▶ Tell students that they are going to listen for the / ng / sound.

▶ Slowly say "wig, wig, wing."

▶ Have the students:

- Try to ring the bell or buzzer before the other team member when they hear the / ng / sound.
- Choral repeat the words.

▶ Repeat with other minimal pairs and the sound / g /. Change the location of the target word when you read out the minimal pairs.

▶ Have students:

- Volunteer to call out the minimal pairs for the teams.

2 Everyday Words

 Students review and practice vocabulary related to feelings and senses.

Review Everyday Words: Feelings

Materials
Squares of paper
Tape

▶ Draw four circles on the board. Write the words **happy, sad, angry,** and **surprised** under the circles.

▶ Have students:
  • Volunteer to draw a face in the circle that expresses the feeling written below it.
  • Say each adjective.

▶ Call out a feeling word.

▶ Have students:
  • Make a face to express the feeling.

Review Everyday Words: The Senses

▶ Review the senses **look, taste, sound, feel,** and **smell** with the students.

▶ Write the words across the board.

▶ Have students:
  • Say and point to the body parts that are associated with each sense.
  • Suggest adjectives that can be used with each sense. For example, delicious, bad, salty, sweet, etc.

▶ Write the adjectives under each sense associated with the adjective. Some adjectives may be used with more than one sense.

▶ For each adjective, have students:
  • Say an item that fits the sense and adjective.
  • Describe the item with the sense and adjective in a complete sentence.

    Example: For the sense **smell** and the adjective **good**, a student might suggest coffee. The student says: Coffee smells good.

What's on My Back?

▶ Give each student a square of paper and tape.

▶ Have each student:
  • Write one of the sensory adjectives on the paper.
  • Tape the word to the back of the student next to them so that the other student can't see it.
  • Walk around the class and give other students clues for them to guess the sensory adjective taped on their back.
  • Use words, phrases, and sentences to give the other students clues.
  • Guess the word written on their own backs.

Example: A student has the word **delicious** on his or her back. Other students might give examples of things that fit this adjective, such as popcorn, a good apple, pizza. More advanced students will be able to say complete sentences, such as Popcorn tastes like this. You say this if you eat something you like.

▸ Continue until all students have correctly guessed their word.

STEP 3

Vocabulary Development

⟹ Students work with the core content vocabulary related to food, clothing, and the evening for everyday conversation.

Review and Introduce: Core Vocabulary

Review: Food

Materials
Student Text
pp. 124–125

▸ Review words for foods that students learned in previous lessons. Write the words **breakfast, lunch,** and **dinner** on the board.

▸ Explain to students that **dinner** is the meal we eat in the evening.

▸ Have students:

  • Suggest foods that are eaten at each of these meals.

  • Write the foods on the board under the correct category.

▸ Direct students' attention to page 125 of the *Student Text*.

▸ Have students:

  • Point out and name the food items in the picture.

Review: Clothing

▸ Review words for clothing items that the students learned in previous lessons.

▸ Have students:

  • Volunteer to stand in front of the class.

  • Say what items of clothing the volunteer is wearing.

▸ Direct students' attention to the evening scenario and list on pages 124–125 of the *Student Text*.

▸ Tell students that they already know some words for things we do in the evening. Tell them they are going to review and learn more words related to the evening.

▸ Point out the times on the clocks in the pictures.

▸ Have students;

  • Tell you the times on the clocks.

▸ Point to each item that appears on the items list on page 125. As you point, say each word out loud.

▸ Have students:

  • Point to each item and repeat each word.

  • Volunteer to act out the action words.

Practice Vocabulary

Guess Who?

▸ Divide the student into pairs.

▸ Direct students' attention to page 124 of the *Student Text*.

Pair/Share

▸ Have students:

- Work in pairs to choose one person in each panel.
- Write a description of where that person is and what the person is doing and wearing.
- Write more information if they can.

  Example: Grandpa in Panel 1. Grandpa is wearing pants and a shirt. He's in the living room. Grandpa is playing a game.

▸ Model an example with the class.

▸ When pairs have finished writing their descriptions, have students:

- Team up with another pair.
- Read the descriptions for the other pair, omitting the name of the person with "this person."
- Guess who the other pair is describing.
- Take turns describing and guessing.

▸ Invite volunteers to:

- Read a description for the class to guess who they are describing.

STEP 4

How English Works

Students are introduced to the dialog. Students participate in the dialog. Students learn and practice **interrogative structures.**

Introduce the Dialog

Picture Walk-Through

Materials

Student Text pp. 126–127

Prepared sentence strips

▸ Have students:

- Look at pictures on page 126 of the *Student Text*.

▸ Ask students simple questions about the pictures to predict the main idea of the dialog.

▸ Point to the picture in each panel. Act out or point to vocabulary words as necessary. Ask:

1. Panel 1: Where is Jessica? in the living room Who is the other family member in the picture? grandfather What are they doing? They are watching television.
2. Panel 2: What is Jessica going to make? fruit salad
3. Panel 3: Who is cooking with Jessica's mom? Jessica's grandmother
4. Panel 4: Where is the town festival? in the street

5. Panel 5: What can Mai, Jessica, and Jacob do at the festival? Answers may vary.

6. Does Grandpa like the food at the festival? yes

▸ Record student responses on the board.

Read the Dialog

▸ Read through the dialog in steps. Have students:

- Track print with you as you read.
- Listen for cognates, or English words that are similar in students' native language.

Grandpa:	How was your math test, Jessica?
Jessica:	It was okay. Some parts of it were hard. I'm glad it's Friday.

▸ Check students' comprehension by asking: "What day is it?" Friday

Grandpa:	Well, tomorrow is a big day. Everyone is excited about the festival.
Jessica:	I am too. I have to make the fruit salad for the barbecue.

▸ Check students' comprehension by asking: "What day is the festival?" tomorrow, Saturday "Where is the festival?" in the street

Grandpa:	Mom and Grandma are going to make pies and cakes for the festival.
Jessica:	I love the town festival. I'm going to wear my new skirt.

▸ Check students' comprehension by asking "What will Mom and Grandma make for the festival?" pies and cakes

▸ Point to the pies and cakes.

▸ Have students:

- Point to the pies and cakes and repeat the words.

▸ Ask students what they like better, pies or cakes.

Grandpa:	Everyone loves the town festival. I like to see the whole town enjoy the sun, the music, and the food.

▸ Check students' comprehension by asking "What does Grandpa like about the town festival?" He likes to see the town enjoy the sun, the music, and the food.

Jessica:	Jacob loves to play the games. Maybe this year he'll win another teddy bear.

▸ Check students' comprehension by asking "What will Jacob do at the festival?" play games "What can he win?" a teddy bear

▸ Have students:

- Point to the teddy bear and say the words.
- Tell you what they would like to do at the festival.

> Grandpa: And I love the food!

▸ Check students' comprehension by asking "How does Grandpa feel about the food? He loves the food.

Practice the Dialog

▸ Divide the class into pairs.

▸ Have students:

- Assign the speaking roles within each pair.
- Read the roles out loud in pairs.
- Volunteer to perform the dialog in front of the class.

▸ Check students' comprehension of the dialog by revisiting the questions from the Picture Walk-Through.

Interrogative Structures

▸ Write the sentence on the board:

Jacob loves games.

▸ Have students:

- Identify the subject and the verb.

▸ Circle the subject and underline the verb in the sentence.

▸ Remind students that in a statement, the subject goes before the verb. Point out the position of the subject and verb.

▸ Review how to make sentences negative with the students. Write the sentence on the board:

Jacob does not love games.

▸ Point out the auxiliary **does** in the negative sentence.

▸ Explain to students that we can use this negative sentence to help us form the question.

▸ Write the question below the negative sentence:

Does Jacob love games?

▸ Draw an arrow from **does** and **Does** in the sentence and the question, and from both subjects in the statement and question.

Oscar does not love games.

Does Oscar love games?

▶ Have students:

  • Point out the position of the word **does** in the statement and questions.

▶ Explain that we use the auxiliary verb **does** from the negative statement to help form the question and that we do not use the word **not** in the question.

▶ Point out that we use the base form of the main verb (the infinitive without **to**) in the interrogative.

▶ Walk the students through further examples with simple subject-verb-object sentences in the present tense.

▶ Give students an example with a subject that requires **do** in the interrogative. For example, use the sentence "Mom and Grandma make pies."

Unscramble the Questions

▶ Prepare sentence strips with simple yes/no questions with verbs other than **be**. Do not include the punctuation or capitalize the first word of the question.

▶ Cut each question to separate the words.

▶ Divide the class into pairs.

▶ Give each pair two cut-up questions:

Pair/Share

▶ Have students:

  • Work in pairs to put the words in the correct order to make two logical, grammatically correct questions.

  • Write their questions on the board.

  • Ask their classmates to answer the questions they formed.

  • Respond to the other pairs' questions.

Revisit the Dialog

▶ Direct students' attention to page 126 of the *Student Text*

On Their Own

▶ Have students:

  • Read the dialog again.

  • Identify the feelings expressed by the characters in the dialog.

  • Explain why they think they characters feel the way they do.

Your Turn

▶ Direct the students' attention to page 127 of the *Student Text*.

▶ Have students:

  • Complete Application A.

  • Share their answers orally with a partner.

  • Find similarities with their partner's responses.

  • Complete Application B.

  • Volunteer to show their illustrations and share their descriptions with the class.

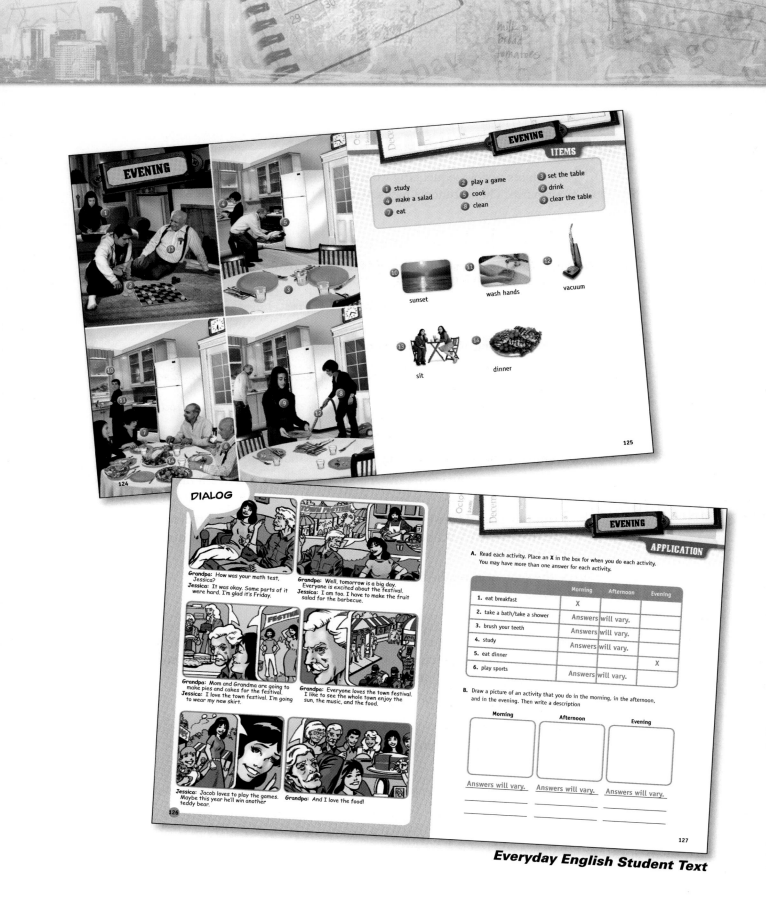

Introduction: Oral Fluency

 Students review sequencing words and are reintroduced to the week's scenario. Then, students focus on one of the areas within the scenario.

Sequence the Sentences

Materials
Student Text
pp. 112–115
Various pictures
or items

▶ Remind students that sequence words help one to understand the order that things and events occur.

▶ Review the sequencing words **first, next, then, last, before** and **after** with the students.

▶ Write the following actions on the board:

go to class   eat breakfast eat dinner go home

go to bed   take a shower go to school study

▶ Have students:

- Number the actions according to the order that these actions would be done.

- Use the sequencing words and their numbered actions to tell the order in which they do these things.

  Example: First, I take a shower. Before I go to school, I eat breakfast. Then, I go to class. After school, I go home. Then, I study. Next, I eat dinner. Last, I go to bed.

▶ Write the sentences on the board.

Review: My Day

▶ Direct students' attention to pages 112–113. Say "my day." Point to the morning, afternoon, and evening sections of the planner and elicit the words **morning, afternoon,** and **evening** from the students.

▶ Point to the **night** section of the planner and say "night."

▶ Have students:

- Point to the **night** section of the planner.

- Repeat the word.

▶ Direct students' attention to pages 114–115. Ask students "Which pictures show nighttime activities?"

▶ Have students:

- Point to the night scenario and repeat the word **night**.

Introduction to Night

▸ Choral repeat the words. Direct students' attention to the night scenario on page 115.

▸ Have students:

- Describe the picture.

▸ Point out the time on the alarm clock (9:30 P.M.).

▸ Have students:

- Tell you what time it is.

STEP 1

Phonemic Awareness

Students practice identifying, differentiating, and producing / *th* / sounds.

The / *th* / Sounds

Materials
Sticky notes in two colors

▸ Write the word **bath** on the board.

▸ Have students:

- Pronounce the word with you.

▸ Underline the ***th*** in the word. Repeat the voiceless / *th* / sound. Show students how to make the sound by putting their tongue between the teeth and pushing the air between the teeth. Put your hand in front of your mouth as you repeat the sound. Tell students they should feel the air coming out as they say this sound.

▸ Have students:

- Put their hands in front of their mouths as they repeat the sound to feel the air.

- Repeat the word **bath**.

▸ Repeat with the words **thermometer** and **theater**.

▸ Write the word **mother** on the board.

▸ Have students:

- Pronounce the word with you.

▸ Underline the ***th*** in the word. Repeat the voiced / *th* / sound. Point out to students that the ***th*** in this word makes a voiced sound. Show students how to make this sound by putting their tongue between the teeth and pushing the air between the teeth as they vocalize the sound. Put your hand on your throat as you repeat the sound.

▸ Have students:

- Put their hands on their throats as they repeat the sound.

- Repeat the word **mother**.

/ *th* / Three-in-a-Row

▸ Draw a grid on the board as shown.

▸ Divide class into pairs. Give each partner sticky notes in different colors. Assign one partner the voiced / *th* / sound and the other partner the voiceless / *th* / sound.

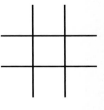

▶ Have students:

- Copy the grid so that it is big enough for each space to fit a sticky note.

- Write a word that has their / *th* / sound on the sticky note.

- Place the sticky note on the grid and say the word.

- Take turns with their partner to try to get three of their sticky notes in a row with words that have their assigned / *th* /. They may get three in a row horizontally, vertically, or diagonally.

- Switch / *th* / sounds and play another round.

▶ When the pairs have finished, compile a list of the words the students came up with for each sound and write them on the board.

▶ Have students:

- Say each word.

STEP 2

Everyday Words

Students review and practice prepositions of placement, colors, and shapes and sizes for everyday conversation.

Review Everyday Words: Prepositions of Placement, Colors, Shapes and Sizes

Materials
Student Text

▶ Review the prepositions of placement, colors, shapes and sizes with the students by pointing out objects in the classroom and asking simple questions about the objects.

▶ Have students:

- Identify the placement, color, shape, and/or size of the objects.

I See

▶ Choose an object in the room to describe to the students.

Example: Describe the door. Say "I see something. I see something big. I see something big and rectangular. I see something big, rectangular, and brown. I see something big, rectangular and brown behind the desks. I can open and close it."

▶ Have students:

- Guess the object.

- Volunteer to describe an object in the room by its location, color, shape, and size.

▶ Divide the class into pairs.

▶ Have students:

- Choose one scenario picture next to the items list page in the *Student Text* to work with within their pair.

- Take turns describing an object in the scenario picture for their partner to guess.

- Each describe five different objects.

You Describe It, I'll Draw It

▸ Describe an object that students know in English. Describe the shape, size, color, and location for the students.

▸ Have students:

- Draw the object according to the description.

- Compare drawings.

- Work in pairs to take turns describing an object for their partner to draw.

  Example: Draw a table. The table is small and round. It is red. It is in front of a big square window.

STEP 3

Vocabulary Development

➡ Students work with the core content vocabulary related to the home and night for everyday conversation.

Review and Introduce: Core Vocabulary

Review: Appliances

Materials

Student Text
pp. 128–129

Prepared cards

▸ Review different household appliances in the home.

▸ Draw a Venn diagram on the board.

work ⬭⬭ *entertainment*

▸ Write **work** next to one circle and **entertainment** next to the other circle.

▸ Have students:

- Tell you which appliances belong in the work category, the entertainment category, or both.

  Example: For work, dishwasher. For entertainment, stereo. For both, computer.

▸ Write the words in the appropriate locations in the diagram.

▸ Have students:

- Explain why they sorted the items in each category.

- Suggest other categories to sort the appliances.

- Copy the Venn diagram in their notebooks.

- Choose two categories to use in sorting.

- Complete their Venn diagrams.

- Share their diagrams with the class and explain why they sorted the items in each category.

Introduce: Night Vocabulary

▸ Direct students' attention to the night scenario and list on pages 128–129 of the *Student Text*.

▸ Tell students that they already know some words for things we do at night. Tell them they are going to review and learn more words related to night.

▸ Point out the time on the alarm clock in the picture.

▸ Have students:

- Tell you the time on the clock.

- Point out and name appliances in the pictures.

▸ Point to each item that appears on the items list on page 129. As you point, say each word out loud.

▸ Have students:

- Point to each item and repeat each word.

- Volunteer to act out the action words.

Practice Vocabulary

Listing for Actions

Model

▸ Write one of the action words from the items list on page 129 of the *Student Text*.

▸ Have students:

- Say words that are associated with this activity.

  Example: You write **sleep**. Students may say: bed, pillow, sheets, blanket, night, etc.

Pair/Share

▸ Have students:

- Each choose three action words from the items list on page 129 of the *Student Text* for their partner to guess.

- Say words that are associated with each activity for their partner to guess the activity.

- Take turns guessing and listing.

When I Go to Bed, I Like...

▸ Tell students that you are very particular when you go to bed. Explain that this means that you need everything to be perfect.

▸ Say "When I go to bed, I like to read a book before I sleep. When I go to bed, I like to have two pillows. When I go to bed, I like to sleep with a blanket. When I go to bed, I like to listen to music. When I go to bed, I like to close the blinds."

▸ Have students:

- Share with a partner the things they like when they go to bed.

How English Works

 Students are introduced to the dialog. Students participate in the dialog. Students learn and practice **imperative** sentence structure.

Introduce the Dialog

Picture Walk-Through

Materials
Student Text
pp. 130–131

▸ Have students:

• Look at pictures on page 130 of the *Student Text*.

▸ Ask students simple questions about the pictures to predict the main idea of the dialog.

▸ Point to the picture in each panel. Act out or point to vocabulary words as necessary. Ask:

1. Panel 1: Where are Jessica and Jacob? in the bathroom
2. Panel 2: What does Jessica have? toothpaste and a toothbrush
3. Panel 3: What does Jacob need? soap
4. Panel 4: What does Jacob have? a towel What does Jessica have? a brush
5. Panel 5: Where are Jessica and Jacob? in the bedroom
6. Panel 6: What is Jacob doing? sleeping

▸ Record student responses on the board.

Read the Dialog

▸ Read through the dialog in steps. Have students:

• Track print with you as you read.

• Listen for cognates, or English words that are similar in students' native language.

Jessica:	Now, Jacob, tomorrow is a big day. We have to get ready for bed.
Jacob:	I'm excited about tomorrow.
Jessica:	First, you have to put on your pajamas.
Jacob:	Put on my pajamas.

▸ Check students' comprehension by asking "How does Jacob feel about tomorrow?" He's excited. "What is Jessica wearing?" pajamas

Jessica:	Before you go to bed, you have to brush your teeth.
Jacob:	Brush my teeth.

▸ Check students' comprehension by asking "What does Jacob have to do before he goes to bed?" brush his teeth "What does he need to do this?" Answers may vary.

> | Jessica: | Then, you have to wash your face and hands. |
> | Jacob: | Wash my face and hands. |

▸ Check students' comprehension by asking "What does Jacob have to wash?"
his face and hands

▸ Have students:

- Point to their **faces** and **hands** and say the words.

> | Jessica: | Now, you have to dry your face. |
> | Jacob: | Dry my face. |
> | Jessica: | I am going to brush your hair. |

▸ Check students' comprehension by asking "What does Jacob have to do?" dry his
face "What does he need to do this?" a towel "What is Jessica going to do?" brush
Jacob's hair "What does she need to do this?" a brush

▸ Have students:

- Point to the **towel** and say the word.
- Point to the **brush** and say the word.

> | Jessica: | Now, I'll read you a story. |
> | Jacob: | Read me a story. |

▸ Check students' comprehension by asking "What is Jessica going to do?"
read a story to Jacob

> | Jessica: | And last, I'll say goodnight. |

▸ Check students' comprehension by asking "What is Jessica going to do last?"
say goodnight

Practice the Dialog

▸ Divide the class into pairs.

Pair/Share

▸ Have students:

- Assign the speaking roles within each pair.
- Read the roles out loud in pairs.
- Volunteer to perform the dialog in front of the class.

Check students' comprehension of the dialog by revisiting the questions from the
Picture Walk-Through.

Imperative Sentence Structure

▸ Tell students that some sentences in English do not have a subject. Write on board:

Go to bed.

- Say "Jessica wants Jacob to go to bed. She tells him 'Go to bed.'" She does not have to say "Jacob" because she is talking directly to him and telling him what to do.
- Underline the verb **go** in the sentence. Point out that when we tell someone what to do, we start the sentence with a verb.
- Point out that we use the base verb (the infinitive without **to**) to give affirmative commands.
- Point out the use of capitalization of the first word and the period at the end. Explain that we can put an exclamation point at the end if we want to express strong feelings or urgency.
- Tell students that we can also give negative commands to tell someone not to do something.
- Write the sentence on the board:

  Don't open the door.

- Underline **don't** in the sentence.
- Explain that we use **don't** at the beginning of negative commands.
- Point out again the use of capitalization of the first word and the period at the end.
- Have students:
  - Say commands they would give to a little brother or sister.

Revisit the Dialog

On Their Own

- Direct students' attention to pages 130–131 of the *Student Text*.
- Have students:
  - Read the dialog again.
  - Find instances in the dialog where Jessica can tell Jacob what to do. For example, You have to put on your pajamas.
  - Write the imperatives that Jessica could use in each instance. For example, Put on your pajamas.
- Check answers.

Your Turn

- Have students:
  - Complete Application A and Application B on page 131 of the *Student Text*.
  - Volunteer to read their paragraphs to the class.

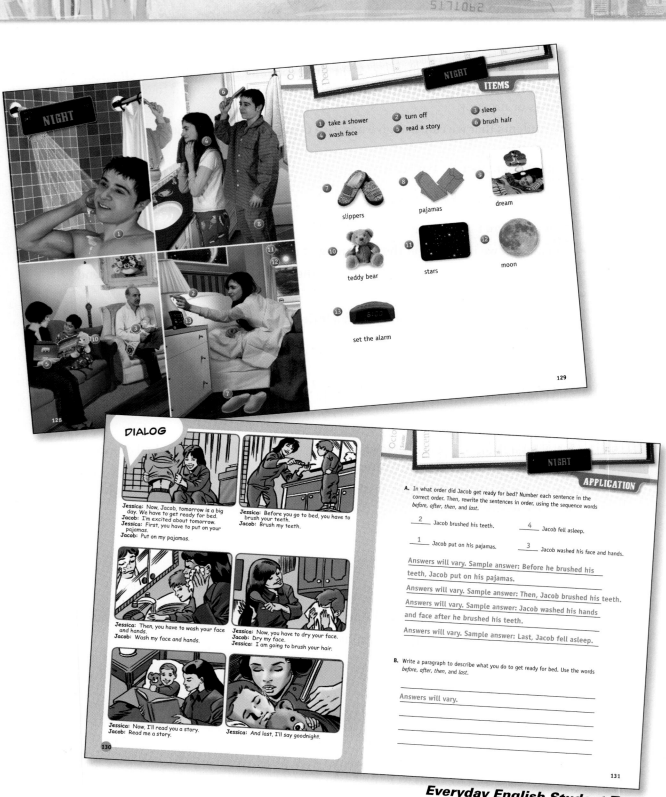

Everyday English Student Text

Introduction: Oral Fluency

 Students review sequencing and how to tell a story. Students revisit the Unit Overview.

Sequencing In a Story

Materials
Student Text
pp. 114–115
Blank cards

▸ Review the sequencing words with the students.

▸ Remind students that sequencing words and the question words **who, what, when, where, why** and **how** can help us tell a clear and interesting story.

▸ Have students:

  • Volunteer to tell one thing they did yesterday.

  • Work together as a class to add information about the event using the question words.

  • Work together as a class to include the sequencing words to put the story events in order.

  • Volunteer to tell the story with the new information.

Unit Review: My Day

▸ Direct students' attention to the pictures on pages 114–115.

▸ Point to each picture and elicit the words **morning, afternoon, evening,** and **night**.

▸ Have students:

  • Chorally and individually repeat the words.

STEP 1

Phonemic Awareness

 Students practice identifying, differentiating, and producing various consonant and consonant cluster sounds.

Review of the Consonant and Consonant Cluster Sounds

Materials
Blank cards
Optional: Paper strips and glue

▸ Review the consonants and consonant clusters learned throughout the course.

▸ Pronounce each sound and write them on the board.

▸ Have students:

  • Repeat each sound.

- Tell you words in English that have the sound.
- Say and repeat each elicited word.
▶ Write the words under each sound under the board.

Sound Chain

▶ Write the word **bath** on the board. Say the word and underline the **th** in the word.

▶ Have students:

- Repeat the word.
- Repeat the voiceless / *th* / sound.
- Think of a word that begins with the voiceless / *th* / sound. For example, thermometer.

▶ Write the word on the board. Underline the **r** in the word.

▶ Have students:

- Say the word and think of another word that begins with the / *r* / sound.
- Continue in the same way until they are unable to come up with a word for the last sound of the previous word.
- Try to make the chain of words as long as possible.

   Example: Start with the word **bath**, ending in the / *th* / sound. Students volunteer the word **thermometer**, starting with the / *th* / sound. Students volunteer the word **roast**, ending in the / *t* / sound, etc.

▶ Record the chain of words that the students make to review with them after they have completed the activity.

Variation:

▶ Have students:

- Individually continue the chain in turn.
- Write the words on long slips of paper.
- Make a paper chain by linking the words together.

Stand Long and Sit Short

▶ Review the long and short vowel sounds with the students.

▶ Divide the class into either five or ten groups, depending on the number of students.

▶ Give each group a stack of blank cards.

▶ If there are ten groups, assign each group one of the ten long and short vowel sounds learned throughout the course. If there are only five groups, assign each group both the long and short vowel sound, for example the / ă / and / ā /.

▶ Have students:

- Write one word on each card that has their vowel sounds.

▶ Collect and shuffle the cards.

▶ Read the word slowly on each card.

▶ Have students:

- Stand up every time they hear a long vowel sound.

- Sit down every time they hear a short vowel sound.
- Repeat each word.

   Example: Say the word **telephone**. Students remain seated for the two / ĕ / sounds and stand up for the / ō / sound.

STEP 2

Everyday Words

Students review and practice everyday words they have learned throughout the course for everyday conversation.

Review Everyday Words: What Do You Know About Your Partner?

Materials
Prepared worksheet

▶ Tell students that they are going to practice the words they have learned throughout the course by finding out information about their partners.

▶ Prepare a three-column worksheet for the students. In the left column, write the information that the students are to find out about their partners. For example: **name, birthday, favorite color, favorite season, favorite food, time the person wakes up and goes to bed, etc**. Write "I think my partner..." at the top of the middle column. In the last column, write "I found out that my partner..."

Information to find out	"I think my partner..."	"I found out that my partner..."

▶ Divide the class into pairs, and give each student a worksheet.

▶ Have students:

- Fill in the middle column about what they think they know about their partner. They may know some of the information. For the information they do not know, they should guess what they think their partner will answer.
- Take turns interviewing each other to confirm or correct the information in the filled out in the chart.
- Write the correct information about their partners in the right column.
- Share with the class any surprising information that they found out about their partners.

STEP 3

Vocabulary Development

 Students work with the core content vocabulary related to a typical day for everyday conversation.

Review: Core Vocabulary

Materials

Pictures of families or family photos

Pair/Share

▸ Gather pictures of families or have students bring in family photos.

▸ Divide the class into pairs.

▸ Assign each pair a time of day.

▸ Have students:

- Identify the family members.

- Write a short paragraph together to tell what the family members do during that time of day.

- Share their photos and paragraphs with the class.

- Listen to the other pairs for any activities that are similar to the activities in their own paragraphs.

▸ Encourage students to specify what time of day the family members do the activities, where they do the activities, and what items they need to do the activities.

STEP 4

How English Works

 Students are introduced to the dialog. Students participate in the dialog. Students review and practice sentence structures.

Introduce the Dialog

Picture Walk-Through

Materials

Student Text pp. 132–133

Prepared and blank cards

▸ Have students:

- Look at pictures on page 132 of the *Student Text*.

▸ Ask students simple questions about the pictures to predict the main idea of the dialog.

▸ Point to the picture in each panel. Act out or point to vocabulary words as necessary. Ask:

1. Panel 1: Where are Charlie and Trang? at the town festival

2. Panel 2: Who is Charlie talking about? the mailman, the librarian, and the doctor

3. Panel 3: What place is Trang talking about? the park

4. Panel 4: Is Trang talking about the mall? no

5. Panel 5: Is Charlie talking about the library? no

6. Panel 6: Where are Trang and Charlie sitting? at a picnic table

‣ Record student responses on the board.

Read the Dialog

‣ Read through the dialog in steps. Have students:

- Track print with you as you read.

- Listen for cognates, or English words that are similar in students' native language.

Charlie:	Thanks for inviting me to the festival, Trang.
Trang:	It's going to be a lot of fun. Do you like living here?

‣ Check students' comprehension by asking "Where are Charlie and Trang?" at the festival "How did they get there?" on their bicycles

‣ Have students:

- Point to the bicycles and say the word.

- Tell you how they get to different places.

Charlie:	Yes, there are a lot of nice people here. The mailman is really nice. Also, Mrs. Simons, the librarian, helps me and my sister a lot. And you were right. Dr. Fielder is a really good doctor.

‣ Check students' comprehension by asking "Who does Trang mention?" the mailman, the librarian, and the doctor "Where do they work?" the post office, the library, and the hospital or doctor's office

Trang:	My favorite place in town is the park.
Charlie:	Yeah. My sister and I like to ride our bikes and go to the park.

‣ Check students' comprehension by asking "What is Trang's favorite place?" the park "What do Charlie and his sister like to do at the park?" ride their bikes and go to the park

‣ Have students:

- Tell you what they like to do at the park.

Trang:	How do you like school?
Charlie:	I like my classes and teachers a lot. I don't like homework though!

‣ Have students:

- Tell you what Charlie likes and doesn't like about school.

- Tell you what they like and don't like about school.

> Trang: Have you and your family been to the mall yet?
>
> Charlie: Yes. My mom and my sister shop there a lot. I think the entertainment store has a lot of cool things.
>
> Trang: Yeah, I saw some video games that I want.
>
> Charlie: When I save some money, I'm going to buy a new video game.

▸ Check students' comprehension by asking "What store does Charlie like at the mall?" the entertainment store "What does Charlie want to buy?" a new video game

▸ Have students:

- Tell you what stores they like at the mall.

> Trang: I'm glad that you moved here. We're going to have a lot of fun.
>
> Charlie: I'm glad we live here.

▸ Check students' comprehension by asking "Does Charlie like his new town?" yes

▸ Have students:

- Tell you what they like about their town.

Practice the Dialog

Pair/Share

▸ Divide the class into pairs.

▸ Have students:

- Assign the speaking roles within each pair.
- Read the roles out loud in pairs.
- Volunteer to perform the dialog in front of the class.

Check students' comprehension of the dialog by revisiting the questions from the Picture Walk-Through.

Sentence Structure Review

▸ Prepare three cards. Write a period (.), a question mark (?), and an exclamation point (!) on the cards. You should have one card for each punctuation mark.

▸ Review the three types of sentence structures that the students have learned in this unit.

▸ Give each student two blank cards.

▸ Have students:

- Write a subject on one card and a verb on another card. The subject and verb do not have to match.

  Example: The student writes the firefighter on the subject card, and sleep on the verb card.

▸ Collect the cards, keeping the subject cards separate from the verb cards. You should now have three stacks of cards.

▸ Explain that the period represents a statement, the question mark represents a question, and the exclamation point represents an imperative.

▸ Have students:

  • Volunteer to choose a card from each of the three stacks.

  • Make a statement, question, or command based on the information in the cards.

  • Remind students that we do not use a subject for imperatives.

▸ Continue until all students have had at least one turn to make a sentence.

Revisit the Dialog

▸ Direct students' attention to pages 132–133 of the *Student Text.*

On Their Own

▸ Have students:

  • Read the dialog again.

  • Find examples of statements and questions.

  • Share answers with the class.

Your Turn

▸ Direct students' attention to Application A on page 133 of the *Student Text.*

▸ Have students:

  • Complete the activity.

  • Share their comic strip with a partner.

▸ Invite volunteers to:

  • Show and read their comic strip to the class.

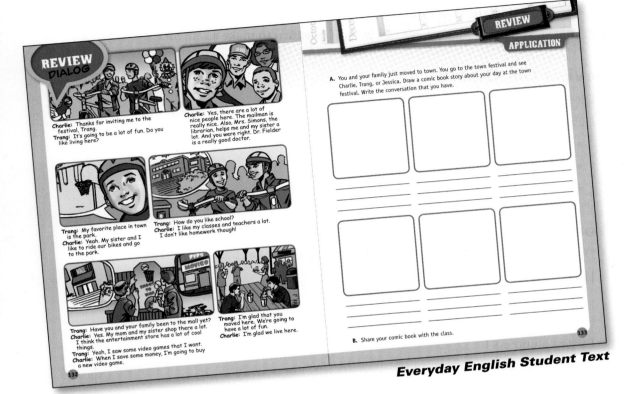

Charlie: Thanks for inviting me to the festival, Trang.

Trang: It's going to be a lot of fun. Do you like living here?

Charlie: Yes, there are a lot of nice people here. The mailman is really nice. Also, Mrs. Simons, the librarian, helps me and my sister a lot. And you were right. Dr. Fielder is a really good doctor.

Trang: My favorite place in town is the park.

Charlie: Yeah. My sister and I like to ride our bikes and go to the park.

Trang: How do you like school?

Charlie: I like my classes and teachers a lot. I don't like homework though!

Trang: Have you and your family been to the mall yet?

Charlie: Yes. My mom and my sister shop there a lot. I think the entertainment store has a lot of cool things.

Trang: Yeah, I saw some video games that I want.

Charlie: When I save some money, I'm going to buy a new video game.

Trang: I'm glad that you moved here. We're going to have a lot of fun.

Charlie: I'm glad we live here.

A. You and your family just moved to town. You go to the town festival and see Charlie, Trang, or Jessica. Draw a comic book story about your day at the town festival. Write the conversation that you have.

B. Share your comic book with the class.

132

133

Everyday English Student Text